The NATIONAL CONSUMER LAW CENTER

GUIDE TO

Consumer Rights FOR Domestic Violence Survivors

Other National Consumer Law Center Publications

BOOKS FOR CONSUMERS

NCLC Guide to Surviving Debt
NCLC Guide to The Rights of Utility Consumers
NCLC Guide to Mobile Homes
Return to Sender: Getting a Refund or Replacement for Your Lemon Car

LEGAL PRACTICE MANUALS

Debtor Rights Library
Consumer Bankruptcy Law and Practice
Fair Debt Collection
Foreclosures
Repossessions
Student Loan Law
Access to Utility Service

Consumer Litigation Library
Consumer Arbitration Agreements
Consumer Class Actions
Consumer Law Pleadings

Credit and Banking Library
Truth in Lending
Fair Credit Reporting
Consumer Banking and Payments Law
The Cost of Credit
Credit Discrimination

Deception and Warranties Library
Unfair and Deceptive Acts and Practices
Automobile Fraud
Consumer Warranty Law

Other Publications for Lawyers
The Practice of Consumer Law
STOP Predatory Lending
NCLC REPORTS Newsletter
Consumer Law in a Box CD-Rom

The NATIONAL CONSUMER LAW CENTER

GUIDE TO

Consumer Rights FOR Domestic Violence Survivors

From

THE NATIONAL CONSUMER LAW CENTER

America's Consumer Law Experts

Chi Chi Wu

John Van Alst

Carolyn Carter

Contributing Authors

Tracy Davis

Chaitra Shenoy

Erika Sussman

Tara Twomey

For reprint permissions or ordering information, contact
Publications, NCLC, 77 Summer Street, 10th Floor, Boston MA 02110,
(617) 542-9595, Fax (617) 542-8028, E-mail: publications@nclc.org

Library of Congress Control No. 2006932128
ISBN-13: 978-1-931697-97-2
ISBN-10: 1-931697-97-3

10 9 8 7 6 5 4 3 2 1

Printed in Canada

HELP US HELP YOU

We appreciate your feedback.
Let us know what you think of the book and
how to make it better by going to
www.nclc.org\publications\dveval.html.

CONTENTS

About the Authors

The National Consumer Law Center (NCLC) is the nation's expert on the rights of consumer borrowers. Since 1969, NCLC has been at the forefront in representing low-income consumers before the courts, government agencies, Congress, and state legislatures.

NCLC has appeared before the United States Supreme Court and numerous federal and state courts and has successfully presented many of the most important cases affecting consumer borrowers. NCLC provides consultation and assistance to legal services, private, and government attorneys in all fifty states.

NCLC publishes a nationally acclaimed series of manuals on all major aspects of consumer credit and sales. (For a complete list of NCLC publications, go to www.consumerlaw.org.) NCLC also conducts state and national training sessions on the rights of consumer borrowers for attorneys, paralegals, and other counselors.

Chi Chi Wu is a staff attorney with the National Consumer Law Center, where she works on consumer credit and credit reporting issues. She is a co-author of NCLC's *Fair Credit Reporting* (6th ed. 2006) and *Credit Discrimination* (4th ed. 2005), and a contributing author to *Truth in Lending* (5th ed. 2003). She was formerly an assistant attorney general with the Consumer Protection Division of the Massachusetts Attorney General's Office and an attorney with the Asian Outreach Unit of Greater Boston Legal Services, where she represented domestic violence survivors.

John Van Alst is a staff attorney with the National Consumer Law Center, where he works on consumer credit issues. Previously, he represented low-income consumers for seven years as a staff attorney and managing attorney at Legal Aid of North Carolina, including representation of domestic violence survivors to obtain restraining orders and in other domestic matters. He has also been a Visiting Clinical Supervisor at the University of North Carolina School of Law.

Carolyn Carter is the Deputy Director for Advocacy at the National Consumer Law Center and co-author of *Repossessions* (6th ed. 2005), *Unfair and Deceptive Acts and Practices* (6th ed. 2004), and *Consumer Warranty Law* (3d ed. 2006). Prior to joining NCLC, she was the Co-Director of Legal Services, Inc., in Gettysburg, Pennsylvania, where a substantial portion of her practice involved representing domestic violence survivors.

CONTRIBUTING AUTHORS

Tracy Davis, the author of Chapter Twenty-Two, is a staff attorney with the Legal Assistance Providers' Technical Outreach Project (LAPTOP), a national project that provides legal and advocacy technical assistance to civil attorneys and advocates for survivors of domestic violence, sexual assault, stalking, and dating violence. She formerly was a staff attorney with Legal Action of Wisconsin providing direct legal services to low-income individuals. This work included serving domestic violence, sexual assault, and stalking survivors through Legal Assistance for Victims and Victims of Crime Act grants. She has worked on a project to remove barriers to employment that included criminal background, driver's license, and child support advocacy. She has trained attorneys and advocates in the areas of protection orders, family law, public benefits, and economic justice. She has a J.D. from American University, Washington College of Law, an M.A. from the University of Cincinnati, and a B.A. from the University of Manitoba.

Chaitra Shenoy, the author of Chapter Ten, is the Legal Resource Administrator at the Legal Assistance Providers' Technical Outreach Project. Her work with survivors of domestic violence, dating violence, sexual assault, and stalking for the past eight years inspired her to go to law school. Originally a Bay Area, California native, she is a graduate of American University, Washington College of Law, and currently resides in Washington, DC.

Erika Sussman, the author of Chapter Nine, is the Senior Attorney of the Legal Assistance Providers' Technical Outreach Project. She also serves as an adjunct professor at Cornell Law School, where she teaches a seminar on Law and Violence Against Women. Previously, she was a staff attorney and teaching fellow at Georgetown University Law Center's Domestic Violence Clinic, where she supervised law students and litigated cases on behalf of survivors in the District of Columbia. She was formerly a litigation associate at Swidler Berlin Sherreff Friedman, L.L.P., where she provided pro bono representation to domestic violence survivors in conjunction with Women Empowered Against Violence (WEAVE) and represented plaintiffs in a civil rights racial profiling class action suit. Ms. Sussman earned her LLM in Advocacy from Georgetown University Law Center and her Juris Doctorate and Bachelor's of Arts degrees from Cornell University.

Tara Twomey, the author of Chapter Eight, is currently "of counsel" to the National Consumer Law Center. She is a Lecturer in Law at Stanford Law School and a former Clinical Instructor at the Hale and Dorr Legal Services Center of Harvard Law School, where her practice focused, in part, on sustainable homeownership for low- and moderate-income homeowners, foreclosure prevention, and chapter 13 bankruptcy. She has previously received appointments as a Lecturer in Law at Harvard Law School and as an Adjunct Faculty member at Boston College Law School, and was formerly a volunteer and member of the Board of Directors for Shelter Legal Services Foundation, Inc., a non-profit organization providing legal assistance to, among others, homeless and low-income women. Ms. Twomey is a contributing author of several books published by the National Consumer Law Center, including *Foreclosures* (2005).

Acknowledgments

The authors would like to thank the many people who offered substantive advice and comment on this volume and a prior edition that focused solely on Massachusetts law: Jane S. Preece, Directing Attorney of Family Law, Legal Aid Foundation of Los Angeles; Susan Morganstern, Legal Aid Society of Cleveland; Leslie Book, Professor of Law and Director, Federal Tax Clinic, Villanova University School of Law; Vicki Turetsky, Center for Law and Social Policy; Caitlin Glass of Legal Aid Services of Oregon; Jody Raphael of the Center for Impact Research; Margaret Drew, a Massachusetts attorney; Deanne Loonin, Olivia Wein, John Howat, Mark Benson, Shannon Halbrook, Jon Sheldon, Charlie Harak, John Rao, and Stuart Rossman of the National Consumer Law Center; Mark Budnitz, Professor at Georgia State Law School; and Douglas Segal of Foley & Lardner. We also acknowledge David Pifer and the work of his Legal Intervention for Employment (LIFE) Project at Legal Action of Wisconsin for the development of many of the strategies discussed in Chapter Twenty-Two.

Thanks also to Gillian Feiner and Mary Kingsley for research and writing, and to the Consumer Federation of America for permission to use a chart of payday loan laws. This guide was made possible with support from the Consumer Protection and Education Fund of the Attorneys General. The original handbook on Massachusetts law was made possible through grants from the John H. and H. Naomi Tomforde Foundation and the George H. and Jane A. Mifflin Memorial Fund. And of course we are also grateful to Dorothy Tan for editing the book, Denise Lisio for editorial supervision, Julie Gallagher for the design and typesetting, and Mary Mclean for indexing.

1

Introduction

When an abuse survivor separates from her abuser, she will likely have physical, emotional, and financial concerns. (Throughout this handbook, the term "survivor" is used for the person who has been subjected to abuse. The term "abuser" is used for the perpetrator of the abuse. Although both men and women suffer abuse, the female pronoun has been used for simplicity.) Immediately after she leaves an abusive situation, physical and emotional needs will probably take precedence. After the immediate crisis, however, she may be left with no income and a stack of bills that she cannot pay. If she is unable to take control of her financial situation she may even be tempted to return to the abuser for financial reasons.

The survivor's fragile financial and emotional situation also makes her vulnerable to predatory behavior. She may be pressured by debt collectors, tempted by high-cost credit products, ripped off by shady car dealers, or feel desperate enough to turn to expensive private child support collectors. If she was married to or shared a household with her abuser, he may have left her with onerous debts that ruined her credit record.

The survivor may have been the target of financial abuse as well. Abusers often control their partners by limiting their access to cash, checking accounts, financial records, and credit cards. As a result, survivors may lack experience dealing with money and basic financial literacy skills. Abusers have even been known to purposefully damage their partners' credit records. The abuse itself may create expenses for the survivor by making her liable for property damage, medical bills, and legal expenses.

This guidebook is intended to assist advocates for domestic violence survivors help survivors who are grappling with these issues. For many years, a major goal for advocates has been helping survivors become economically independent and secure. Advocates have worked toward this goal principally by focusing on raising or preserving the income of survivors.

While income is critical to economic independence, focusing solely on income addresses only part of the equation. Ensuring the economic security of a survivor requires both maximizing income and minimizing expenses. Consumer law advocacy helps survivors minimize their expenses through effective budgeting, obtain access to credit, avoid debts that should be the abuser's liability, and avoid scams and predatory creditors.

Before counseling a survivor who is experiencing financial distress it is important to let her know that it is all right (and common) to have money problems after leaving or escaping an abusive situation. Nearly everyone in this country—including some very prominent people—experiences some type of financial difficulties at one time or another. Many of them did not also have to go through the harrowing ordeal of abuse at the same time. It is important to emphasize to the survivor that there is nothing to be ashamed of or embarrassed about.

As an early step, the survivor should get an overall picture of her financial situation. An advocate or counselor can help the survivor develop a budget. Budgeting is discussed in the next chapter of this guidebook.

The advocate may also assist the survivor in invoking her consumer rights under various federal and state laws to stop debt collection harassment or clean up her credit record. The survivor may also need advice to steer her away from scams that would drain her limited resources.

This guidebook provides an introduction for advocates to many of the most critical consumer issues faced by low-income survivors of domestic violence. More extensive resources are cited throughout. In addition, this guidebook discusses some common scams and scams that particularly affect domestic violence survivors. It also addresses ways that the survivor can increase her income, or shift debts to the abuser, through child support orders, orders requiring the abuser to pay certain debts or expenses, and victim compensation funds. In addition, it addresses tax and driver's-license issues that can affect the survivor.

One caution about using this guidebook is that some of the remedies discussed must be viewed with the survivor's safety in mind. For example, before a court action is initiated that would involve contact with the abuser, the survivor and her advocate must consider how such an action could jeopardize the survivor's safety. The abuser may view certain actions, such as cancellation of a joint credit card, as a direct threat and retaliate against the survivor. Sometimes the contact alone, even through a third party such as a lawyer or creditor, might lead to an abusive response. Survivors and their advocates must consider such possibilities when deciding what actions to take. The possibility of retaliation should be included in the survivor's safety planning.

If the survivor's whereabouts are not known to the abuser, she must consider whether a particular action might result in disclosure of her location. If the location of the survivor is known to the abuser, or if the survivor otherwise decides that a particular course of action is best, she might consider obtaining a protective order or requesting that police step up surveillance of her residence immediately prior to any notice to the abuser of action that could impact him financially.

Advocates must remember that the ultimate safety decisions are made by the survivor. She knows best the behavior of the abuser. The thoughtful advocate will present the options and concerns to the survivor so that a meaningful decision may be made.

As the survivor becomes aware of her options as described in this guidebook, she will understand that her situation is far from hopeless. The options presented can be empowering for the survivor. Thoughtful consideration of the remedies available will enhance the survivor's independence and her recovery.

HELP US HELP YOU

We appreciate your feedback.
Let us know what you think of the book and how to make it better by going to www.nclc.org\publications\dveval.html.

2

Budgeting

REASONS TO SET UP A BUDGET

Setting up a budget is a key element for a survivor trying to get out or stay out of financial trouble. Particularly for a survivor who shared a household and/or finances with an abuser, a budget is essential for the following reasons:

- A survivor who has left her abuser may be experiencing a dramatic change in her income and expenses. The abuser may have been providing most of the income in the household. Even if the survivor is working, overall resources may be considerably reduced, especially if she is taking care of minor children. Budgeting can help the survivor avoid overspending and getting into unmanageable debt by helping the survivor come to a better understanding of her financial situation.
- If the survivor is seeking child support from the abuser, a budget may assist her to demonstrate the true extent of expenses for the children. She can use the budget to avoid getting shortchanged on child support.
- If the survivor is having trouble meeting all her bills, she may want to work with her creditors and propose a payment plan or modification of the debt. The survivor's ability to qualify for these programs will be based on her budget. If the survivor has already done some of the work to develop a budget, she will have a sense of what she can afford to offer creditors. She will also be able to provide basic information to creditors that will make negotiating with them easier and give her additional credibility.

HOW TO SET UP A BUDGET

Here are some suggestions to help a survivor set up a budget:

1. Start with a current budget using existing income and expenses, without anticipating future changes. A sample budget form is included at Appendix C.

➡ **POINTER:** If the survivor does not have bills, documents, or other information about her debts because she had to flee quickly, one way to obtain information about these accounts is to obtain a copy of her credit report. Information about how to obtain a credit report is discussed in Chapter Twelve.

2. For the income budget, include all sources of income that the survivor receives on a regular basis, including wages, child support, or public assistance. Make sure that the survivor can realistically expect the receipt of income from these sources. For example, only include child support payments if the survivor can reasonably expect to receive them.
3. For the expense budget, include all food, shelter costs, utilities, clothing, transportation, and medical expenses. Food bills should include, for example, grocery bills, estimated trips to the convenience store for special needs, and the occasional restaurant or fast food meal. If possible, a review of the survivor's checkbook and credit card bills may be helpful.
4. It is important to determine which debts are the survivor's debts. Survivors should not include in their budget debts for which they have no personal liability. For a more through discussion of liability for joint debts, see Chapter Six.
5. If the survivor is having trouble making ends meet, do not include credit card bills and other unsecured debt (see Chapter Three for an explanation of unsecured debt) in the expense budget. Do not even include minimum payments if it means the survivor cannot pay her housing costs or car loan. Explain to the survivor the reasons for not paying credit card bills using the principles of debt prioritization discussed in the next chapter. For more information on credit cards, see Chapter Fifteen.
6. Evaluate what the survivor expects for the near future. This is often a difficult task and even harder for survivors whose situations may be still in turmoil. Ask if the survivor's income is likely to go up or down over the

next few months. See if there is anything she can do to reduce expenses. Will there be new expenses not included in the current budget?

7. After completing the budget, review it again with the survivor. Can she afford the future budget that she has set up? If not, don't despair. There are ways for the survivor to reduce or eliminate obligations.
8. The survivor should try to live on the budget for a month to see if it works. At the end of the month, adjust the budget based on the experience.

MAXIMIZING INCOME

Advocates for survivors must be adept at helping survivors become aware of various federal and state government benefits for which the survivor might be eligible. Advocates can also assist survivors in applying for these benefits and other private assistance programs. Advocates should help survivors investigate their eligibility for Food Stamps, WIC (a federal nutrition program for Women, Infants, and Children), TANF (Temporary Assistance for Needy Families), unemployment benefits, and other programs to assist those in need.

There are other programs that are sometimes overlooked. There are a number of utility assistance programs that can help, including the federal Low Income Home Energy Assistance Program (LIHEAP) and Lifeline telephone assistance program. More information on these programs is included in Chapter Seven. The survivor may also be eligible for the Earned Income Tax Credit. For more information on tax issues for survivors, see Chapter Twenty-One.

In addition to public assistance, survivors may be eligible for assistance from private institutions. Advocates can help survivors seek child support from the abuser or any other non-custodial parent. For more information on child support see Chapters Eleven and Seventeen. Survivors may also be able to improve their financial situation by seeking compensation from the abuser. For more information, see Chapter Nine.

MINIMIZING EXPENSES

An important means of lowering expenses is to reduce or eliminate the debts that a survivor owes. Consumer law can be extremely helpful in reaching this goal. Consumer law may reduce or eliminate debt by providing

- defenses against mortgage foreclosure and car repossession;
- defenses against unconscionably priced loans and goods;
- protections from overreaching creditors and collectors, including abusive debt collectors;
- access to reasonably priced energy and credit;
- discharges of student loans or reduction of the monthly payment; and
- reduction of debt through bankruptcy.

This guidebook includes chapters that cover many of the above issues. These issues are also addressed more extensively in the *NCLC Guide to Surviving Debt* (2006) (hereinafter *"Surviving Debt"*), written for consumers and published by the National Consumer Law Center. This publication can be ordered by calling the NCLC Publications Department at 617-542-9595 or going to www.consumerlaw.org.

3

Prioritizing Debt

A recent survivor may have trouble keeping all of her debts up to date. This is not surprising since she has just emerged from a difficult crisis that may have changed her life situation. The survivor may find her income reduced or expenses increased so that she cannot always pay all of the household expenses each month. This leaves the survivor with no choice but to delay or not pay some debts.

Once the survivor determines that not all of the household bills can be paid as they come due, she will have to make hard choices about which bills to pay first. Unfortunately survivors and other debtors often pay particular bills because of a harassing debt collector rather than deciding which bills are most important and paying those. The home or apartment, the utility service, the car, and even household possessions may be at risk if survivors fail to prioritize their debts. Following the rules described below may make the difference between keeping and losing important property.

UNSECURED VERSUS SECURED DEBT

The most important principle in setting bill-paying priorities is to understand the concept of "collateral." Collateral is property that a creditor has the right to seize if the survivor does not pay a particular debt. The most common forms of collateral are the family home in the case of a mortgage and the car in the case of most car loans. A creditor may also have collateral in household goods, business property, bank accounts, or even wages. When a creditor has taken collateral for a loan, it has a "lien" on the property.

Creditors who have collateral are usually referred to as "secured" creditors. They may be entitled to take the collateral and sell it to get their money if the debtor fails to pay as agreed. Creditors without collateral are often referred to

EXAMPLES OF UNSECURED VERSUS SECURED DEBTS

The following is a list of common unsecured and secured debts. Remember that secured debts have some type of collateral, such as a house, attached to them.

SECURED DEBTS:
Mortgages
Car loans
Loans secured by household goods

UNSECURED DEBTS:
Credit and charge cards
Legal or medical bills
Loans from friends or relatives
Department store and gasoline cards (unless the card specifically says that it is a "secured credit card")

as "unsecured." It is usually hard for unsecured creditors to collect what they are owed unless a consumer pays voluntarily. The survivor should determine which of her debts are "secured" and which are "unsecured." Survivors should almost always pay secured debts first.

Instead of delaying or eliminating certain debt repayments, survivors may be tempted to take on more debt to repay old debts. This is generally a bad idea. The best strategy in dealing with too much debt is deciding which debts to pay first, which debts the survivor can refuse to pay, and which debts can be put off until later. The most important creditor to pay is not necessarily the creditor that screams the loudest or the most often.

If the survivor is not paying all of her debts, she will probably experience creditor harassment. Chapter Four provides important information on how to deal with and even stop debt-collection harassment. In terms of priority-setting, it is important to remember this axiom: creditors who yell the loudest often do so only because they have no better way to get their money than to intimidate the survivor into paying. Of more concern are creditors who not only threaten but also actually can take quick action against the residence, utility service, car, or other important assets.

Survivors should direct their limited resources to what is most necessary for their families—typically food, clothing, shelter, and utility services. Unfortunately, there is no magic list indicating the order in which debts should be paid. Everyone's situation will be different. Instead, what follows are sixteen rules about how to set priorities. Information about the consequences of not paying certain types of debts is also discussed in *NCLC Guide to Surviving Debt.*

Always Pay Family Necessities First. Usually this means food and unavoidable medical expenses.

Pay Housing-Related Bills Next. The survivor must keep up the mortgage or rent payments for the home where the survivor lives, if at all possible. If she owns or has possession of the family home, real estate taxes and insurance must also be paid unless they are included in the monthly mortgage payment. Similarly, any condo fees, payments toward the purchase of a mobile home, or mobile-home-lot payments should be considered a high priority. Failure to pay these debts can lead to loss of the home. If the survivor previously had a household with the abuser and no longer lives in that home, the mortgage or rent on that home would not be as important as the payments for the home or apartment where the survivor currently lives. To learn more about a survivor's liability under a mortgage or lease with the abuser, see Chapter Six.

Pay the Minimum Required to Keep Essential Utility Service. While full and immediate payment of the entire amount of the bill may not always be necessary, the minimum payment necessary to avoid disconnection should be made if at all possible. Working hard to keep the house or apartment makes little sense if the survivor's family cannot live there because there are no utilities.

Pay Car Loans or Leases Next If the Car Is a Necessity. If the survivor needs the car to get to work or for other essential transportation, the car payment must be the next priority after food, housing costs, unavoidable medical expenses, and utilities. The survivor may even want to pay for the car first if the car is necessary to keep her job. The car insurance must be paid as well. Otherwise the creditor may buy costly insurance for the car at the survivor's expense. And, in most states, it is illegal not to have automobile liability coverage.

Child Support Debts Must Be Paid If the Survivor Owes Them. If the survivor owes child support, she must pay it. If she feels the award of support is unjust, she needs to seek the assistance of a family lawyer. Ignoring child support debts will not make them go away and can result in very serious problems.

Income Tax Debts Are Also High Priority. Survivors must pay any income taxes owed that are not automatically deducted from wages and must file federal income tax returns even if they cannot afford to pay any balance due. The government has many collection rights that other creditors do not have, particularly if the survivor does not file a return.

Loans Without Collateral Are of Low Priority. Most credit card debts, attorney bills, doctor and hospital bills, other debts to professionals, open accounts with merchants, and similar debts are of low priority. Survivors have not pledged any collateral for these loans, and there is rarely anything that these creditors can do to harm survivors in the short term. Many professionals will not bother to try to collect in the long term, either.

Loans with Only Household Goods As Collateral Are Also of Low Priority. Sometimes a creditor requires the survivor to place some household goods as collateral on a loan. This loan can generally be treated in the same way as an unsecured debt—as a low-priority debt. Creditors rarely seize household goods because they have little market value, it is hard to seize them without involving the courts, and it is time-consuming and expensive to use the courts to seize them.

A Debt Should *Not* Be Moved Up in Priority Because the Creditor Threatens Suit. Many threats to sue are not carried out. Even if the creditor does sue, it will take a while for the collector to seize any property, and much of the survivor's property may be exempt from seizure. On the other hand, nonpayment of rent, mortgage, and car debts may result in immediate loss of the home or car.

Do Not Pay When There Are Good Legal Defenses to Repayment. Some examples of legal defenses are that the goods were defective when purchased or that a creditor is asking for more money than it is entitled to. A survivor whose agreement to a loan was coerced or forged may have a viable legal defense. If there is a defense, the survivor should obtain legal advice to determine whether the defense will succeed. In evaluating these options, remember that it is especially dangerous to withhold mortgage or rent payments without legal advice.

Court Judgments Move Up in Priority, But Often Less Than One Would Think. After a collector obtains a court judgment, that debt often should move up in priority because the creditor can enforce that judgment by asking the court to seize certain property, wages, and bank accounts. Nevertheless, how serious a threat this really is will depend on the law in the state where the survivor resides, the value of the survivor's property, and the survivor's income. As discussed in Chapter Five, there are a number of protections for consumers even after a judgment has been obtained. It may be that all of the survivor's property and wages are protected. If so, the survivor should pay off more pressing obligations first and then come back and pay this debt.

Student Loans Are Medium-Priority Debts. They should generally be paid ahead of low-priority debts but after top-priority debts. Most delinquent student loans are backed by the United States. The law provides special collection remedies to the government that are not available to other creditors. These include seizure of tax refunds, special wage garnishment rules, and denial of new student loans and grants. More information is included in Chapter Thirteen.

Debt-Collection Efforts Should *Never* Move Up a Debt's Priority. Survivors should be polite to the collector but make *their* own choices about which debts to pay based on what is best for the family. Debt collectors are unlikely to give good advice. Survivors can easily stop debt-collection contacts and have legal remedies to deal with collection harassment.

Threats to Ruin One's Credit Record Should *Never* Move Up a Debt's Priority. In many cases, when a collector threatens to report a delinquency to the credit bureau, the creditor has already provided the credit bureau with the exact status of the account. And, if the creditor has not reported the delinquency, a collector hired by the creditor is very unlikely to report it.

Co-Signed Debts Should Be Treated Like One's Other Debts. Sometimes a survivor may be a co-signor on a loan with her abuser. The priority of that debt depends primarily on the same factors that are involved if the loan were her own. If the loan is secured by the survivor's home or car, that is a high-priority debt, especially if the abuser is not keeping the debt current. If the survivor has not put up such collateral, or if the abuser has possession of the home or car, she should treat the co-signed debts as a lower priority.

Refinancing Is Rarely the Answer. Survivors should always be careful about refinancing. It can be very expensive and can give creditors more opportunities to seize important assets. A short-term fix can lead to long-term problems.

More detailed information on these topics can be found in *NCLC Guide to Surviving Debt.*

4

Debt Collection Harassment

Abuse survivors trying to get their lives together, particularly those re-entering the work force or trying to rent an apartment or buy a home, often find that past debts continue to cause them problems. If they have prioritized their debts as discussed in Chapter Three, and made difficult choices about which debts to pay first, they have had to let some debts go unpaid. As a result, they may be the target of harassing letters and phone calls from debt collection agencies.

The discussion below contains a brief summary of important debt collection rights. In particular, survivors should be counseled to avoid letting debt collectors pressure them into making the wrong choices about which debts to pay first.

WHAT CAN A DEBT COLLECTOR REALLY DO?

A debt collector can do little more than demand payment. If the creditor has not taken the survivor's house, car, or other property as collateral on a loan, then legally the creditor can only do three things:

1. Stop doing business with the survivor.
2. Report a default to a credit bureau (see Chapter Twelve on credit reports).
3. Sue the survivor in court. This threat may not be as serious as many consumers think. Many creditors do not follow through on their threats. Even if they do, consumers can raise defenses to paying the debt. Even if the creditor obtains a judgment, this judgment still does not force the

survivor to pay the debt. It is simply a court order that she owes the creditor a certain amount. After obtaining a judgment, a creditor may then be entitled to start the process of trying to seize part of her wages or property. During this process, many protections apply (see Chapter Five on dealing with collection lawsuits).

WHAT IS A DEBT COLLECTOR PROHIBITED FROM DOING?

Federal law and the law of many states prohibit harassment by collection agencies. The federal law is the Fair Debt Collection Practices Act (FDCPA) and can be found at 15 U.S.C. § 1692–1692o. Most states also have fair debt collection laws. In many cases, the state laws provide additional protections. For example, the federal law applies only to third-party collectors, but some states have laws that govern creditors collecting their own debts. For more information about fair debt collection laws and other ways to challenge debt collector harassment, see NCLC's manual *Fair Debt Collection* (5th ed. 2004 and Supp.), which also contains an appendix summarizing the state debt collection laws.

Debt collectors are required by law in all circumstances to respect the survivor's privacy and avoid using deceptive, abusive, or harassing collection tactics.

The FDCPA requires collection agencies to take certain actions, including the following:

- The collection agency must stop contacting the survivor if she makes a request in writing or disputes the debt in writing.
- The collection agency, in its initial communication or within five days of that communication, must send the survivor a written notice. That notice must identify the debt and the creditor and must explain the survivor's right to dispute the debt or to request the name and address of the original creditor, if it is different from the current one. If the survivor raises a dispute, the collector must suspend collection efforts on the disputed portion of the debt until the collector responds to the request.
- Any lawsuit by a collector must usually be brought in the same county or other judicial district where the survivor lives or where she signed the contract.

- The FDCPA also prohibits a wide range of harassing and deceptive collection agency behavior, including the following:
  —Communicating with third parties (such as the survivor's relatives, employers, friends, or neighbors) about a debt unless she or a court has given the collector permission to do so. Several narrow exceptions to this prohibition apply. Collectors may contact creditors, attorneys, credit reporting agencies, cosigners, and the survivor's parents (if she is a minor). Third-party contacts are also permitted if the contacts are solely for the purpose of locating the survivor and do not reveal in any way that the contact is regarding an unpaid debt.
  —Communicating with the survivor at unusual or inconvenient times or places. The times 8:00 A.M. to 9:00 P.M. (in the time zone where the survivor lives) are generally considered convenient; but, if the collector knows that a survivor works a night shift, daytime contacts may be inconvenient.
  —Contacting the survivor at work if the collector knows that the employer prohibits personal calls or at other inconvenient places, such as a friend's house or the hospital.
  —Contacting the survivor who is represented by a lawyer, unless the lawyer gives permission for the communication or fails to respond to the collector's communications.
  —Contacting the survivor after she sends a letter asking the collector to cease communications. The collector is allowed to acknowledge the letter and to notify her about actions the collector may take, however.
  —Using obscene, derogatory, or insulting remarks.
  —Publishing the survivor's name.
  —Telephoning repeatedly and frequently.
  —Telephoning without disclosing the collector's identity.
  —Making communications that intimidate, harass, or abuse the survivor, such as a threat to conduct a neighborhood investigation or telling the survivor that she should not have children if she cannot afford them.
  —Making false, misleading, or deceptive representations in collecting debts, such as pretending that letters carry legal authority.
  —Falsely representing the character, amount, or legal status of a debt or of services rendered or compensation owed.

—Falsely stating or implying a lawyer's involvement, such as a form letter written on an attorney's letterhead and bearing an attorney's signature that in fact came from a collection agency and was not reviewed by a lawyer.

—Threatening arrest or loss of child custody or public assistance benefits.

—Stating that nonpayment will result in arrest, garnishment, or seizure of property or wages, unless such actions are lawful and the collector fully intends to take them.

—Threatening to take actions that are illegal or that are not intended. Determining that the action a collection agency threatens to take is illegal is often easier than determining whether it intends to follow through with a threat. To verify a collector's intention to file suit, the survivor could ask the local court clerk to help check the plaintiff's index to see whether the company making the threat has a history of filing similar suits. A lawsuit is less likely if the debt is small (for example, less than $500), if the collector is distant, and/or if survivor's dispute of the debt is strong. Other common threats that the creditor may have no intention of carrying out are that the collector will refer the action to a lawyer, harm the survivor's credit rating, or repossess household goods.

—Using any false representation or other deception to collect or to attempt to collect a debt or to obtain information about the survivor.

—Failing to disclose in communications that the collector is attempting to collect a debt.

—Using unfair or unconscionable means to collect debts.

—Collecting fees or charges unless expressly authorized by the agreement creating the debt and permitted by law.

—Depositing post-dated checks before their date. The collector must also give at least three days', but not more than ten days', notice before depositing the postdated check or using the check for the purpose of threatening or filing criminal charges.

—Threatening self-help repossession without the legal right or present intent to do so.

—Creating the false impression that the collector is an affiliate or agent of the government.

—Using any communication, language, or symbols on envelopes or postcards that indicate that the sender is in the debt-collection business.

HOW TO AVOID HARASSMENT

In general, a survivor being harassed by debt collectors should follow these eight steps:

Head Off Harassment Before It Starts. She should call the creditor and explain her situation. Explain that she has to pay the mortgage or landlord and utilities first and that she will pay her other bills when she can. If she feels comfortable and is willing to discuss the matter, the survivor or advocate should explain that the survivor's financial situation has become difficult because of the abuse, but she will pay what she can when her situation improves. The survivor should not over-promise—it is better to be realistic about prospects for paying. By contacting the creditor first, the survivor may avoid having the debt turned over to a collection agency, which will usually be less flexible than the creditor in working out a payment plan.

Write a Letter Requesting the Collector to Stop Collection Efforts. This is often called a "cease communication" letter. Collection agencies must stop contacting the consumer after receiving this letter, with only a few limited exceptions. The most important exception is that the collector will still be able to sue the survivor. While entities that are collecting their own debts are not required to stop contacting the survivor even after receiving a letter from her, they often will. It is a good idea to include in the letter why the survivor cannot pay right now and what her expectations are for the future, though this is not necessary. She should also note in the letter any billing errors or abusive tactics the debt collector has used in its contacts with her. She should send the letter by certified mail with a return receipt and keep a copy of the letter. A sample letter is included at the end of this chapter.

Have a Lawyer Write a "Cease Communication" Letter. A lawyer is not necessary to write a cease communication letter, but if the letter from the survivor does not stop the harassment, a letter from a lawyer usually will. Also, collection agencies must stop contacting the survivor once they know she is represented by a lawyer and speak only with the lawyer.

Work Out a Payment Plan. Probably the most common strategy to deal with debt harassment, though not always the best, is to work out a deal with the collector. Generally, the survivor should try to figure out a way to make monthly payments to a creditor. Tips for negotiating payment plans are discussed below. Keep in mind that she can negotiate with creditors about other terms as well. For example, the creditor may agree to "re-age" the account, which means that the account is treated as if it is current even though the total amount owed is unchanged. A creditor might also be persuaded to restructure payments or reduce the interest rate on a debt.

Regardless of the type of deal negotiated, the survivor must be careful about offering too much. It is extremely important to prioritize debts. Even a small payment to an unsecured creditor is unwise if this prevents payment of the survivor's mortgage or rent. Better ways to stop debt harassment can be found throughout this chapter.

The survivor must decide if she can offer a lump sum or must offer to make monthly payments. In a lump-sum settlement, the creditor accepts a portion of the amount owed to fully resolve the debt. Often a creditor will accept as little as one-half or even less of the amount owed in return for fully releasing the survivor. A lump sum will often be a better deal, but the survivor may not be able to raise the money. She should be cautioned against making choices, such as applying for payday loans, that may raise some money in the short term but will likely cause more problems not too far down the road.

If the survivor decides instead to negotiate a payment plan, it is critical to be sure that her payments will make a dent in the debt. Especially with credit card debts, a modest monthly payment can easily be eaten up by interest and fees such that the balance owed barely decreases at all. If the creditor will not reduce the interest rate and waive fees so that the survivor's payments make a dent in the debt, a payment plan may not be worthwhile. An exception to this rule might apply if she is desperate to avoid collection efforts that may harm her.

In general, she should be aware that she has some power in negotiating with a collector. Just knowing her rights in this situation can empower her. Credit card companies in particular may be willing to lower or eliminate interest or fees for a period of time simply because the survivor requests a reduction or in exchange for agreeing to a payment plan. Getting an agreement often depends on whether the creditor believes the survivor will honor the agreement. Chances of obtaining a payment plan are likely to decrease considerably if she has set up a plan with this creditor in the past and failed to keep making those payments. When negotiating with a creditor, the survivor should avoid over-promising, be realistic about what she can pay, and offer that amount.

The survivor should always be sure to get any deal in writing. She may also find it useful to negotiate with the creditor for a favorable, or at least neutral, credit report.

Complain About Billing Errors. Collection letters are sometimes in error. If a letters contains a mistake, the survivor should write and request a correction (and keep a copy of the request). If she disputes the debt in writing within thirty days of receiving notice of the right to dispute, the collector must stop collection efforts while it investigates. If the account is an open-end account, like a credit card, she can dispute a charge within sixty days of receiving the bill.

Complain to a Government Agency. Another strategy is for the survivor to write to government agencies—such as the Federal Trade Commission or the attorney general's office in the state where the survivor lives—that are responsible for enforcing laws that prohibit debt collection abuse. A government agency is not likely to investigate immediately unless it has other complaints against the same collector. Even so, she should send a copy of the letter to the collector, as this often produces good results.

Letters of complaint may be sent to the Federal Trade Commission's Consumer Response Center at Federal Trade Commission, CRC-240, Washington, D.C. 20580. The survivor can also call the Commission toll-free at 1-877-FTC-HELP (382-4357) or file a complaint on-line at www.ftc.gov. Copies of the letter should also be sent to the consumer protection division within the state attorney general's office (usually in the state capitol) and to any local office of consumer protection listed in the local telephone book or on the Internet. The survivor can get these addresses from a local better business bureau or office of consumer affairs.

File Bankruptcy. If the survivor files for bankruptcy, the "automatic stay" is instantly triggered in most cases. This is a very powerful tool because it will stop all collection activity against her from collectors, creditors, or even government officials. No further collection activity can proceed unless a particular collector obtains permission from the bankruptcy court. The bankruptcy court will not grant this permission to most collectors seeking unsecured debts. For this reason, filing for bankruptcy can be a very effective means of stopping debt harassment. If the survivor has filed other bankruptcy cases that were dismissed within the previous twelve months, however, she may not get an automatic stay or it may only last for the first thirty days of the bankruptcy case.

Nevertheless, as a general rule, a bankruptcy filing is not the survivor's best strategy when the only concern is debt harassment. Harassment can usually be stopped without having to resort to bankruptcy. In fact, be wary of any attorney offering to file bankruptcy when the only problem is debt harassment. See Chapter Eight for more information about bankruptcy.

Sue the Debt Collector If Appropriate. The federal Fair Debt Collection Practices Act allows consumers to sue debt collectors who violate the Act's provisions. Statutory damages up to $1000, actual damages, costs, and attorney fees are available to individuals who bring successful actions. The survivor should consult an attorney to discuss such litigation.

ADDITIONAL HELP IN DEALING WITH CREDITORS

If an abuser is being prosecuted criminally, an additional resource may be available. In some states, the survivor may have a victim witness advocate assigned to her case by the prosecutor's office. In many states, the role of the victim witness advocates includes offering "creditor intercession" services. This means that the victim witness advocate will contact creditors on behalf of a crime victim to explain that the victim cannot pay her bills immediately because of a crime. Sometimes having a victim witness advocate from the prosecutor's office call a creditor may be more effective than if the survivor herself calls the creditor.

SAMPLE LETTER

[date]

[name of collection agency]

[address]

Name
Account Number

Dear Agency:

I am writing to request that you stop contacting me about account number __________ with [name of creditor] as required by the Fair Debt Collection Practices Act 15 U.S.C. section 1692c(c).

[*Author's Note:* Delete reference to the Act when the letter is to a creditor instead of to a collection agency. Document any harassing contact by the collection agency. In some cases, provide information about why consumer cannot pay bill or, if appropriate, does not owe the money.]

This letter is not meant in any way to be an acknowledgment that I owe this money. I will take care of this matter when I can. Your cooperation will be appreciated.

5

Dealing with Collection Lawsuits

If the survivor has determined that she cannot pay all her debts, she may be concerned that her creditors will sue her. Threats by a creditor or collection agency to sue on a debt can be very frightening. However, most threats of lawsuits are just that—threats. Threats should not lead the survivor to make special efforts to pay a debt.

This chapter discusses how, even if a survivor is sued, she may have defenses which, if she asserts them, will reduce or even eliminate the debt. This chapter also discusses how the survivor should know when she may be "judgment-proof." Judgment-proof is a term used to describe a debtor whose income and assets cannot be taken by the creditor even if the creditor wins a judgment. Information about protections for income and assets is discussed in the second part of this chapter. The chapter concludes with a discussion of the creditor's right to question a debtor at a "debtor's examination."

HOW TO RESPOND TO A LAWSUIT BY A CREDITOR OR COLLECTOR

The following is basic advice for responding to a collection lawsuit. Responding to a collection lawsuit is especially important if the survivor has a good reason why she has not paid the creditor. Creditors do not expect consumers to put up a fight in collection lawsuits, and a survivor can improve her outcome simply by responding to the lawsuit. More detailed information about how to fight back in a collection lawsuit is available in *NCLC Guide to Surviving Debt.*

The survivor should always pick up her certified mail and accept notices about court actions. She will not escape the consequences of a lawsuit by hiding from notices about that action. This includes notices of arbitration. The consequences of arbitration can be just as serious as those of a court action. More information on arbitration is provided later in this chapter.

The survivor should get professional legal advice if she thinks she does not owe the money or if she may have a defense. In many cases, a lawyer can take steps that will significantly improve the outcome for the survivor. Court procedures can be confusing and technical, especially in courts other than small claims courts, so a survivor without an attorney may make mistakes that will prevent the court from giving full consideration to her defenses. If the survivor cannot afford an attorney, she may be eligible for assistance from Legal Aid. Information about Legal Aid programs may be found in Appendix A at the back of this guidebook.

The survivor should carefully read all court documents. The creditor must file at least one document with the court in order to start a lawsuit. The first document is usually called a "complaint" or "petition" and asks the court to enter an order or judgment that the survivor owes the creditor a certain amount of money. In more formal courts, there is a second document, which is often called a "summons" or "original notice." The summons informs the survivor that a lawsuit has been filed against her. In some states, in small claims court, the two documents are combined into one form. The complaint and summons may be delivered personally or by certified mail, depending on the court. The survivor should not hide from a court summons. She should always read it carefully, follow the instructions, meet all deadlines, and attend all hearings. The summons usually tells the survivor the proper steps to take to respond to the lawsuit. She should be especially careful to meet any deadlines.

➡ **Pointer:** If the documents filed by the creditor reveal the survivor's address, she may want to go to the court immediately to request that her identifying information be sealed. She should take a copy of her protective order with her if she has one.

The survivor should answer the summons if required. If the survivor fails to respond to a lawsuit, often the creditor will be entitled to a judgment without any hearing on the merits of the case. When the creditor obtains a judgment because the survivor failed to respond, it is usually called a "default" judgment. To avoid a default judgment, the survivor *must* follow any instructions to appear at hearings or file written responses. In more formal courts, a summons will instruct a defendant to file a written "answer" (sometimes called an "appearance") within a certain number of days. In small claims courts, it is usually unnecessary to file a written response or answer, but a written response may be required if the survivor wants to raise certain types of defenses or counterclaims.

The survivor should submit defenses and counterclaims to the court. By presenting a defense, a counterclaim, or both, the survivor can tell the court why the creditor should not collect on a debt. A defense is a reason why a consumer does not owe the creditor anything or owes less than the creditor claims. A counterclaim is a claim that the creditor owes money to the consumer, regardless of whether the consumer owes the creditor on the debt. It is often very effective to raise defenses and counterclaims in debt collection lawsuits, particularly if the amount at stake is small. Creditors know that the vast majority of consumers who are sued never file answers and count on winning by default. *The creditor is counting on the survivor to give up; creditors often drop lawsuits if the consumer puts up a fight.*

The survivor should attend all court proceedings and respond to all papers she receives. If a hearing is scheduled and the survivor does not show up, a default judgment may be entered against her even if she filed an answer or appearance earlier. If she cannot attend, she should ask the creditor or the creditor's attorney to agree to a postponement of the hearing (usually called a "continuance"). If they agree, she should inform the court—well before the hearing date—and ask the court to reschedule the hearing. If they do not agree, she should ask the court in writing for a postponement and explain the reasons why she cannot attend the hearing that day. Then, before the hearing date, she should check with the court to find out if the hearing has been postponed. If the court refuses to postpone the hearing, she may want to send someone else to the hearing to explain again why she cannot be there and repeat the request for a postponement.

Any settlement should be clearly documented. If the survivor reaches a payment plan or other settlement with the creditor, it should be in writing. An agreement about what will happen to the lawsuit should be negotiated as part of the settlement and included in the written document. If the creditor agrees to dismiss the lawsuit, check with the court to make sure it has been dismissed. This should be done before the hearing date or the deadline for filing a written response. If the creditor does not follow through on dismissing the lawsuit, the survivor should resume fighting the case by showing up at any hearings or filing and written responses that are required. If a settlement is worked out with a creditor, it is helpful for the survivor to have an attorney who can make sure it is properly documented. In some cases, it is a good idea to file a copy of the written agreement with the court clerk to be entered into the court record.

CAN A CREDITOR WHO WINS A COLLECTION LAWSUIT TAKE MONEY OR PROPERTY FROM THE SURVIVOR?

Even if a creditor does obtain a court judgment against a survivor, there are a number of protections for the survivor. A judgment is simply a court order that states that the survivor owes a certain amount of money. If the survivor is in a difficult financial situation, the judgment may have no real practical effect.

The court order does let creditors use several special collection tools to try to squeeze money from the survivor. The most commonly used methods involve seizing and selling personal property or real estate belonging to the survivor or taking money out of the survivor's wages, benefits, or bank accounts. However, in every state there are "exemption" laws that protect a certain amount of this property from seizure.

Whether the creditor can take anything from the survivor will depend not only on how much income and property the survivor has but also on the *types* of income and property she has. In some cases, these collection tools are effective in recovering money and may even result in loss of the survivor's home. In other cases, these special tools will have *no* impact on the survivor. Even a court order cannot make the survivor pay a debt if all the survivor's income and property are exempt from seizure.

When a judgment cannot be enforced against the survivor, the survivor is called "judgment proof" or "collection proof." This means that the survivor's assets and income are small enough that they are protected by federal and state "exemption" laws from seizure by creditors. In that case, the survivor does not really have to worry about the judgment unless her financial situation substantially improves. If the survivor's financial situation improves, the creditor may still be able to collect money from the survivor in the future. Even if her income stays the same, she may no longer be judgment proof if she acquires more property, her property increases in value, or she pays down a lien on property such as a home or a car.

If the survivor is faced with a collection lawsuit, she should determine in advance whether she is judgment proof. If the survivor can be harmed by a judgment, there is even more incentive to defend against the lawsuit.

If a survivor is notified that a creditor is attempting to take specific property of hers or attach her wages, it is important to get help from a lawyer if possible. Even if the survivor believes she is judgment proof, it may be necessary to file papers in court or attend hearings to protect the assets. If there is a real threat of losing important assets, the survivor may want to evaluate whether bankruptcy can help. (See Chapter Eight for a discussion of the basics of bankruptcy law.)

The types of property, wages, benefits, and other income that are protected from seizure are discussed in the next part of this chapter.

PROTECTING THE SURVIVOR'S PERSONAL PROPERTY

How Seizure of Personal Property Works and How to Fight It. A creditor with a court judgment can arrange for a court official such as a sheriff to seize certain items of the survivor's personal property. The sheriff can seize the survivor's personal property even though the creditor had not taken that property as collateral for its loan. A common term for this is "attachment and execution."

This creditor right is sharply limited by federal and state exemption law, as discussed in later in this chapter. In some states, the survivor will need to file papers with the sheriff or a public official by a certain deadline in order to get the benefit of an exemption. In other states, the sheriff gives the survivor permission to set aside exempt items at the time of seizure or sale.

Additionally, the sheriff cannot seize property in the survivor's possession that does not belong to the survivor. To stop its seizure, the property's rightful owner may have to file a declaration of ownership with the appropriate office.

If the sheriff is able to seize the survivor's property, it will then be sold at public auction, with the proceeds going to the creditor to help pay off the judgment. These auctions are usually poorly attended and bring low bids. For this reason, creditors rarely seize used household goods, which will have minimal resale value. If property is sold at auction, the survivor or the survivor's friends can attend the auction and re-purchase the possessions at a bargain price.

After a sale, the creditor may seek the remainder due on the debt if the sale price is less than the amount the survivor owed.

State Exemption Laws. State exemption laws protect certain types of personal property from seizure after a court judgment and permit the survivor to keep the basic necessities of life. However, exemption statutes do not prevent a creditor from seizing property that the survivor put up as collateral for the debt. For example, if the survivor agreed to put up a home or car as collateral on a loan, exemption laws do not prevent the creditor from seizing the home or car if she gets behind in her loan payments.

Some exemption statutes specify dollar amounts of personal property that are exempt from seizure. For example, the statute may specify that $8000 worth of the survivor's personal property is exempt. This would allow her to choose which items of personal property she wants to keep, as long as what the survivor keeps is worth $8000 or less.

Some states list certain types of personal property that are totally exempt from seizure, no matter how much money they are worth. A list of totally exempt property typically includes items such as tools and supplies required for the survivor's occupation, clothing, a car (usually with a value under a specified amount), a bible, and household goods.

If the survivor files for bankruptcy in some states, the amount of property exempted from seizure may increase because she can choose federal bankruptcy exemptions rather than state exemptions. The federal bankruptcy exemptions may or may not be better than her state's exemptions. But some states have "opted out" of the federal exemptions, meaning that even in a bankruptcy, the federal exemptions are not available and the survivor must rely on her state exemptions.

The protections created by state exemption laws cannot be waived in the contract that the survivor signs with the creditor. Nonetheless, some creditors may try to force her to turn over property that the law exempts from seizure. The creditor will point to small print in the contract that says she agreed to waive rights under state exemption laws. Do not give in to these aggressive creditors.

State exemption laws can be very complicated. The survivor may want to get professional legal advice to understand the exemption laws available in her state. At a minimum, she should try to find a publication that explains her state's laws. This type of publication may be available from the local bar association, a legal services office, or a nonprofit consumer credit counselor. A summary of the most important features of each state's exemption laws is included as Appendix E at the back of this guidebook, but these laws are amended often and the survivor should use this appendix only to get a sense of the general range of exemptions in her state.

PROTECTING THE SURVIVOR'S HOME FROM SALE TO PAY A COURT JUDGMENT

How Judgment Liens Work. Any unpaid judgment generally becomes a lien on any real estate the survivor owns in the county where the judgment is entered (or statewide in some states). Creditors also may have the right to transfer judgments so that they cover the survivor's real estate in other locations.

Unless the real estate is legally exempt from execution, as discussed below, creditors can force its sale in much the same way as they can force the sale of other property. Even if the real estate is exempt from execution, the creditor's lien on the survivor's property usually remains in effect until the survivor sells it.

In most states, when the survivor sells the property, mortgages are paid off first. Then the survivor gets to keep what is left, up to the maximum exemption amount in the state where she resides. Anything over that amount goes to satisfy all or some of the creditor's judgment against the survivor. Even if the survivor's property is exempt from seizure today, if the property's value increases enough in the future, it may no longer be exempt from seizure.

One possible way of getting rid of judgment liens is to file for bankruptcy. To the extent the property is exempt when the survivor files for bankruptcy, the lien can be permanently removed. Bankruptcy is discussed in Chapter Eight.

Homestead Exemptions. Homestead exemptions can protect the survivor's residence and can be as high as $100,000 or more in some states but also significantly less in others. Under some states' laws, property that is jointly owned by husband and wife is entitled to special protection from the debts of one spouse or the other (but not from joint debts). Joint owners, whether married or not, usually may each obtain a separate exemption that covers their share of the property and doubles the amount of protection.

To benefit from the homestead exemption in some states, a declaration of the homestead must be filed with the property registry in the survivor's community. In a few states, this paper must be filed before the credit is granted. The survivor should always file this declaration as early as possible if she lives in a state where a declaration is required. In other states, protection is automatic.

Most state homestead exemptions allow the survivor to exempt only a certain dollar amount of the equity in her home. However, a relatively small exemption amount may be enough to protect property worth a lot more.

Example One:
The survivor lives in a state with a homestead exemption of $30,000. Her home is worth $150,000. She has a first mortgage of $100,000 and a $20,000 home equity loan. The total liens on her property = $120,000. Equity equals the value of the home minus the liens. In this case, $150,000 – $120,000 = $30,000 in equity.

In this example, since the homestead exemption is $30,000, the survivor's home is fully protected from execution by a judgment creditor. She does not have to worry that a creditor can force a sale of her home.

Example Two:
If the survivor's home increases in value to $200,000, her equity also increases. The new amount of equity would be $200,000 – $120,000 = $80,000. The homestead exemption of $30,000 no longer protects all of the survivor's equity.

The creditor in example two could force a sale. The first $100,000 from the sale would go to the mortgage holder. The next $20,000 would pay off the home equity loan. The survivor would get to keep $30,000, the amount of the homestead exemption. This leaves $50,000 of the sale proceeds available to pay off the creditor that initiated the sale. If the creditor is owed less than $50,000, the survivor will get any balance left.

A creditor can force a sale in example two but will not necessarily do so. Forcing a sale is expensive. The creditor may instead wait to collect on the lien until the survivor sells the property.

PROTECTING THE SURVIVOR'S WAGES, BENEFITS, AND BANK ACCOUNTS FROM GARNISHMENT

How Garnishment Works. "Garnishment" usually refers to taking wages, benefits, bank accounts, or other property that belong to the debtor but are in the hands of a third party such as an employer, a government agency, or a bank. A creditor with a court judgment against the survivor may have the right to garnish money belonging or owed to her that is in the hands of a third party. Most often, garnishment will take money from her wages or bank account.

Garnishment can only take place *after* the creditor obtains a judgment against the survivor. (One exception is the collection of student loans and other debts owed to the government, in which garnishment is allowed without a judgment but only after a notice and hearing process. For more information on student loans see Chapter Thirteen.)

After obtaining a judgment, the creditor can file a request for garnishment with the court clerk, sheriff, or another local official depending on state practice. A notice is then issued to the "garnishee" (a bank, an employer, or another third party holding the survivor's money or property), directing that party to turn over the property at a specified time.

The survivor must be given notice of the garnishment. She can then request a hearing to prove that state or federal law protects her money from garnishment.

A Portion of the Survivor's Wages Is Protected from Garnishment. Current federal law provides that the first $154.50 of weekly take-home pay, after taxes and Social Security are deducted, cannot be garnished at all. This $154.50 is based on a formula that is linked to the minimum wage. If the minimum wage goes up, the amount of wages protected from garnishment also goes up.

If the debtor's weekly take-home pay is more than $154.50, an employer, in response to a garnishment order, must pay the *smaller* of the following amounts to a sheriff:

- The weekly take-home pay (after deductions) minus $154.50; or
- 25% of that take-home pay.

For example, if the survivor's weekly income after deductions are taken out is $200, her employer would be required to calculate the amount due under the two formulas:

(1) ($200 – 154.50 = $45.50) or

(2) (25% of $200 = $50) and pay the creditor the smaller amount.

In this case, the survivor's employer would pay the creditor $45.50 from the survivor's take-home pay. A higher amount can be garnished if the debt is for child support or alimony.

The standard described above is based on federal law and sets out minimum wage protections for debtors in all fifty states. In some states, the survivor has even greater protections against wage garnishment. Some states prohibit all wage garnishment or allow a smaller amount of wages to be garnished than the federal standard.

Federal law forbids employers from firing employees solely because their wages are being garnished for a single debt. Some states have similar laws.

Certain Types of Income, Primarily Government Payments, Are Completely Exempt from Garnishment. Certain sources of income are *completely* protected under federal or state law. For example, federal law exempts Social Security payments, Supplemental Security Income, and veterans' benefits in almost all circumstances. States with TANF (Temporary Assistance for Needy Families) and unemployment insurance programs usually exempt those benefits from garnishment as well.

In most cases, these funds are exempt from seizure even if the survivor keeps them in a bank account. However, problems sometimes arise when her bank account contains both exempt and nonexempt money because it is hard to trace which portion of the funds is exempt.

In many cases, creditors will improperly seize money, such as Social Security payments, which should be exempt. The survivor will then need to fight back and show that the seizure was illegal and that those funds were protected. In some states, she may receive a form describing how to claim that the funds are exempt. If so, she should act immediately and follow the steps explained in the form. If she does not receive any forms to claim this property as exempt, or if she is unclear about the steps she should take, she should seek legal advice as soon as possible. If she is threatened with a court judgment, she must weigh the benefits of opening or keeping a bank account against the risk of having the money seized.

More information on garnishments and available defenses is contained Chapter Nine of National Consumer Law Center's *Fair Debt Collection* (5th ed. 2004 and Supp.). This book also provides information about situations in which the bank is trying to take money from the survivor's bank account to pay a debt owed to the bank. This is called a bank's right of "set-off" and there are special rules that apply.

Social Security Offsets. A 1996 law takes away some of the protection for Social Security benefits, but only when federal agencies are collecting debts owed to them. Examples include money owed to the Department of Education for student loans and money owed to the Department of Agriculture for food stamp overpayments. Certain amounts of other federal benefits may also be taken under this law, including certain Railroad Retirement Benefits and Black Lung benefits. Supplemental Security Income (SSI) cannot be taken under this law.

Even if the survivor's Social Security payments may be taken through this program, she does not have to worry that the government will take her entire check. The government cannot touch the first $750 of the survivor's per-month benefits payment ($9000 over the course of a year). In addition, no matter how much money the survivor gets, the government cannot take more than 15% of the total benefit.

The survivor is supposed to get a number of notices warning that her benefits are going to be taken. These notices give the survivor information about her right to request a hearing with the agency that is collecting the money. She should especially consider this strategy if she thinks she has defenses to repayment or if she is facing financial hardship that may make her eligible for a reduction in the amount of the offset.

The IRS can also take Social Security benefits to collect tax debts. The rules are different for this program. Not all of the same protections apply. The survivor should contact a tax professional for more information.

DEBTOR'S EXAMINATIONS

After obtaining a judgment, another step a creditor can take is to ask a judge to order the survivor to appear in court to answer questions about her income and assets. The purpose is to find income or property that is not protected by law and which the creditor may seize.

In some states this procedure is called a debtor's examination, but the procedure goes by other names in other states. Some creditors routinely request a debtor's examination. Others never do. There are two important things to remember about a debtor's examination:

- *It is a court-ordered appearance.* Failure to show up can result in arrest (often called a body attachment, bench warrant, or writ of *capias*), citation for contempt, and a jail sentence. A notice to appear for a debtor's examination should *never* be ignored. The survivor should always appear or make a written request to the court for a postponement. The court will usually grant a postponement if the creditor agrees to the request or if the survivor has a good reason. Before deciding that it is safe not to attend the examination, the survivor should check with the court to find out if the request for a postponement has been granted.
- *The survivor's answers are made under oath and often are recorded by a court reporter.* Lying under oath is perjury, a crime punishable with a jail sentence.

If a survivor receives a notice of a debtor's examination she should consult with an attorney if possible. Their first step in responding to the notice should be to review her assets *well before the examination.* It is important to determine if all of her property is protected by law and if all her income is exempt from garnishment. If so, it may be useful to tell the creditor. This may be sufficient to get the creditor to drop the request for an examination since it will just be a waste of everyone's time. If the examination is canceled, be sure to get this in writing. Do not rely on the creditor's oral promise that it will drop the examination.

If there is property important to the survivor that a creditor can seize, she can approach the creditor about a "workout" agreement. She can offer to pay all or a portion of the amount due over a period of months or even years. The amount she offers to pay should be directly related to what the creditor could seize after the debtor's examination. Do not offer to pay $3000 over twelve months when the only items the creditor could seize have a market value of $500.

If the survivor negotiates a workout agreement, she should always get it in writing. The written agreement should excuse her from attending the debtor's examination if it has not already been held and should contain the creditor's promise not to use wage garnishment or execution on her property as long as she continues to make payments. She can also ask for an agreement to waive the remainder of the debt if a part of it is paid. Some creditors will accept partial payment if they know they cannot get payment in full. From the creditor's perspective, some payment is better than none.

6

Joint Debts and Bank Accounts

Understanding jointly incurred debts is important for survivors who were married or who shared a household or expenses with their abuser. Survivors also need to know if they have any liability for the abuser's individual debts. Division of *joint property*, including joint bank accounts, is discussed briefly at the end of this chapter but is best handled in consultation with a family law attorney.

The first step for the survivor is to determine what kinds of debts she has incurred. She may have to check her files or call her creditors. She needs to determine whether the debts are

- individual debts,
- authorized user accounts, or
- joint debts.

See Chapter Seven for advice about accounts for utility service.

INDIVIDUAL DEBTS

Different states treat individual debts incurred by spouses in different ways. In non-community property states, a spouse is usually not liable for the individual debts of the other spouse. In these states, creditors have no claim to a spouse's separate property or separate interest in joint property for individual debts of the other spouse. In states with community property laws, spouses may be liable for the debts incurred by their spouse depending on when the debt was incurred. (States with community property laws, at least in part, are Arizona,

California, Idaho, Louisiana, Nevada, New Mexico, Texas, Washington, and Wisconsin.) Some states look to the date of separation or the date of divorce to decide what debts are owed by both spouses.

It is important for the survivor to determine her liability under the laws of her state. State laws regarding liability for spouses can be very complicated. The survivor may need an attorney's advice to understand the laws in her state. At a minimum, the survivor should try to find a publication that explains her state's laws. This type of publication may be available from the local bar association or a legal services office. Make sure any source the survivor relies on is up-to-date.

In some states, a "family expense" or "necessaries" law makes spouses liable for debts incurred for "necessaries," such as food, shelter, and medical bills. This means for example that, if the abuser incurs a hospital bill, the hospital could try to seek payment from the survivor. However, in some states the survivor may have a defense if she was separated from the abuser when he incurred the debts for necessaries. In some states the survivor can claim this defense only if the provider of the necessary item or service was aware or had access to information that the parties were separated.

If a creditor or debt collector attempts to collect on the abuser's debt from the survivor and the necessaries law does not apply, the survivor should be advised not to pay it. The survivor should point out that the creditor or collector may be in violation of state and federal fair debt collection and consumer protection laws. See Chapter Five for advice if the creditor sues the survivor.

AUTHORIZED USER ACCOUNTS

In some cases, one person will open an individual account, such as a credit card account, and will allow another person to use the account. This is called an "authorized user" account. The person who is the account holder will be fully liable for any charges incurred by the authorized user.

Survivors should immediately remove the abuser from any of her credit card accounts on which he is an "authorized user" by calling the credit card company and then following up in writing. Otherwise, the abuser can run up charges on that card and the survivor will be liable for payment. However, before removing the abuser, the survivor should consider any risk that the abuser could become angry and retaliate. The decision to remove the abuser as an authorized user should always be up to the survivor. If the survivor decides to remove the abuser as an authorized user, she and her advocate should then decide on a plan to help protect the survivor should the abuser attempt to retaliate.

If the abuser is the account holder and the survivor is the authorized user, the survivor should consider taking herself off the account. While the survivor probably is not liable for the abuser's charges as an authorized user, the credit history of the account will be reflected on her credit record as long as she is listed on the account. Thus, any post-separation credit problems that the abuser has will show up on her credit report until she removes herself from the account. In addition, keeping the card and continuing to use it may anger the abuser and create a risk of further violence. On the other hand, the survivor may need the credit card to cover expenses as she is separating from the abuser. If she decides to take herself off the account, she should call the credit card company and then follow up in writing. She should keep a copy of this letter. She should also cut up any cards that she possesses and send them with her letter.

JOINT DEBTS

Joint debts are any debts that were incurred together by both the abuser and the survivor. A debt that was incurred by the abuser, but co-signed or guaranteed by the survivor, should also be treated as a joint debt. Survivors are fully liable on joint debts. *This is true even if a divorce agreement or judgment provides that the abuser is responsible for paying the debt, because the creditor is not bound by the agreement or judgment.* The survivor can write to the creditor to ask the creditor to release her from liability based upon the divorce agreement or judgment. However, the creditor need not agree to do so, in which case the survivor is still legally responsible for the debt. To prevent herself from being liable for even more debt, the survivor should close any joint credit accounts that are still open, for example, credit cards. This topic is discussed in more detail below.

Sometimes a survivor will have signed a joint loan under duress from the abuser. Abusers have even been known to forge a survivor's signature on loan documents. If a survivor has any claims of forgery or duress, she should not pay the debt but should raise her defenses whenever she has an opportunity.

For example:

- If the survivor is contacted by a debt collector, she should raise any forgery or duress claims with the debt collector. She should do so in writing and within thirty days of being contacted by the debt collector, because federal law provides her with certain protections if she does. If a collector ignores the claims, it may be violating debt collection or consumer law.
- If the joint debt goes into default and shows up on her credit report, she should raise the forgery or duress claims in a written dispute to the credit bureau (see Chapter Twelve). The credit bureau will be required to investigate the dispute with the creditor. If the creditor fails to cooperate in the investigation, it may be liable under the federal law governing credit reports.
- If the survivor is sued over the joint debt, she should raise the claims of forgery or duress as defenses to the lawsuit.

The survivor should consult an attorney under each of the above circumstances.

If there are no special defenses or claims, the survivor should treat joint debts the same as individual debts and apply the sixteen rules of debt prioritization discussed in Chapter Three.

If the abuser declares bankruptcy, other problems may arise. The survivor may be left solely responsible for joint debts. The abuser's bankruptcy filing may also show up on the survivor's credit history. For tips on how to deal with a negative credit history and begin rebuilding a good one, see the tips in Chapter Twelve.

The following are some helpful suggestions about certain types of joint debts.

Unsecured Joint Debts. Any unsecured debts should be considered a low priority. Also to be considered a low priority should be any debts that are secured by property in the possession of the abuser. This includes debts secured by the abuser's car or a house retained by the abuser unless the survivor wants to regain possession of that collateral. The survivor can ask the creditor to release her from liability because the collateral is no longer in her possession. However, the creditor may not agree to do so, in which case the debt should be considered a low priority.

The survivor should be advised against refinancing or consolidating any joint debts, especially by taking out a loan secured by a home or car. Refinancing is rarely helpful and adds extra costs to the debt. Also, the survivor may end up solely liable for what was formerly a joint debt; in essence, she will be letting her abuser off the hook for this debt.

Joint Open Lines of Credit. Sometimes, a survivor and an abuser will have a joint open line of credit. Examples of open lines of credit are credit card accounts and home equity lines of credit. The survivor should close any joint open lines of credit immediately by calling the creditor and then following up in writing. Again, before closing the account, the survivor should consider any risk that the abuser could retaliate and should plan accordingly.

To close an account, the survivor should send a letter to the creditor and, if it is a credit card account, shred the credit card and send the pieces back to the credit card company. The survivor will still be liable for any amounts still owed on the account that are not paid back, but at least the abuser cannot charge any more to the account.

It is especially important to close any home equity lines of credit if the survivor and her family are in the home. Otherwise, the abuser might be able to borrow money against the home, putting the survivor at risk of losing the home. If there already is debt secured by the home, and the survivor is having problems keeping current with payments, she should follow the advice found later in this chapter.

Home-Secured Loans. A special category of joint debts is mortgages or loans secured by the family home. If a survivor owns her home or has possession of a jointly-owned home, it is critical to make sure she can stay in the home whenever possible. If the abuser is responsible for paying off the loan, the first line of defense is to force him to make payments. The survivor will need the assistance of a family law attorney to do this. Before deciding on a course of action, the survivor should consider the risk of retaliation by the abuser.

If foreclosure is a potential problem, here are some steps that advocates can recommend. More detailed information about dealing with foreclosures is provided in NCLC's book *NCLC Guide to Surviving Debt*:

- *Get Legal Assistance.* If her home is in jeopardy, it is critical that the survivor seek legal assistance quickly. The survivor may be unaware of legal defenses that she has. Too often, homeowners postpone consulting a lawyer until after the time to assert their legal rights has passed.
- *Keep Current on Home Payments.* As discussed in Chapter Three on prioritizing debt, the survivor should not pay credit card debts, doctor bills, or other low-priority debts ahead of home mortgage payments. Sometimes the default can be cured by simply paying the amount in arrears.

- *Negotiate a Temporary Delay in Payments.* One of the most important strategies for homeowners in financial trouble is to work out with the lender a temporary delay in payments or a period of reduced payments. A lender may be willing to let the survivor skip a payment, extend the grace period for making late payments, or accept reduced payments for a short period of time. The survivor may want to seek the assistance of a housing counselor certified by the Department of Housing and Urban Development. Contact information for the HUD housing counseling program is included in Appendix A at the back of this guidebook.
- *Negotiate a Permanent Loan Restructuring.* Although a temporary forbearance is easier to negotiate, for some survivors the financial problem is longer in term. Some lenders realize that permanently receiving less interest may be a better solution than foreclosing on the home. A few homeowners report success in getting their lenders to lower their interest rates for a temporary period or even permanently. Other homeowners have been able to negotiate long repayment periods for delinquent amounts. If the home is jointly owned with the abuser or the abuser is a co-debtor, the abuser's consent or a court order will normally be required for restructuring.
- *Sell the House Herself.* When foreclosure is threatened, a survivor may wish to list the home for sale. Selling the house may be painful, but it is always a better solution than letting a bank sell the house. The survivor may even want to consider this before foreclosure if she cannot afford to stay in the home. If the abuser is still part owner of the house, he must be notified of the intention to sell and in most circumstances the abuser must agree to the sale. The survivor must give careful consideration as to how this notification is made. Since contact with the abuser can often escalate the violence, the survivor and her advocate must determine the safest means of communication with the abuser as well as the best way to proceed legally.
- *Consider Filing for Bankruptcy.* Homeowners who are about to lose their homes should carefully consider filing a petition in bankruptcy. See Chapter Eight on bankruptcy for more information. Bankruptcy can stop the foreclosure process and allow the survivor time to regroup and try to work out a plan to keep the home. Bankruptcy may also help the survivor cure past defaults and make future payments. However, the bankruptcy option is complicated, and it is a good idea

to seek professional assistance from an attorney specializing in bankruptcy.

JOINT BANK ACCOUNTS

If the survivor has a joint bank account with the abuser, the usual rule is that either party can withdraw any or all of the money from the account. (The customer agreement that the account holders sign with the bank can set different rules, however.) If the survivor needs the money in the account, she should consider withdrawing it or withdrawing the portion that she reasonably considers to be hers. Otherwise, the abuser may withdraw all the money. Even if a court later rules that the money belonged to the survivor, it will be hard to retrieve that money if the abuser has already spent it.

In the alternative, the survivor may want to remove the abuser's name from the account so that he no longer has access to it. Or the abuser may attempt to take the same step. Whether one party can unilaterally remove the other's name from the account depends on the terms of the agreement with the bank. Even if the agreement does not allow this, however, virtually the same thing can be accomplished by withdrawing all the funds in the account and depositing them into a new account.

If the survivor closes a joint bank account, she should make sure to redirect all automatic deposits—paychecks, government benefits, dividend checks, and the like—so that they are no longer sent to the closed account. Even if she does not close that account but opens a new one in her name, she should redirect her automatic deposits so that they go into her new account. In addition, she may need to give new instructions for automatic withdrawals for bills such as mortgage payments and utility bills.

Before withdrawing money from an account or removing the abuser's name from it, the survivor should consider whether this will place her at risk of further abuse. The survivor may want to consider withdrawing only the portion of the funds that the abuser would agree is hers. Another alternative is to withdraw all or most of the money but hold it in another account for safekeeping so that the abuser knows that it will not disappear.

It is best for the survivor to consult a family law attorney in her state before withdrawing funds from a joint bank account. A court may ultimately issue a ruling about who is entitled to the money in the account, and it is important that the survivor be prepared to comply with whatever the court orders.

7

Utility Assistance

Utility service is crucial for survivors. Everyone needs electricity, heat, and water. A survivor at risk may especially need telephone service. Yet utility services can be very expensive, and utility providers have powerful methods to force customers to pay their bills. They can deny new service or terminate existing services to force payment of old bills.

This chapter provides advice on how to obtain and keep utility service. When going over the strategies suggested, it may be useful for the survivor to find out what entity, if any, regulates the utility she is dealing with. Many states closely regulate certain utilities such as privately-owned electric, natural gas, and local telephone service. States rarely regulate municipal utilities and cooperatives.

Typically states have utility commissions or departments that are responsible for regulating utilities. Often commissions will have a consumer division as well as divisions for electricity, natural gas, telephones and water. Even though utilities are being increasingly deregulated, most states still regulate utility providers who provide service to residential consumers. It is often helpful for the survivor to speak with the consumer division of the state utility commission about what rights she has and any assistance the agency can provide.

➡ **Pointer:** You can find your state utility commission's website through the National Association of Regulatory Utility Commissioners at www.naruc.org or in the Blue Pages of the phone book (which cover government listings).

GETTING ACCESS TO UTILITIES

Utilities are crucial to a survivor who leaves an abuser and needs to set up a new household. The survivor cannot make the transition to a new home without utilities. Yet sometimes it will be difficult for her to get access to utility service because of money owed for previous service.

WHEN THE ABUSER OWES BACK PAYMENTS

Sometimes a utility company will deny service to a survivor in her own name because of a previous utility bill owed by the abuser. In some states, the utilities can seek payments for a back-bill from anyone who lived in a household, even if that person is not the account holder. In other states only the consumer listed on the account can be held responsible for the bill. As discussed in the previous chapter, in some states, if the abuser and survivor were married, the utility may try to hold the survivor responsible for the bill under a "family expense" or "necessaries" law.

WHEN THE SURVIVOR OWES BACK PAYMENTS

A survivor may also find it difficult to get utilities for a new household because there is an old bill in her name. She may be surprised to find her name on the old bill because she had no access to the bills or to the funds when she was with the abuser.

The first step the survivor must take is to get her name off the account for the prior household. Otherwise she will be responsible for any further utility debts incurred by the abuser, even though she is no longer living with him. She should notify all of the utilities in writing that she has left the household and should be taken off the account. She should also consider the risk that the abuser will become angry at her action and retaliate, and she should plan for this possibility.

The next step is to deal with the old bill so that she can get utilities at her new household. Some strategies to do so are discussed below.

Payment Plans. One method to deal with back bills is for the survivor to ask the utility to allow her to pay off the old bill in installments. A state-by-state list of laws and regulations that require utilities to offer payment plans is included as Table 4 in Appendix F. All the tips regarding payment plans found in Chapter 4 are helpful in dealing with utilities.

Payment Assistance. See *Strategies for Becoming Current on Utility Bills*, below, for a range of payment assistance programs that may be available to help pay down the old debt.

Bankruptcy. Another option is for the survivor to file for bankruptcy. Information on filing for bankruptcy is included in Chapter Eight. Generally, filing for bankruptcy will immediately entitle the survivor to service at the new address. The old bills will be discharged in bankruptcy. The utility company will have to provide new service but, in several states, utilities can require the survivor to provide a deposit as reasonable assurance of the ability to make future payments. She will still be responsible for current bills as they come due.

Payment of a Security Deposit. In general, if a survivor owes back-bills to the utility, the company may request a security deposit before it will agree to provide new service. However, state utility laws and regulations may limit the amount of the security deposit that the utility company can require, the situations when a utility may require a deposit (for example, if the survivor has a poor payment history with the utility), and situations in which deposits must be returned (for example, once a good payment history is established). These laws are summarized in Table 5 in Appendix F.

Avoiding Utility Company Restrictions on New Service. When a survivor cannot pay a prior bill with the utility, there are still ways to obtain utility service. She can look for a house or apartment that includes utilities in the rent. Some states allow those with bad credit history or no credit history to use a "guarantor"—someone who is willing to be co-responsible for the account—in place of a utility deposit. However, since the guarantor becomes legally responsible for any unpaid bills, the survivor should consider this approach carefully and make sure to disclose to the guarantor all the risks involved. Also, see the discussion below of sources that can help pay for utility bills.

STRATEGIES FOR BECOMING CURRENT ON UTILITY BILLS

A survivor may already have utility service but may have trouble paying her current bills. The discussion below provides some strategies to help her.

Federal Fuel Assistance. The federal Low Income Home Energy Assistance Program (LIHEAP), administered by the states, helps low-income families pay their winter heating bills and, in some states, summer cooling bills. LIHEAP benefits can also go to renters, including some public and subsidized housing tenants whose heat is included in the rent. A survivor who is eligible for LIHEAP will also generally be eligible for assistance in weatherizing her home and receiving a range of energy efficient services that will reduce her monthly bills. However, there may be waiting lists for these weatherization services. The survivor should still consider putting her name on the waiting lists, as those services can help her save over the long term.

➡ **Pointer:** To get information on LIHEAP availability in a particular state, call the toll-free numbers 1-866-NRG-NEAR or 1-866-674-6327 or e-mail energyassistance@ncat.org.

Utility Fuel Funds. Many utility companies participate in special funds, sometimes directly subsidized by other customer contributions, to give loans or grants to those who cannot pay their utility bills.

Discounted Rates. Some electric, gas, and water utilities have special discounted rates for low-income, elderly, or disabled households.

Level Payment Plans. A level payment plan may help a survivor who is paying her utility bills on time but who is having trouble paying her bills at certain times of the year. A level payment plan can help the survivor avoid running up debts in the winter, when heating bills are high. If she chooses a level payment plan, her projected yearly bill is divided into equal monthly installments; monthly bills reflect this amount rather than each month's actual costs. For example, a survivor whose total gas bill for a year is $1200 would pay $100 each month, instead of paying $200 to $300 a month in the winter and $30 to $40 a month in the summer. At some point in time, for example once a year, her account will be reconciled with the actual amount owed.

Budget Payment Plans. A survivor in financial distress can quickly get so far into the hole with her utility bills that a level payment plan may not be enough. She cannot catch up on past-due payments (called arrears) and also keep up current utility bills. One solution is for the survivor and the utility company to negotiate a budget payment plan in which she makes a fixed monthly payment and the utility promises not to shut off service. A state-by-state list of state laws and regulations that require utility companies to offer payment plans is included as Table 4 in Appendix F. The plan can be designed so that the survivor pays current usage but only slowly catches up on the amount in arrears.

To make a successful payment plan, the survivor, preferably with the help of a counselor or advocate, must develop a budget as described in Chapter Two. The survivor or her advocate must be willing to push her plan with the utility company employee who negotiates the agreement. The utility company is likely to want a payment plan that requires larger payments than the survivor can afford. She should not agree to these payments simply because she believes she has no other choice. In many states, if she agrees to a payment plan and then fails to keep up with it, she will lose a range of protections and will be in danger of disconnection.

Energy Conservation Programs. As mentioned in the *Federal Fuel Assistance* discussion above, there are federal and, in many cases, state and utility funds to help homeowners and tenants weatherize their homes and install energy efficient appliances so as to reduce heating and cooling costs. The survivor may want to find out more about weatherization and energy conservation services, which are often provided free to low-income households.

Charities and Other Private Sources. Many charities, churches, and other private organizations help people pay their utility bills. These groups provide assistance only when they have funds available and sometimes only at certain times of the year. In some areas, community action programs can refer the survivor to such private energy-assistance programs.

FIGHTING A TERMINATION OF SERVICE

The threat of immediate termination of service, and the need to restore service that has already been terminated, can be two of the most urgent problems faced by a survivor. In many states, statutes and public utility commission regulations provide a variety of significant protections against privately owned utility terminations. Each of the fifty states has a Public Utilities Commission. A survivor and her advocate should check with the utilities directly regarding consumer rights and obligations for municipal utilities and cooperatives.

➡ **Pointer:** State utility commissions often have separate divisions for electric, natural gas, and water utilities as well as a consumer division. You can find the website for state utility commissions through the National Association of Regulatory Utility Commissioners at www.naruc.org or in the Blue Pages of the phone book.

Limitations on Termination. Because utility termination can profoundly affect a household, many states restrict termination. Some providers even self-impose termination restrictions. Often these restrictions are designed to protect elderly, ill, or disabled individuals. Some states require a doctor's opinion that the utility is medically necessary (such as for a health aid that uses electricity or water). Many states also limit termination at particular times of the year (for example, winter terminations of utilities). Others limit terminations based on temperature. State-by-state charts of these restrictions are included at the back of this guidebook as Table 2 in Appendix F. In general, utilities cannot terminate utility service during non-business hours, sometimes on the day before the weekend and before holidays, or on a day when the utility will be closed to the public.

Tenant Protection. When a landlord fails to pay for utility service, the tenants are at risk of losing their utility service. A survivor in this situation may have special protections. In some states, she must receive a special shutoff notice if the landlord is delinquent. In most states, she will have the option of having the utility service continue under her name and deducting those payments from her rent. If a survivor is planning to withhold rent, she should consult with a lawyer familiar with housing law because some states do not allow rent withholding or have special procedures that must be followed.

Advance Notice of Utility Termination. State law prohibits utility companies from terminating service without first giving the customer notice of the pending termination. These laws are summarized in Appendix F. In such situations, the survivor should expect the utility to give her an opportunity to dispute or contest the reasons for the shutoff.

Contesting the Termination. If the survivor disputes the utility's right to terminate her service, she should first talk to the utility about the problem and try to resolve the dispute (the utility commission will often require this first). The survivor should take notes about the call(s) (for example, who she spoke to, their title, when she called, what the utility said, etc.). This is not to say that she should just accept whatever the company offers. It is important to negotiate for an *affordable* payment plan. Agreeing to impossible terms will only make matters worse in the long run. It is a good idea for her to be prepared to discuss a payment plan before she calls the utility. This includes working out the household budget to figure out an affordable monthly payment amount ahead of time. Be prepared to ask to speak with the customer service representative's supervisor or a "billing or credit" specialist if the first person the survivor speaks to cannot help.

If the utility cannot resolve the dispute to the survivor's satisfaction, she should complain to the state utility commission. In many states, the utility commission's Consumer Division responds to complaints by residential customers.

Complaints about municipal utilities are handled differently, however. They are generally not regulated by the utility commissions. Instead, if the survivor is a customer of a municipal utility, she has a constitutional right to notice and a hearing and should request one if there is a dispute. An actual in-person hearing is not necessary in all cases. While the survivor does not need to have a lawyer represent her at the hearing, she may find it helpful to have an attorney, paralegal, or experienced utility counselor to assist her. It is important for her to bring all relevant documentary evidence supporting her claim, such as a physician's affidavit or cancelled checks. It may also be helpful to have witnesses such as friends and neighbors present.

Dealing with the utility or the utility commission can be intimidating, and it may be a helpful for the survivor to find an advocate who can help with this process. Legal services offices, councils on aging, fuel assistance programs, or other non-profits may be able to help.

Bankruptcy Protection. As discussed above, generally the filing of a bankruptcy petition automatically requires the utility to restore service or cease a threatened termination, but the survivor will often have to put down a deposit and make ongoing monthly payments to maintain the utility service.

TELEPHONE SERVICE

Another utility bill that survivors sometimes have trouble paying is the telephone bill. Yet telephone service may be critical to her safety. The following are some ways to help preserve and pay for telephone service.

Shop Around. One of the simplest ways for a survivor to minimize telephone expenses is to review her phone bills to see if a cheaper telephone service is available. The survivor should pay attention to any monthly fees, minimum charges, time restrictions, long-distance charges, and other fine print.

Assistance to Help Pay for Telephone Bills. There are two federal programs designed to help those with low incomes pay for local telephone service. These two programs, Link-Up and Lifeline, are federal programs and are administered by the Universal Service Administrative Company. Link-Up can provide discounted rates for the survivor's household to connect to service and can allow deferred payments for costs that she must pay. Lifeline lowers the cost of local service for one telephone conection per household by providing a monthly discount on the local phone bill. In most cases, the Lifeline program covers landline service (as opposed to wireless).

➡ **Pointer:** Information about the phone companies that participate in the Lifeline program by state can be found on the Universal Services Administrative Company website at www.universalservice.org/li/low-income/lifelinesupport/default.aspx.

Eligibility for These Services Varies from State to State As Does the Application Process. In some states, the survivor may apply through a particular agency while, in others, she may apply through her local phone company. She should contact the local phone company or the state utility commission for more information on eligibility and how to enroll.

➡ **Pointer:** The Universal Services Administrative Company administers the federal funds for the telephone assistance program. Their website has information about the phone companies that participate in the Lifeline program by state (www.universalservice.org/li/low-income/lifelinesupport/default.aspx).

Avoid Phone Sharks. Phone sharks are businesses that target low-income neighborhoods, selling pre-paid local telephone service. They "resell" local telephone service to consumers, encouraging them to believe that they have no other way of getting local phone service. Rates for these resellers are usually two to three times as high as the local telephone company, often for services that are not so complete or convenient. The survivor should be warned to avoid phone sharks. She should contact the state utility commission to find out which companies participate in the federal Lifeline and Link-Up assistance program. If she has unpaid bills that are barring her from receiving service, review the discussion above, *Strategies for Becoming Current on Utility Bills*. If the unpaid bills are for out-of-state long-distance charges, there may be rules requiring—or it may be possible to negotiate—for local service with toll-limitation service (to prohibit long-distance calling or to limit long-distance charges to a fixed amount).

➡ **Pointer:** If the survivor qualifies for federal Lifeline assistance for discounted phone service, toll-limitation service charges are covered by the Lifeline program.

Pre-Paid Phone Cards. Pre-paid phone cards can sometimes help to save money on long-distance phone expenses. They may also be a great convenience for survivors who are in a temporary housing situation. However, survivors should be warned that phone card companies sometimes go out of business or engage in deceptive practices, charge exorbitant rates, or provide poor quality service. Because the survivor will pay up front for the phone card, she will be out of pocket—and out of luck—if the company goes out of business or she discovers a problem trying to use the card. She should either stick with pre-paid phone cards that are recommended by people she knows or try out new cards in small denominations so that, if there is a problem, the amount of money lost is minimal.

Phone Service for Emergencies. A survivor should know that she can often keep 911 service in some states even if her phone service is terminated for non-payment of bills. In addition, there are programs that provide cell phones to survivors for emergency use.

ADDITIONAL INFORMATION ON UTILITY ACCESS

The National Consumer Law Center publishes a guidebook for consumer advocates and consumers entitled *NCLC Guide to the Rights of Utility Consumers.* NCLC also publishes a manual for consumer attorneys entitled *Access to Utility Service* (3d ed. 2006), which provides current utility and energy law developments, including customer service and utility termination issues, special utility payment plans and rates for low-income consumers, and federal LIHEAP and weatherization developments. Information on utilities is also available in *NCLC Guide to Surviving Debt.*

8

Bankruptcy Basics

Bankruptcy is an important option for survivors facing unmanageable debts. Bankruptcy can help a survivor eliminate most of her debts and get a fresh start. It can also stop a foreclosure on a home, restore utility service, or undo a wage garnishment.

This chapter is intended to give a basic explanation of bankruptcy, so that advocates can help survivors determine whether they should consider it as an option. This chapter does not explain every aspect of the bankruptcy process. It is meant to give general information and not to give specific legal advice. If the survivor still has questions after reading it, she should speak with an attorney familiar with bankruptcy or a paralegal working for an attorney.

There have been many news reports suggesting that changes to the bankruptcy law passed by Congress in 2005 will prevent many people from filing bankruptcy. It is true that these changes have made the process more complicated. But the basic right to file bankruptcy and most of the benefits of bankruptcy remain the same for most survivors.

The survivor should decide to file for bankruptcy only after determining that bankruptcy is the best way to deal with her financial problems. Each case is different. This determination will require careful analysis and depend on a number of factors discussed below.

Furthermore, the survivor should consider whether the abuser might view her filing for bankruptcy as a direct threat to him and retaliate. Especially if the survivor files a chapter 7 bankruptcy, the abuser may be left solely responsible for joint debts.

WHAT IS BANKRUPTCY?

Bankruptcy is a legal proceeding in which a person who cannot pay his or her bills can get a fresh financial start. The right to file for bankruptcy is provided by federal law, and all bankruptcy cases are handled in federal court. In most cases, filing bankruptcy immediately stops all of a debtor's creditors from seeking to collect debts from her, at least until her debts are sorted out according to the law.

WHAT CAN BANKRUPTCY DO FOR THE SURVIVOR?

Bankruptcy may make it possible for the survivor to do the following:

- Eliminate the legal obligation to pay most or all of her debts. This is called a "discharge" of debts. It is designed to give debtors a fresh financial start.
- Stop foreclosure on a house or mobile home and allow the survivor an opportunity to catch up on missed payments (bankruptcy does not, however, automatically eliminate mortgages and other liens on property).
- Prevent repossession of a car or other property, or force the creditor to return property even after it has been repossessed.
- Stop wage garnishment, debt collection harassment, and similar creditor actions to collect a debt.
- Restore or prevent termination of utility service.
- Allow the survivor to challenge the claims of creditors who have committed fraud or who are otherwise trying to collect more than she really owes.
- Prevent a government agency from recouping public assistance or Social Security overpayments, unless the receipt of the overpayment was deliberate.

WHAT BANKRUPTCY CANNOT DO

Bankruptcy cannot cure every financial problem. Nor is it the right step for every individual. In bankruptcy, the following are usually *not* possible:

- Eliminate certain rights of "secured" creditors. As discussed in Chapter Three, a "secured" creditor is one who has taken a lien on property as collateral for the loan. Common examples of secured loans are car loans and home mortgages. The survivor *can* force secured creditors to take payments over time in the bankruptcy process, and bankruptcy *can* eliminate the obligation to pay any additional money if the property is taken. Nevertheless, the survivor generally cannot keep the collateral unless she continues to pay the debt.

- Discharge types of debts singled out by the bankruptcy law for special treatment. These include child support, alimony, most student loans, court restitution orders, criminal fines, and some taxes.
- Protect co-signers on a debt. If the survivor's relative or friend has co-signed a loan, and the survivor discharges the loan in bankruptcy, the cosigner may still have to repay all or part of the loan.
- Discharge debts that arise after bankruptcy has been filed.
- Prevent a landlord from evicting the survivor, *if the landlord has already obtained a judgment for possession against the survivor and she does not satisfy certain requirements set forth in the bankruptcy law.*

CAN AN ABUSER FORCE THE SURVIVOR INTO BANKRUPTCY?

The abuser might sometimes threaten the survivor by saying that he will "force her into bankruptcy." The survivor should understand that this is an empty threat. Except in very unusual circumstances, bankruptcy cannot be involuntarily imposed onto a debtor by a third party—the debtor must initiate the bankruptcy. Furthermore, this type of threat seeks to exploit unfounded fears and myths about bankruptcy. Bankruptcy is not an oppressive or harsh process. Instead, it may be a useful option for debtors who are overburdened and need a fresh start.

However, there are some risks to the survivor if the abuser files for bankruptcy. For more information on the effect of an abuser's bankruptcy on the survivor, see the discussion at the end of this chapter.

WHAT DIFFERENT TYPES OF BANKRUPTCY CASES ARE THERE?

There are four types of bankruptcy cases provided under the law:

- *Chapter 7* is known as "straight" bankruptcy or "liquidation." It requires a debtor to give up property that exceeds certain limits called "exemptions" so the property can be sold to pay creditors.

- *Chapter 11,* known as "reorganization," is used by businesses and a few individual debtors whose debts are very large.
- *Chapter 12* is reserved for family farmers.
- *Chapter 13* is called "debt adjustment." It requires a debtor to file a plan to pay debts (or parts of debts) from current income.

Most people filing bankruptcy will want to file under chapter 7 or chapter 13.

Chapter 7 (Straight Bankruptcy). In a bankruptcy case under chapter 7, the survivor files a petition asking the court to discharge her debts. The basic idea in a chapter 7 bankruptcy is to wipe out (discharge) debts in exchange for giving up property, except for "exempt" property that the law allows the survivor to keep. In most cases, all of the survivor's property will be exempt. But property that is not exempt is sold, with the money distributed to creditors.

If the survivor wants to keep property like a home or a car and she is behind on the payments on a mortgage or car loan, a chapter 7 case probably will not be the right choice for her. This is because chapter 7 bankruptcy does not eliminate the right of mortgage holders or car loan creditors to take her property to cover her debt. On the other hand, a chapter 7 bankruptcy can offer some help on secured debts if the survivor has decided she cannot keep the home or car. After a chapter 7 discharge, a secured creditor has no right to seek a deficiency judgment or to collect money from her beyond seizing the collateral.

Chapter 13 (Reorganization). In a chapter 13 case, the survivor files a "plan" showing how she will pay off some of her past-due and current debts over a period of up to five years. The most important thing about a chapter 13 case is that it will allow her to keep valuable property—especially her home and car—that might otherwise be lost, if she can make the payments that the bankruptcy law requires to be made to her creditors. In most cases, these payments will be at least as much as her regular monthly payments on her mortgage or car loan, with some extra payment to get caught up on the amount she has fallen behind.

The survivor should consider filing a chapter 13 plan if she

(1) owns her own home and is in danger of losing it because of money problems;

(2) is behind on debt payments, but can catch up if given some time; or
(3) has valuable property that is not exempt, but she can afford to pay creditors from her income over time.

The survivor will need to have enough income in chapter 13 to pay for her necessities and to keep up with the required payments as they come due.

WHEN SHOULD THE SURVIVOR FILE BANKRUPTCY?

Like the decision to file for bankruptcy itself, the issue of when to file also depends on the survivor's unique circumstances. It is often stated that bankruptcy should only be considered as a "last resort" for financially troubled consumers. This advice is oversimplified. In some cases, legal rights can be lost by delay. The survivor should be especially careful to get early advice about bankruptcy if she is hoping to use the process to help save her home or car.

In some cases, the survivor might have to file bankruptcy on an emergency basis to prevent a foreclosure, repossession, eviction, execution sale, or utility shut-off. Bankruptcies in an emergency can be filed very quickly with little preparation, although there must be additional follow-up later on. A good discussion of how to do this is set out in § 7.2.2 of NCLC's *Consumer Bankruptcy Law and Practice* (7th ed. 2004 and Supp.). But, as discussed later in this chapter, the survivor must complete a credit counseling briefing before filing for bankruptcy or have sufficient grounds to request a temporary or permanent waiver of the credit counseling requirement.

In other cases, the survivor might want to delay filing bankruptcy in anticipation of further *unavoidable* debt, such as new medical, utility, or unpaid rent bills. Debts incurred after a bankruptcy filing are not discharged in that case, so delaying a filing will give her the maximum benefit from the case. As a general rule, bankruptcy should not be filed until the survivor's debts have peaked. However, she must avoid the temptation to buy goods or services on credit that she does not intend to pay for. In a chapter 7 bankruptcy, debts incurred this way can be declared non-dischargeable. Expenses for medical bills and other essentials are rarely challenged.

In cases in which the survivor needs to file bankruptcy and is in hiding from the abuser, it may be possible to request that the bankruptcy court not release to the public identifying information in the bankruptcy documents.

The survivor and her advocate should check with an attorney about local practice.

WHAT DOES IT COST TO FILE FOR BANKRUPTCY?

It now costs $299 to file for bankruptcy under chapter 7 and $274 to file for bankruptcy under chapter 13. The court may allow the survivor to pay this filing fee in installments if she cannot pay all at once. If she is unable to pay the filing fee in installments in a chapter 7 case and her household income is below 150% of the official poverty line, a bankruptcy court may waive the filing fee.

If the survivor hires an attorney, she will also have to pay the attorney fees that she agrees to.

Pre-filing credit counseling is a requirement for most people filing for bankruptcy and will cost between $30 and $50. If the survivor cannot afford the fee, approved credit counseling agencies are required to reduce or waive the fee. In addition, she will need to complete a post-filing financial education course in order to receive a discharge. The cost for the financial education course is also between $30 and $50 and may be reduced or waived if the survivor does not have the ability to pay.

In a chapter 13 reorganization case, the trustee is usually entitled to a commission of about 10% of the payments made through the plan. These payments must be included with the amount that the debtor pays the trustee under a plan.

WHAT PROPERTY CAN THE SURVIVOR KEEP?

In a chapter 7 case, the survivor can keep all property that the law says is "exempt" from the claims of creditors. State law or, in some cases, the federal bankruptcy law will specify which property is exempt. The question of which exemption law applies can be complex. A good bankruptcy attorney can help ensure that the survivor claims all the exemptions to which she is entitled.

Exemption laws vary widely from state to state. Some states will allow the survivor to choose between the federal bankruptcy exemptions or state law exemptions and federal non-bankruptcy exemptions. Other states have "opted out" of the federal bankruptcy exemption scheme. In these "opt-out" states, the survivor will be required to use her state law exemptions and federal non-bankruptcy exemptions. However, even in these states, a special federal bankruptcy exemption may be used to protect retirement funds in pension plans and IRAs.

Usually, the survivor's state of residence determines the applicable exemption law. However, if she has moved to a different state within the two years before filing for bankruptcy the exemption laws of a state she previously lived in or federal bankruptcy exemption law may apply.

In determining whether property is exempt, the survivor must keep a few things in mind. First, the value of property is not the amount she paid for it, but what it is worth now. Especially for furniture and cars, this may be a lot less than what she paid or what it would cost to buy a replacement.

The survivor also only needs to look at her equity in property. This means that she counts her exemptions against the full value minus any money that she owes on mortgages or liens.

For example:
If the survivor owns a $50,000 house with a $40,000 mortgage, she has $10,000 in equity. Only that $10,000 counts against her exemption.

While the exemptions allow the survivor to keep property even in a chapter 7 case, the exemptions do not stop a mortgage holder or car-loan creditor from taking the property to cover the debt if she is behind on her payments. In a chapter 13 case, she can keep all of her property if her plan meets the requirements of the bankruptcy law. In most cases, she will have to pay the mortgages or liens as she would if she did not file bankruptcy.

WHAT WILL HAPPEN TO THE SURVIVOR'S HOME AND CAR IF SHE FILES BANKRUPTCY?

In most cases, the survivor will not lose her home or car during her bankruptcy case as long as her equity in the property is fully exempt. Even if her property is not fully exempt, she will be able to keep it if she pays its non-exempt value to creditors in a chapter 13 case.

However, bankruptcy does not make security interests go away. There are several ways that the survivor can keep collateral or mortgaged property after she files bankruptcy. She can agree to keep making her payments on the debt until it is paid in full. Or she can pay the creditor the amount that the property she wants to keep is worth. In some cases involving fraud or other improper conduct by the creditor, she may be able to challenge the debt. If she put up her household goods as collateral for a loan (other than a loan to purchase the goods), she can usually keep her property without making any more payments on that debt.

CAN THE SURVIVOR OWN ANYTHING AFTER BANKRUPTCY?

Yes! Many people believe they cannot own anything for a period of time after filing for bankruptcy. This is not true. The survivor can keep her exempt property and anything she obtains after the bankruptcy is filed. However, if she receives an inheritance, a property settlement, or life insurance benefits within 180 days after filing for bankruptcy, that money or property may have to be paid to her creditors if the property or money is not exempt.

WILL BANKRUPTCY WIPE OUT ALL DEBTS?

Yes, but with some exceptions. Bankruptcy will not normally wipe out

(1) money owed for child support or alimony, including attorneys fees related to support proceedings (property settlements, however, may be dischargeable);
(2) most taxes;
(3) debts not listed on the bankruptcy petition;
(4) loans the survivor got by knowingly giving false information to a creditor, who reasonably relied on it in making her the loan;
(5) debts resulting from "willful and malicious" harm;
(6) most student loans, except if the court decides that payment would be an undue hardship;
(7) fines and certain restitution obligations;
(8) loans from a retirement plan or pension; and

(9) mortgages and other liens that are not paid in the bankruptcy case (but bankruptcy will wipe out her obligation to pay any additional money if the property is sold by the creditor).

HOW WILL BANKRUPTCY AFFECT A SURVIVOR'S CREDIT?

There is no clear answer to this question. Unfortunately, if the survivor is behind on her bills, her credit may already be bad. Bankruptcy will probably not make things any worse. The fact that she has filed a bankruptcy can appear on her credit record for ten years. In contrast, defaults only appear for up to seven years. However, since bankruptcy wipes out her old debts, she is likely to be in a better position to pay her current bills, and she may be able to get new credit because she no longer has a number of debts in default.

The survivor should not assume that, because she filed bankruptcy, she will have to get credit on the worst terms. If she cannot get credit on decent terms right after bankruptcy, it may be better to wait. Most lenders will not hold the bankruptcy against the survivor if, after a few years, she can show that she has avoided problems and can manage her debts.

The survivor should be cautioned about auto dealers, mortgage brokers, and lenders who advertise their business by saying "Bankruptcy? Bad Credit? No Credit? No Problem!" They may give her a loan after bankruptcy, but at a very high cost that can make it impossible for her to keep up the loan payments. Getting this kind of loan can ruin her chances to rebuild her credit. The survivor should also avoid credit offers that are aimed at recent bankruptcy filers or are from her former creditors. These may be an attempt to collect discharged debt.

OTHER CONSIDERATIONS

Sometimes a survivor may have a feeling of moral obligation that makes her hesitant to file bankruptcy. This feeling needs to be balanced by other considerations, such as the need to provide herself and her children, if she has any, with food, clothing, and shelter. Advocates may want to remind her that the U.S. Constitution includes a provision for bankruptcy and that many big corporations and famous people have chosen to file for bankruptcy. The survivor may take comfort in that fact that the Bible mentions the need for debt-forgiveness that sounds very similar to bankruptcy:

> At the end of every seven years thou shalt make a release. And this is the manner of the release: every creditor shall release that which he has lent unto his neighbor and brother; because the Lord's release hath been proclaimed.
>
> (Deut. 15:1–2)

The survivor may also be concerned about the effects of bankruptcy on her reputation. She should be reassured that most people who file for bankruptcy find that their reputations suffer no perceptible harm. Bankruptcies are not generally announced in newspapers. They are a matter of public record, but it is unlikely that friends or neighbors will look at those records.

WHAT ELSE IS IMPORTANT TO KNOW?

Utility Services. Public utilities (such as the electric company) cannot refuse or cut off service because the survivor has filed for bankruptcy. However, the utilities can require a deposit for future service, and the survivor does have to pay bills that arise after the bankruptcy is filed.

Discrimination. The bankruptcy law offers the survivor some protection against discrimination on the basis of bankruptcy. Government agencies cannot deny her any benefits because of a previous bankruptcy discharge of debts to the agency. This includes agencies such as welfare offices, unemployment agencies, housing authorities, licensing departments, and student loan guarantee agencies. Employers are not permitted to discriminate against her for filing for bankruptcy, except in cases of some sensitive jobs that involve money or security.

Driver's License. If the survivor lost her license solely because she could not pay court-ordered damages caused in an accident, bankruptcy will allow her to get her license back.

Co-Signers. If someone has co-signed a loan with the survivor and she files for bankruptcy, the co-signer may have to pay her debt. If the survivor files a chapter 13, she may be able to protect co-signers, depending on the terms of her chapter 13 plan.

HOW DOES A SURVIVOR FIND A BANKRUPTCY ATTORNEY?

As with any area of the law, it is important for the survivor to carefully select an attorney who will respond to her personal situation. In bankruptcy, as in all areas of life, remember that the person advertising the cheapest rate is not necessarily the best. Many of the best bankruptcy lawyers do not advertise at all.

The best way to find a trustworthy bankruptcy attorney is to seek recommendations from family, friends, or other members of the community, especially any attorney the survivor knows and respects. She should carefully read retainers and other documents the attorney asks her to sign. She should not hire an attorney unless the attorney agrees to represent her throughout the case. She should select an attorney who is not too busy to meet her individually and to answer questions as necessary.

Some legal services organizations or local bar associations may have attorneys that will take bankruptcy cases *pro bono* (that is, free of charge) for low-income clients. The National Association of Consumer Bankruptcy Attorneys maintains a website, www.nacba.org, with a searchable index of bankruptcy attorneys. Additional resources are listed in Appendix A at the back of this guidebook.

CREDIT COUNSELING REQUIREMENTS

Bankruptcy law requires that debtors receive pre-filing budget and credit counseling and take a post-filing financial education course. These requirements may be temporarily or permanently waived in a very limited number of circumstances. Organizations providing the required credit counseling and/or education course must be approved by the United States Trustee Program (or Bankruptcy Administrator in North Carolina and Alabama). However, approval does not endorse or ensure the quality of the provider's service.

Agencies must provide the bankruptcy counseling and necessary certificates to those without ability to pay. If the survivor cannot afford the fee, she should ask for a fee waiver or reduced fee.

To be eligible to file bankruptcy, the survivor usually must receive budget and credit counseling within the 180 days before the bankruptcy case is filed. Approved agencies are allowed to provide the counseling in person, by telephone, or over the Internet. The counseling session usually takes less than an hour. The agency will prepare and review with the survivor a budget that examines her income and expenses. The agency will review possible alternatives to filing a bankruptcy, including a debt management plan. Such debt management plans are generally a bad idea unless the survivor has a significant amount of money left over each month to pay credit card debt.

Credit counseling agencies are not permitted to give legal advice. Therefore, it may be a good idea for the survivor to meet with a reputable attorney before participating in the pre-filing credit counseling. A good attorney will generally provide counseling on whether bankruptcy is the best option and, if it is not right, will offer a range of other suggestions.

In addition, to receive a discharge in a chapter 7 or chapter 13 case, the survivor must complete a financial education course. This course is different from the budget and credit counseling that must be completed prior to filing. The financial education course is about two hours long and may be completed in person, by telephone, or over the Internet. It will include instruction on budget development, money management, the wise use of credit, and other consumer information.

WATCH OUT FOR BANKRUPTCY-RELATED SCAMS

There are many people and companies that advertise bankruptcy-related services in order to take advantage of vulnerable, financially distressed consumers. Some of these enterprises charge enormous fees. Others make promises that they cannot possibly keep. The survivor should be careful to avoid scams and offers of high-rate debt consolidation loans as a way out of debt. Most of these deals will only make her situation worse.

The survivor should not pay money for debt counseling or bankruptcy without being sure she is dealing with a reputable business. Bankruptcy counseling from a for-profit business (as opposed to a nonprofit organization) is almost never a good idea. These entities more likely to take advantage of the survivor and they cannot give her the certificate she would need to file for bankruptcy in the event she decided to do so (only nonprofit organizations can be approved to provide the required bankruptcy counseling).

Document preparation services also known as "typing services" or "paralegal services" involve non-lawyers who offer to prepare bankruptcy forms for a fee. Problems with these services often arise because non-lawyers cannot offer advice on difficult bankruptcy cases and they offer no services once a bankruptcy case has begun. Shady operators, who give bad advice and defraud consumers, are prevalent in the field, and the survivor should be counseled to avoid these scams.

CAN THE SURVIVOR FILE BANKRUPTCY WITHOUT AN ATTORNEY?

Although it may be possible for the survivor to file a bankruptcy case without an attorney, it is not a step to be taken lightly. The process is difficult and the survivor may lose property or other rights if she does not know the law. It takes patience and careful preparation. Chapter 7 (straight bankruptcy) cases are easier. Very few people have been able to successfully file chapter 13 (reorganization) cases on their own.

WHAT IF THE ABUSER OWES THE SURVIVOR MONEY AND HE FILES FOR BANKRUPTCY?

In some instances, the survivor may find herself in the role of a creditor. This is especially true if the abuser owes child support payments to the survivor. In this situation, the abuser might threaten to file for bankruptcy to eliminate his child support obligations or even claim that a bankruptcy has already wiped out child support debts.

The survivor should know that such claims are false and cannot be carried out. Child support debts are not dischargeable in a chapter 7 bankruptcy and normally must be paid in full in a chapter 13 bankruptcy. Domestic support orders are now first priority under the new Bankruptcy Code. This means that they must be paid before any other claims. The following debts cannot be discharged in chapter 7 bankruptcy and normally must be paid in a chapter 13 bankruptcy:

- Restitution ordered as part of a conviction in a criminal case.
- Child support owed to the state because the child is receiving public assistance.
- Criminal fines.

If the survivor and the abuser still have joint debts, the abuser's bankruptcy puts the survivor at risk. The survivor might end up solely liable for these debts. However, if the abuser is required to pay a joint debt because of a divorce agreement or order, this requirement usually will not be affected by his bankruptcy filing. The abuser will remain liable for the debt (as will the survivor—remember that the divorce order cannot prevent the creditor from holding the survivor liable as well).

Another risk to the survivor is that a debt incurred because of a property settlement in a divorce case can sometimes be discharged. If she is served with court papers when a former spouse is asking that a property settlement be discharged, it is important that she seek legal advice and file a response.

The abuser's bankruptcy may also show up on the survivor's credit record. If that happens, the survivor has a good argument to have it removed. She should dispute having the abuser's bankruptcy on her credit record and should consult an attorney. For more information on how to dispute an item on a credit report, see Chapter Twelve.

FOR MORE INFORMATION

For a more detailed overview of bankruptcy, consult *NCLC Guide to Surviving Debt* (2006). For a comprehensive review of consumer bankruptcy law, see NCLC's *Consumer Bankruptcy Law and Practice* (7th ed. 2004 and Supp.).

9

Using Civil Protection Orders As a Tool for Economic Justice

[*Endnotes can be found at the end of the chapter*]

Civil protection orders provide survivors of domestic violence with a tool for accessing safety and economic justice. Unlike the criminal justice system, in which the state wields control over initiation and pursuit of the case, the civil protection order system was intended to provide domestic violence survivors with control over whether and how to initiate the case, the specific relief requested, and enforcement of the relief. Civil protection orders are injunctive in nature and include provisions that require perpetrators of domestic violence to refrain from or engage in certain proscribed acts for a temporary period of time.

Relief available through civil protection orders is expansive. The most common examples include: orders to "stay away" from the survivor's home, school, employment, and/or her person; orders directing the abuser to refrain from contacting the survivor directly or indirectly; orders directing the respondent to refrain from abusing, harassing, or committing further criminal acts against the survivor; and temporary orders of child custody.[1]

Though greatly underutilized, most state civil protection order statutes include provisions that enable survivors to pursue economic relief, including access to material resources. The statutory intent of civil protection order statutes is, simply put, safety. Virtually every state protection order statute emerged from legislative history or contains comments that indicate a legislative purpose to promote future safety or prevent violence.[2]

Safety for survivors of domestic violence requires economic security. Domestic violence impoverishes survivors and exposes them to increased risks of violence.[3] Survivors may incur direct economic harms, including medical damages, property destruction, theft, and lost wages.[4] Survivors may also incur enormous preventive costs to minimize the abuser's access to them and to establish a free and independent life. The costs of future safety may include housing, health insurance, childcare, transportation, clothing, utilities, and tuition.[5] Indeed, access to economic resources is the most likely predictor of whether a survivor will permanently separate from her abuser.[6]

For civil protection order statutes to achieve their legislative mandate, courts must honor requests for economic justice. Specific statutory provisions offer direct authority for obtaining economic relief, while "catch all" provisions offer expansive, creative mechanisms for obtaining monetary payments or access to resources required for short- and long-term economic security. If guided by strategies that balance both physical and economic safety risks, civil protection orders offer tools to recompense survivors for past economic damages and provide prospective relief necessary for future safety and independence.

The following sections describe the landscape of economic relief in protection orders and offer practical strategies for the issuance and enforcement of those economic relief provisions.

THE LANDSCAPE OF ECONOMIC RELIEF IN PROTECTION ORDER STATUTES

Specific Types of Economic Relief Available. Many state civil protection order statutes include specific provisions that provide direct authority for orders of monetary payment, access to material resources, or injunctive relief designed to facilitate the survivors' economic well-being. Below are some common examples:

Restitution for Medical Expenses, Property Damages, and Other Compensatory Losses. Many statutes authorize courts to grant restitution for costs stemming directly from the respondent's abuse of the survivor. Many state protection order statutes specifically authorize payment and/or reimbursement for medical costs resulting directly from the abuse. Medical expenses may be physical or psychological in nature, and they may include an emergency hospital visit as well as follow-up medical visits related to the abuse. Similarly, courts in many states are authorized to award reimbursement and/or payment for property damages resulting from the respondent's abuse. Frequently, states authorize a list of compensatory losses, including attorney fees, shelter, and lost wages.[7]

Housing Access and Payments. Survivors of domestic violence cite the need for housing as a substantial obstacle to their safety. Civil protection order statutes provide housing access in a variety of different ways.[8]

Many protection order statutes specifically authorize orders to vacate a previously shared residence. Several states enable courts to issue vacate orders regardless of ownership of the residence. For example, the Alaska statute authorizes the court to "remove and exclude the respondent from the residence of the petitioner, regardless of ownership of the residence."[9] Other statutes limit the scope of "vacate provisions" to circumstances in which the property is jointly owned, leased, or rented. For example, the District of Columbia statute authorizes the court to order the abuser to vacate the residence if the residence is "marital property; jointly owned, leased, or rented; or Petitioner individually owns, leases, or rents."[10] Still other statutes limit "vacate orders" to circumstances in which the survivor individually owns, leases or rents the previously shared residence.[11]

An order to vacate a residence may not offer adequate assistance, if a survivor lacks the monetary resources to pay for the rent or mortgage. Therefore, many state statutes explicitly direct the abuser to make rent or mortgage payments.[12] Other statutory provisions require the abuser to provide suitable alternative housing to the victim and/or children.[13] Protection order statutes may condition these types of relief upon marital status or having a child-in-common (that is, a duty to support). For example, Missouri's protection order statute provides explicit authority for the court to issue an order requiring the respondent to "pay the petitioner's rent at a residence other than the one previously shared by the parties if the Respondent is found to have a duty to support . . . and the petitioner requests alternative housing."[14] However, many statutes do not require support, other than that stemming from the economic justice needs related to the prior abuse.

Property Use, Transfer, and Protection. Civil protection orders in many states contain specific provisions that grant the survivor the temporary use of a vehicle or other personal property. For example, Georgia's civil protection order statute enables the court to "[p]rovide for possession of personal property of the parties."[15] Statutes may condition temporary possession of a vehicle upon ownership or alternative means of transportation. For example, the Alabama protection order statute allows the court to grant temporary possession of a vehicle "if the plaintiff has no other means of transportation of his or her own and the defendant either has control of more than one vehicle or has alternate means of transportation."[16] In contrast, Alaska specifically authorizes a protection order that grants the survivor "possession and use of a vehicle and other essential personal items, regardless of ownership of the items."[17]

Some statutory provisions aim to protect property from damage or misappropriation by the abusive partner. For example, the Illinois statute authorizes an order that "forbids the respondent from taking, transferring, encumbering, concealing, damaging, or otherwise disposing of any real or personal property."[18]

Many state statutes provide for the exchange of personal property between the parties. Several state statutes include provisions that require the police to accompany the victim or the abuser to retrieve his or her belongings from a shared residence.[19]

By explicitly addressing the details of the exchange in the order—identifying specific items, the date, time, and method of transfer—courts are able to assist domestic violence survivors in ensuring that the property transfer actually takes place and that it occurs without further incident.

Liens, Debts Due, Economic Burdens. Many civil protection order statutes offer an opportunity to address routine financial obligations that continue throughout the duration of the protection order. For example, California authorizes "the payment of any liens or encumbrances coming due during the period the order is in effect."[20] Minnesota specifically grants "the continuance of all currently available insurance coverage without change in coverage or beneficiary designation."[21]

Support Payments. The majority of state protection order statutes offer specific authority for requiring the abuser to pay child support for children-in-common or to pay spousal support when married. For example, the Pennsylvania statute allows an order "directing the defendant to pay financial support to those persons the defendant has a duty to support."[22] The New Jersey statute provides that "compensatory losses shall include, but not be limited to, loss of earnings or other support, including child or spousal support."[23] A New Jersey court recognized the connection between domestic violence and the need for support in *Mugan v. Mugan*, in which it held that, "when a defendant's violent acts result in his removal from the marital residence and bar contact with his wife, this may well cause the loss to her of the funds necessary to maintain herself and the house. Such consequences are as direct as removal."[24] The court added a policy justification for the provision of support, stating that survivors of domestic violence should not be discouraged from attempting to separate from their abusers by a threat of financial distress.[25]

"Stay Away" and "No Contact" Provisions. Virtually every state protection order statute contains "stay away" and "no contact" provisions. Typically associated with physical protection from abuse, "stay away" and "no contact" orders also can have a direct impact on a survivor's economic security. For example, an order to stay away from a survivor's place of employment may mean the difference between employment and unemployment.[26] An abuser who stalks a survivor at work may cause her to lose her job—due to an employer's unlawful decision to fire her or to the survivor's fear of abuse and thus inability to go to her workplace. Similarly, "stay away" orders restricting the abuser from the survivor's home may enable her to remain in her home (and thus avoid the costs of relocation) or may prevent her from experiencing eviction, which, though unlawful, is commonly faced by survivors of domestic violence.[27] Survivors can request "stay away" and "no contact" provisions as a means of restricting the abuser's ability to inflict substantial economic damages in the future.

Punitive Damages and Compensation for Pain and Suffering. The New Jersey protection order statute offers extraordinarily comprehensive economic relief for survivors of domestic violence. In addition to a wide array of financial measures found in various other state protection order statutes, the New Jersey statute specifically authorizes "compensation for pain and suffering" and, "where appropriate, punitive damages."[28] In *Sielski v. Sielski*, the court awarded $6000 in punitive damages to the survivor, after the court found that the abuser had acted viciously and sadistically when he yanked her out of bed by her hair, slapped her about the face and neck, attempted to push her face in the toilet, yanked at her pubic hair, threw cold water at her, violently broke a lamp, and cut the phone connection so that the plaintiff could not summon assistance.[29] The court held "it cannot be argued that torture such as reported here is not an evil-minded act warranting both the protection of the Prevention of Domestic Violence Act of 1990 and punitive damages."[30]

Catch-All Relief Provisions. Catch-all provisions enable survivors to recoup economic damages that resulted from the abuser's violence and/or cover the costs of future safety and independent living. The specific language of catch-all provisions varies from state to state but is consistently equitable in nature.[31] Courts have interpreted statutory catch-all provisions to authorize creative and particularized remedies that are needed to prevent future abuse.

In its Civil Protection Order Study, the National Institute of Justice found that the majority of jurisdictions "explicitly grant judges the latitude to grant any constitutionally defensible relief that is warranted."[32]

In *Powell v. Powell*, the District of Columbia Court of Appeals held that the court had the authority to grant monetary relief in a civil protection order proceeding, even though such relief was not specifically provided for in the protection order statute.[33] The D.C. statute's catch-all provision enabled the court to award relief "appropriate to the effective resolution of the matter."[34] The survivor argued that, because her financial dependency on her husband was a major factor in the perpetuation of violence in the family, the only effective means of stopping the abuse and protecting her in the future was for the abuser to vacate the home and make it financially and physically secure. The court looked to the legislative history of the domestic violence statute and concluded that the statute was to be read expansively.[35] In light of that expansive reading and remedial purpose, the court held that the intent of the catch-all provision was to enable courts to grant individualized solutions, tailored to meet the safety needs of each case.[36]

Thus, attorneys for survivors and *pro se* litigants should use catch-all provisions creatively and opportunistically in order to access specifically tailored monetary payments and resources needed for their future safety and restoration.

PRACTICAL STRATEGIES FOR ACCESSING ECONOMIC RELIEF

Despite the clear link between economic security and safety, judges are often reluctant to grant economic relief in protection orders. Therefore, attorneys and advocates for survivors must carefully assess, advocate, and fully litigate the economic issues before the court.

Intake and Assessment. Survivors and advocates should consider economic security at the initial stages of the civil protection order process. They can explore the universe of potential economic relief in two steps. First, identify the prior economic harms. Consider individual instances of physical and sexual violence to identify direct economic damages including property damage, medical damages, lost wages, etc. Consider the respondent's economic abuses of the survivor, including identity theft, stolen money, etc. Second, consider the costs of future safety. Brainstorm relief tailored to meet the cost of independent living, including things like housing, transportation, child care, health care, food, clothing, tuition, etc.

Requests for economic relief must be grounded in the survivor's own risk assessment.[37] Advocates should work with survivors to explore various economic options that might address the prior harms and future economic costs. While the civil protection order may provide powerful tools for economic justice, such requests have the potential to trigger retaliatory violence by the abuser against the survivor.[38] Therefore, assessment must engage the survivor in carefully considering how economic orders might impact her safety. Both economic risks and physical safety risks must be analyzed, with an eye toward crafting solutions that provide access to economic security while minimizing safety risks. In some instances, survivors may decide that the risk of physical abuse or retaliation (or the risk of accessing the justice system) outweighs the potential economic benefit, or that other options outside of the protection order system involve a lower risk of retaliatory abuse. Only the survivor can determine whether economic relief through a civil protection order is desirable in her particular circumstance.

Strategies to Promote Safety. The desirability of a request for economic relief will depend entirely upon a survivor's own particularized circumstances. The following are strategies that may (or may not) minimize the risks for physical harm:

- Survivors may feel that bifurcating the protection order proceeding, or separating the liability phase from the damages phase of the case, will minimize risk.
- A survivor may wish to include payment methods that minimize contact with herself and her children or other family members. She might consider requesting that the court require the abuser to send his payments to the court or that the court withholds monetary payments from his wages as is often done with child support awards.
- Survivors may wish to request that the court require monetary payments in installments, as opposed to one lump sum. Such smaller amounts may seem less threatening to an abuser and less likely to spur retaliation.
- A survivor may decide to pursue some types of economic relief, based upon her knowledge of the abuser, while refraining from seeking others. Advocates can assist survivors in this complex strategizing by offering alternative sources of economic relief to complement those

forms of economic relief that she obtains through the civil protection order process (for example, victims compensation funds).

Strategies to Promote Enforceability. As with all civil protection order provisions, economic relief provisions should be crafted with specificity with regard to the method and amount of payment, thus maximizing the likelihood of enforceability. Ask the court to include specific details about the property to be exchanged, the prohibited or required actions of the abuser, and/or the monetary amounts, the dates on which monetary payments are to be paid or actions to be carried out, and the methods for doing so. For items that are non-monetary in nature, such as property, ask the court to list the various items to avoid future dispute.

STRATEGIES TO ACCESS RELIEF WHEN THE DAMAGES AMOUNT IS UNKNOWN

Because civil protection order hearings are expedited proceedings, survivors often do not know the cost of economic damages at the time of the hearing. For example, a survivor who sought medical treatment may not have received the bill specifying the amount at the time of the hearing. Such timing issues need not preclude survivors from accessing economic justice. Under these circumstances, the survivor can ask the court to litigate liability (that is, whether the abuser is liable) but leave the amount of damages (that is, how much) for a status hearing at a later date. The survivor may request that the court issue an order requiring the respondent to appear at the status hearing, specifying the date and time within the civil protection order itself. Then, at the status hearing, the survivor can present the proper evidence and the court can determine the amount and specific method of payment at that time.

Alternatively, if the court is unwilling to set a status hearing date or if the survivor wishes to avoid having to appear for future hearing dates, the survivor may request that the court require the abuser to pay the medical bills once they become available. Typically, the survivor or her advocate will need to forward the bills to the abuser. Note that such a strategy, though necessary under certain circumstances, is open to manipulation by the abuser and is more difficult to enforce than damages ordered by the court.

If the survivor discovers an economic injury that was unknown at the time of the initial hearing (for example, medical conditions are subsequently discovered) or if the damages are more extensive than prescribed by the original order (for example, follow-up medical visits are required), the survivor may file a motion to modify the civil protection order, arguing that the newly discovered damages constitute "good cause" or a "change in circumstances" that justify a modification.[39]

Proving the Case. Even sympathetic judges who wish to read their protection order statutes broadly and award remedial economic relief cannot do so unless the survivor presents the court with the evidence and arguments to do so.

Physical Evidence.

- Evidence of Liability—Present the court with physical evidence of economic damages. Evidence of economic harm resulting from physical abuse might include photos of physical injuries or property damage, destroyed clothing, broken furniture, and medical records. Evidence of harm resulting from economic abuse might include forged checks, credit card bills, or credit reports.
- Evidence of Damages Amount—After proving liability, the survivor will also have to offer evidence to prove the amount of damages. Evidence of the costs of prior harm might include medical bills, receipts for property purchases, or repair receipts. Evidence of the costs of future safety might include a residential lease, a childcare bill, an automobile lease or monthly bus pass, or a utility bill.

Testimonial Evidence. Survivors must present testimony in court to illustrate the nexus between the violence and the need for economic relief. While judges may readily see the need for a "stay away" order, they may need some assistance in understanding how the economic relief is critical to this survivor's short- and long-term safety. For example, in a case seeking reimbursement for damage to work clothes, a survivor might testify, "Without replacement of my suit, I cannot go on a job interview and will not be able to provide a safe home for myself and my child." Testimony should be specific not only about the need for the relief, but also about how the particular request—amount, timing, method of payment or access—are tailored to meet this survivor's individual safety needs.

Arguments. The overarching aim in arguing for economic relief is to articulate the *nexus* between the economic relief requested and the legislative purpose of the protection order statute—safety. To illustrate that connection, cite to social science to educate judges on the importance of economic independence for survivors and explain how economic relief will impact this survivor's life in particular.

- If your state protection order statute contains explicit provisions that specifically authorize the type of economic relief requested, rely upon that provision.
- Use catch-all provisions when the statute does not specifically provide for the relief requested.
- Rely upon the legislative purpose of the statute to support requests for liberal relief.
- Argue that short-term economic relief is essential. Many courts are reluctant to offer economic relief, because they believe that such relief can more properly be obtained in family law proceedings or through tort actions. Be sure to explain how immediate economic relief is essential to the survivor's short-term safety. Without it, she may not be able to separate or remain separated from the abuser. Such a result would be at odds with the goal of the civil protection order statute. Moreover, in cases in which the survivor and the abuser are not married, the civil protection order case may be the only venue for economic justice.
- Request that the economic terms be specific to enhance enforcement.
- Explain how the particular requests—amounts, items, timing, and method—"make sense" in light of her larger safety plan.
- Request that the court make written findings of economic harm and the need for economic relief.

Enforcement Advocacy. Civil protection orders are not self-implementing. Obtaining the court's order is only part of the process. For civil protection orders (or any order) to be effective following their issuance, advocates and survivors must take various steps to facilitate the abuser's compliance.

- Third Parties—Survivors should consider whether to enlist third parties as allies in the enforcement of the economic terms of a protection order.
  Example: Imagine a protection order that directs the abuser to re-pay the survivor for $1000 worth of credit card debt that he incurred as an authorized user on her card. A survivor or her advocate might use the civil protection order as a tool for advocating with the credit card

company to either waive the debt or develop a lenient payment plan that coincides with the terms of the protection order.
Example: Imagine a protection order that directs the abuser to stay away from her place of employment. Provided that she feels safe in doing so, a survivor might share a copy of her protection order with her employer so that he/she can aid in enforcing that "stay away" provision in the event that the abuser appears at the workplace.

- The Abuser—Advocates for survivors should consider taking various steps to enforce the economic terms of protection orders. If the abuser fails to make a payment, the advocate might write a letter to him or his attorney to remind him of the specific terms of the court order and to document his non-compliance.

Civil Contempt Proceedings. When an abuser fails to comply with the economic relief provisions of a civil protection order, a survivor may choose to file a civil contempt action against him.[40] While criminal contempt actions punish the violator for past disobedience, civil contempt actions are intended to encourage compliance with the order and will generally be more efficacious when economic relief is needed.[41] Survivors will want to present evidence of the abuser's non-compliance. In instances in which monetary payments were to be directed to the courthouse, the survivor might provide official copies from the court financial office to prove his failure to pay. Similarly, when payments were to be made directly to a creditor, the survivor might offer an official business record from that institution to prove non-payment.

ENDNOTES

1. *See generally* Fredrica Lehrman, Domestic Violence Practice & Procedure §§ 4:1-4:41 (West 1996) (providing an overview of civil protection order law).

2. *See, e.g.*, Ala. Code § 30-5-1(b) ("This chapter shall be liberally construed and applied . . . (1) to assure victims of domestic violence the maximum protection from abuse that the law can provide."); Ark. Code Ann. § 9-15-101 ("The purpose of this chapter is to provide an adequate mechanism whereby the State of Arkansas can protect the general health, welfare, and safety of its citizens by intervening when abuse of a member of a household by another member of a household occurs or is threatened to occur, thus preventing further violence."); Cal. Fam. Code § 6220 (West) ("the purposes of this division are to prevent the recurrence of acts of violence and sexual abuse and to

provide for a separation of the persons involved in the domestic violence for a period sufficient to enable these persons to seek a resolution of the causes of the violence"); Colo. Rev. Stat. § 13-14-102(1) ("protection orders are of paramount importance . . . because protection orders promote safety, reduce violence, and prevent serious harm and death"); Idaho Code Ann. § 39-6302 ("It is the intent of the legislature to expand the ability of the courts to assist victims by providing a legal means for victims of domestic violence to seek protection orders to prevent such further incidents of abuse."); 750 Ill. Comp. Stat. § 60/102 ("This Act shall be liberally construed and applied to promote its underlying purposes, which are to . . . (4) support the efforts of victims of domestic violence to avoid further abuse . . . so that victims are not trapped in abusive situations by fear of retaliation, loss of a child, financial dependence, or loss of accessible housing or services"); Ind. Code § 34-26-5-1 ("This chapter shall be construed to promote the (1) protection and safety of all victims of domestic or family violence in a fair, prompt, and effective manner; and (2) prevention of future domestic and family violence").

3. *See* Martha F. Davis, *The Economics of Abuse: How Violence Perpetuates Women's Poverty, in* Battered Women, Children and Welfare Reform: The Ties That Bind (Ruth A. Brandwein ed., 1999) (Sage Series on Violence Against Women).

4. *See* Lawrence A. Greenfield et al., U.S. Dep't of Justice, Violence by Intimates: Analysis of Data on Crimes by Current or Former Spouses, Boyfriends, and Girlfriends 21 (1998); Ted R. Miller et al., U.S. Dep't of Justice, Victim Costs and Consequences: A New Look (1996); Barbara J. Hart, *Legal Road to Freedom, in* Battering and Family Therapy: A Feminist Perspective 18 (Marsali Hansen et al. eds., 1993).

5. *See* Barbara J. Hart & Erika A. Sussman, *Civil Tort Suits and Economic Justice for Battered Women,* 4(3) The Victim Advocate, at 3–4 (Spring 2004).

6. *See* Edward Gondolf & Ellen R. Fischer, Battered Women As Survivors: An Alternative to Treating Learned Helplessness 95 (1988).

7. *See, e.g.,* Del. Code Ann. tit. 10, § 1045(a)(7) ("compensation for losses suffered as a direct result of domestic violence committed by the respondent, including medical, dental, and counseling expenses, loss of earnings or other support, cost of repair or replacement of real or personal property damaged or taken, moving or other travel expenses and litigation costs, including attorney's fees").

8. Indeed, the District of Columbia Court of Appeals affirmed the courts' power to order abusers to vacate their home in *Robinson v. Robinson,* 886 A.2d 78 (D.C. 2005). Finding it inadequate for the respondent to vacate the marital home but live right next door, the court held that the broad remedial purposes of the civil protection order act allowed "safety concerns to trump property rights." *Id.* at 86.

9. Alaska Stat. § 18.66.100(3).

10. D.C. Code § 16-1005(c)(4).

11. *See, e.g.,* Kan. Stat. Ann. § 60-3107(d); Md. Code Ann., Fam. Law § 4-506(d)(4) (West); N.H. Rev. Stat. Ann. § 173-B:5; Ohio Rev. Code. Ann. § 3113.31(E)(1)(b) (West).

12. *See, e.g.,* Ind. Code § 34-26-5-9(c)(3)(b); Nev. Rev. Stat. § 33.030(2)(b)(2).

13. *See, e.g.,* 23 Pa. Cons. Stat. § 6108(a)(2).

14. Mo. Rev. Stat. § 455.050.

15. Ga. Code Ann. § 19-13-4(8).

16. Ala. Code § 30-5-7(d)(6).

17. Alaska Stat. § 18.66.100 (B)(10).

18. 725 Ill. Comp. Stat. § 5/112A-14(11).

19. *See, e.g.*, Kan. Stat. Ann. § 60-3107(8) ("making provision for the possession of personal property of the parties and ordering a law enforcement officer to assist in securing possession of that property, if necessary"); Or. Rev. Stat. § 107.718 (1)(d) ("that a peace officer accompany the party who is leaving or has left the parties' residence to remove essential personal effects of the party").

20. Cal. Fam. Code § 6324 (West).

21. Minn. Stat. § 518B.01(6)(11).

22. 23 Pa. Cons. Stat. § 6108.

23. N.J. Stat. Ann. § 2C:25-29(4) (West).

24. 555 A.2d 2, 3 (N.J. Super. Ct. App. Div. 1989).

25. *Id. See also* Powell v. Powell, 547 A.2d 973 (1988) (holding that the catch-all provision of the District of Columbia civil protection order statute authorized an award of child support).

26. *See generally* Wendy R. Weiser & Deborah A. Widiss, *Employment Protection for Domestic Violence Victims*, Clearinghouse Rev. J. of Poverty Law and Policy, 3–11 (May–June 2004).

27. *See generally id.* at 708–718.

28. N.J. Stat. Ann. § 2C:25-29(b)(4) (West).

29. Sielski v. Sielski, 604 A.2d 206, 207 (N.J. Super. Ct. Ch. Div. 1992).

30. *Id.* at 210.

31. *See, e.g.*, D.C. Code § 16-1005(c)(10) ("directing the respondent to perform or refrain from other actions as may be appropriate to the effective resolution of the matter"); N.C. Gen. Stat. § 50B-3(a)(13) ("include any additional prohibitions or requirements the court deems necessary to protect any party of any minor child"); 23 Pa. Cons. Stat. § 6108(a)(10) ("granting any other appropriate relief sought by the plaintiff").

32. Peter Finn & Sarah Colson, National Inst. of Justice, Civil Protection Orders: Legislation, Current Court Practice, and Enforcement 33 (1990).

33. *See* Powell v. Powell, 547 A.2d 973 (1988).

34. D.C. Code § 16-1005(c)(10).

35. *See* Powell v. Powell, 547 A.2d 974–75 (1988).

36. *See id.*

37. *See generally* Jill Davies, Safety Planning with Battered Women: Complex Lives/Difficult Choices (1998).

38. *See* Desmond Ellis & Walter S. DeKeseredy, *Marital Status and Woman Abuse: The DAD Model*, 19 Int'l J. of Sociology of the Family 67–87 (1989) (finding that "post separation abuse" correlates with women's assertion of independence); James Ptacek, Battered Women in the Courtroom: The Power of Judicial Responses 80–81 (Claire Renzetti, ed. 1999) (finding that 80% of women interviewed indicated that their partners made threats or attempts at physically forcing them to return to the relationship).

39. *See, e.g.*, D.C. Code § 16-1005(d) ("modify the order for good cause shown");

Mo. Rev. Stat. § 455.060(1) ("showing a change in circumstances sufficient to warrant the modification").

40. *See* Fredrica Lehrman, Domestic Violence Practice & Procedure § 4:35 (West 1996).

41. *See, e.g.*, D.C. Code § 16-115(f).

10

Crime Victim Compensation Funds

Survivors of abuse often suffer physical, economic, and emotional harms associated with the batterer's behavior. Often these harms correlate to high medical, psychological, and living bills that a survivor usually does not have the means to pay. Due to this trauma and loss of wages, all fifty states and U.S. territories have set up crime victim compensation funds to help support victims of crime.

Victims of domestic violence, dating violence, stalking, and sexual assault, which are all crimes, can seek assistance from compensation fund programs. Any person who has suffered a crime under federal, state, military, or tribal jurisdiction is eligible to apply for compensation funds. These funds are available to provide substantial economic assistance to the survivor.

COMPENSABLE COSTS

Though it varies from state to state, the survivor can seek crime victim compensation funds to pay for a wide variety of expenses. These expenses include loss of job compensation due to the injury suffered or for recovery from the injury, child care, funeral and burial costs, mental health counseling, travel expenses to receive treatment, dental work, and hospital and medical care. Some funds cover moving or relocation expenses, rehabilitation, and modification of homes for victims who are wheelchair-bound.

The cost of property that was lost or damaged as a result of the crime may not be covered. Costs for replacing or repairing certain medical aids or devices—such as hearings aids or eyeglasses—that are broken during the crime are usually recoverable. Depending on the state, costs related to the crime are reimbursable anywhere from $2000 up to $25,000.

COLLATERAL RESOURCES

Crime victim compensation funds are utilized as a place of "last resort." Collateral resources include public or private health insurance, car insurance, disability insurance, public program benefits, and workers' compensation. Compensation programs will not allocate funds to an applicant who has not attempted to seek these other means of economic recovery. If the survivor does receive money from the perpetrator or any other liable party, most states require that the survivor return any monies that the program has covered.

REQUIREMENTS

Each state has its own set of eligibility requirements for the crime victim compensation fund. But all programs share similar criteria that the victim must generally meet. These include

- Reporting the crime promptly to law enforcement officials (generally within seventy-two hours after the crime occurred, although there are "good cause" exceptions);
- Cooperating with the police and District Attorney's Office in the investigation and prosecution of the crime (although there may be exceptions to this);
- Being innocent of criminal activity that contributed to the victim's injury;
- Submitting a timely application to the compensation board (anywhere from one to two years after the crime occurred); and
- Incurring a cost or suffering a loss that is not covered by other collateral sources (for example, Medicare, insurance, disability).

The survivor should keep in mind that, in some states, if it is a family-violence crime, getting a civil protection order or order of protection might be sufficient to apply for the compensation fund, replacing the requirements for the survivor to take part in the criminal justice system. Some compensation programs allow a survivor's temporary restraining order as a basis to receive monies.

Survivors who are residents of the state are eligible to apply to the state's compensation fund. Also, if the crime occurred in another state, the survivor can apply to that state's compensation fund. For some state funds, the survivor's immigration status must be known, and generally the survivor must be a United States citizen.

It is not a requirement that the perpetrator of the crime be apprehended and/or prosecuted for a survivor to be eligible to apply for compensation. Therefore, if she meets all the eligibility requirements for the state's crime victim compensation fund, and has safety planned accordingly (see below) she should apply.

APPLICATION PROCESS

Applications are generally found at local law enforcement or victim assistance program offices. States typically have a compensation board that reviews the applications and determines the amount of money to award. Survivors applying for compensation should be aware that these boards typically determine the truthfulness of the submitted application by doing the following:

- Interviewing police and analyzing police reports;
- Interviewing hospital staff for any reported medical issues;
- Discussing the case with mental health counselors;
- Speaking with the funeral home (if the victim is deceased); or
- Contacting the employer (if work loss is claimed).

Therefore, it is important for an advocate to discuss safety planning and privacy issues prior to deciding whether or not to submit an application to the crime victim compensation fund. The survivor should think through any concerns if any of the above parties are notified and how she might be able to address these concerns.

APPLICATION DEADLINES

Generally, the survivor needs to file an application within one year of the crime incident. Some states have a two-year limitation if the applicant shows "good cause" for the delay. If the survivor is under the age of 18, some compensation boards will allow her to apply up to five years after the incident if the abuser is a parent or living in the same household as the victim. Timeliness is generally determined by the postmark date.

EMERGENCY AWARDS

Some states allow an emergency award to a victim who is in a difficult monetary situation. For example, if a survivor has paid for medical bills or has a loss of earnings due to the crime and now cannot pay for food or utilities, she may be able to get money from the compensation program to help pay for necessities. The survivor and her advocate should keep in mind that the process takes time and it may still take several weeks before she actually receives the money. She should also be aware that the police, any mental health counselors or hospital staff connected to her case, or her employer may be contacted during this process, so she should plan for her safety, if necessary.

APPEALS

If an applicant is denied compensation, she should seek the help of a victim's advocate or domestic violence advocate and try to get more information as to why her application was denied (if it is not supplied in the rejection letter). The survivor should also collect information from the sources from which the board gathered information—for example, the police, relevant medical professionals, mental health counselors, or her employers—some of whom may not have responded to the board on time, resulting in the rejection of her application.

Depending on the ruling, the survivor may have grounds to appeal the decision. The rules and statutes regarding appealing the compensation fund denial vary from state to state. The survivor and her advocate should check the rules of appeal specific to her state.

REFERENCES

The National Association of Crime Victim Compensation Boards has more information about crime victim compensation funds on its website at www.nacvcb.org. This website also contains links to all of the states' crime victim compensation fund websites. A list of addresses, telephone numbers, and websites for each state's crime victim compensation board can be found in Appendix D at the back of this guidebook.

11

Child Support

It is difficult for most survivors with minor children in the household to make ends meet if they do not receive reliable child support payments. When a survivor has custody of minor children, whether from the relationship with the abuser or another relationship, establishing and maintaining child support payments is one of the most important things the survivor can do to help herself succeed financially.

In order to obtain reliable child support, the survivor should do two things: first, she should establish the child support obligation; and second, she should make sure that the obligation is met through enforcement. Help is often available for survivors throughout this process.

ESTABLISHING THE CHILD SUPPORT OBLIGATION

Child support payment requirements are usually set out as part of a state court order. Although the parents may have agreed on a child support amount as part of a separation agreement, such an agreement can be much more difficult to enforce than a court order. Child support orders are usually available as part of a court order establishing custody of the child. The survivor may be able to obtain at least a temporary child support order as part of a civil domestic violence case (see Chapter Nine).

Each state has its own laws regarding child support requirements. Generally, in order to be entitled to a child support order, the survivor must either have either joint or sole physical custody of the child. Often there is a requirement that the parent seeking support provide the majority of the care for the child.

If the survivor was not married to the child's father when the child was born, she may have to prove that the person from whom she is seeking child support is the parent of the child. A genetic test, often called a paternity test, may be necessary if there is disagreement about who the father of the child is.

Next, the amount of child support will be decided. In many states, there are guidelines that either determine or suggest the amount of support. Some states base the amount on factors such as each parent's income and how many other children each parent has. Other states consider the needs of the child rather than, or in addition to, the parent's income. Many states permit courts to enter orders for amounts other than those found on the guidelines under special circumstances. In some states, the court can require the parent who is receiving the support payment to account for how the money is being used.

CHILD SUPPORT ENFORCEMENT

After the survivor obtains a court order establishing the support obligation, the required payments should begin. If payments are not made as ordered, the survivor has several options available.

Income withholding is available for child support orders. Withholding is available from paychecks as well as retirement, workers' compensation, and some other types of income. Assuming the person paying child support is employed or receives one of these other types of income, withholding makes collection much easier. The child support payment is simply deducted from the paycheck. This way, payment is automatic.

If income withholding does not work because the parent paying child support is unemployed or self-employed (or for other reasons), there are several alternatives available. Tax refunds can be seized. Depending on the state where the parent paying child support lives and the amount owed, driver's licenses can be revoked or suspended or passports not issued. A lien may be placed on certain property owned by the parent paying child support. In many states, parents who willfully refuse to pay may even be jailed.

CHILD SUPPORT AND GOVERNMENT BENEFITS

If the survivor is receiving certain types of government benefits, she will be required to pursue child support and to assign to the government her rights to child support payments. When and if child support is collected, it will be paid to the government program as reimbursement for the government benefits the survivor received.

A survivor of domestic violence may be afraid to seek government benefits because she knows she will be required to pursue child support. If she thinks it would be dangerous to name the father in cases in which paternity has not been established, she may seek relief from this requirement by showing the danger of involving the abuser. She may also ask that a family violence indicator be placed in her records. This should restrict access to the survivor's personal information.

HELP IN OBTAINING CHILD SUPPORT

Title IV-D of the Social Security Act established child support enforcement offices throughout the nation. Child Support Enforcement Offices (CSEs) are found in each state. Any parent with a child support need may apply for services. Survivors receiving government assistance described above will be automatically referred to the program without having to pay a fee. Those not receiving public assistance may be charged up to $25. Depending on the state, there may be other charges as well for those not receiving public assistance. These fees may include attorney fees, lab testing for paternity, and costs for locating parents.

The CSE program can help the survivor in establishing child support. It can help locate the other parent and establish paternity. It also has resources to help enforce payment of child support orders.

➡ **Pointer:** Information about applying to the CSE program for help can usually be found at the local department of social services. Contact information for local offices and other information can also be found online at www.acf.hhs.gov/programs/cse.

Survivors may be tempted to seek help from private, for-profit collection agencies. Problems with such agencies are discussed in Chapter Seventeen.

12

Credit Reports

Credit history is extremely important to a survivor hoping to establish a new life. Credit reports may be used by landlords when the survivor is looking for an apartment, employers when she is looking for a new job, insurance companies when she applies for car or homeowners insurance, and creditors when she is trying to get access to affordable credit.

Survivors face many credit history problems. They may lack credit history. Often any credit accounts or loans were in the abuser's name and do not show up on the survivor's credit report. A survivor fleeing her abuser may have had to change her identity, leaving her with no credit history.

A survivor may have a negative history as a result of an abusive relationship. The abuser may have damaged the survivor's credit history by having her co-sign debts on which he has defaulted or by leaving unpaid credit card bills from an account on which the survivor was an authorized user. The abuser may declare bankruptcy on his own, which may show up on the survivor's credit history as well as leaving her solely responsible for joint debts. A survivor or an advocate working with a survivor should be aware that these signs of abuse may appear on her credit report, remind the survivor of the abuse, and bring back painful memories.

This chapter discusses ways in which an advocate can advise or help a survivor with problems on her credit report. For more information on credit reporting, NCLC publishes a manual entitled *Fair Credit Reporting* (6th ed. 2006). NCLC also publishes a consumer brochure entitled "The Truth About Credit Reports" (also available in Spanish, Chinese, Vietnamese, Russian, and Korean—see the order form at the end of this guidebook to order).

CREDIT REPORT BASICS

What Is a Credit Report? A credit report is a record of how a consumer has borrowed and repaid debts. Creditors usually look at this report to decide whether or not to grant credit.

What Kinds of Information Are Included in a Credit Report? Most commonly a credit report includes:

- name, current and former addresses, birth date, and Social Security number;
- employment information;
- payment history on all accounts;
- a listing of all creditors who have recently requested copies of the credit report; and
- public records information (such as bankruptcies, foreclosures, court judgments).

Sample credit reports are available from the websites of all three major credit bureaus.

Who Can See a Credit Report? Under federal law, not everyone is permitted to look at a credit report. In general, people or businesses that have legitimate business reasons can look up a credit report. These include:

- *Creditors*, when the survivor applies for credit or for a loan
- *Potential employers*, but only under certain circumstances and only if the survivor gives them authorization
- *Insurers*, when the survivor applies for insurance
- *Government agencies* trying to collect child support
- *Landlords*, deciding if they will rent to the consumer

An abuser will usually not have a reason that is permitted by federal law to look at a survivor's credit report. This is generally true even if the survivor is involved in a divorce case with the abuser, unless a judgment for support has been entered against the survivor.

HOW DOES A SURVIVOR GET A COPY OF HER CREDIT REPORT?

The first step in learning about the survivor's credit report is to order copies from the three main credit bureaus and read these reports carefully. This will allow the survivor to see what information is listed in the report. This section tells the survivor how to get a copy of her report. A later section discusses what the survivor can do if the survivor does not like what she sees on the report.

Because there can be differences in the reports kept by each of the three major national credit bureaus, the survivor should order her report from all three, either online, in writing, or by telephone. To obtain a report, the survivor will be required to provide certain information. Each company provides sample reports online and has a toll-free number that the survivor can call for more information. The current toll-free phone numbers and web addresses for ordering credit reports are listed below. The survivor can also order by mail, but these addresses change frequently and it is best to call or e-mail to get the current mail address.

One Free Credit Report per Year from Each Credit Bureau. Federal law requires the three major credit bureaus to provide one free credit report per year. The survivor can get her free credit reports from a centralized request service by

- going to www.annualcreditreport.com (if the survivor has access to the Internet);
- calling 877-322-8228; or
- completing the Annual Credit Report Request Form and mailing it to:
  Annual Credit Report Request Service
  P.O. Box 105281
  Atlanta, GA 30348-5281.

If she has Internet access, the survivor can download the request form at www.ftc.gov/credit.

The credit bureaus should not be contacted individually for the free annual report. They are only providing free annual credit reports through the centralized resource listed above. The survivor should be able to get all three reports, or just one at a time if she prefers, at no cost when she goes to the centralized resource. Once the survivor has received her free credit report from each of the three major credit bureaus, she will not be eligible for another free report for twelve months under these rules. As discussed below, however, under certain circumstances she may be entitled to additional free reports.

The survivor needs to provide her name, address, Social Security number, and date of birth. If she has moved in the last two years, she may have to provide her previous address. To maintain the security of the survivor's file, each credit bureau may ask the survivor for some information that only the survivor would know, like the amount of her monthly mortgage payment, or it may ask the survivor for different information.

Other Ways to Get a Free Credit Report. In addition to the free annual credit report the survivor is entitled to receive under federal law, the survivor should be able to get the report for free if she lives in a state that allows its residents to get one free report each year. These states are Colorado, Georgia, Maryland, Massachusetts, New Jersey, and Vermont. These special state law rights should be in addition to the right to a free report that is available under federal law.

The credit bureaus are also required to give the survivor a copy of the report for free if she has been denied credit within the past sixty days. Even if the survivor has not been denied credit, she can get one free report in any twelve-month period if she

- is unemployed and will be applying for a job within the next sixty days;
- is receiving public assistance; or
- has reason to believe that the file at the credit bureau contains inaccurate information due to fraud.

In addition, credit bureaus must provide the survivor with a free report if she has requested a fraud alert. Such alerts are discussed later in this chapter.

$10 Maximum Charge for Credit Reports. If the special circumstances entitling a person to a free report do not apply, and if the survivor has already accessed the free annual report, credit bureaus can currently charge the survivor no more than $10 per report. This is a maximum charge, not a required charge, and some states have passed laws limiting the amount credit bureaus can charge consumers for reports. The survivor should check with her state consumer affairs department or legal services office to see what the limits are, if any, in her state.

If the survivor buys a copy of her credit report directly from a credit bureau, she should be careful not to buy other products and services she does not want. Credit bureaus make it hard for consumers who visit their websites *not* to sign up for other expensive products and services.

CREDIT BUREAU CONTACT INFORMATION

Equifax	Experian	Trans Union
800-685-1111	888-EXPERIAN (888-397-3742)	800-916-8800
www.equifax.com	www.experian.com	www.transunion.com

CREDIT REPORTS AND ABUSERS

Keeping Credit Report Information Safe from the Abuser. An abuse survivor may be concerned about preventing her abuser from getting a copy of her credit report, especially if she is keeping her location a secret from her abuser. The abuser usually will not have a legal right under federal law to obtain a copy of the credit report.

However, there are circumstances in which an abuser could obtain a copy of the survivor's credit report by using illegitimate means. For example, he could have a friend who works for a debt collector or lender order a copy. Furthermore, if the abuser and survivor were married, the abuser may be able to obtain a *joint* credit report showing information on both parties. Therefore, the survivor should not assume that the abuser can not obtain her credit report. She should check to make sure that her location is not listed on the credit report if she is keeping that information from her abuser. In order to keep this information from appearing on her report, she should be sure not to use her confidential address on any credit applications.

A survivor who has changed her identity in order to escape her abuser should be especially careful. Unfortunately, the tendency of the credit reporting agencies is to favor cross-reference and merging of files whenever there is any indication that two persons may be the same individual (even when they are not). Consequently it is important that a survivor who has changed her identity avoid using any credit history from her prior identity and monitor her report to ensure that no prior identifying information is present.

Threats to Ruin a Credit Record. Sometimes an abuser may threaten a survivor by saying he will "ruin her credit." The abuser may threaten to do this by abusing joint credit or by identity theft. This is a real possibility. Any joint open-ended lines of credit should be closed *immediately*, whether or not the abuser has made any threats. If the survivor leaves the home, she should remove her name from the utility service. Ways to deal with joint debts are discussed in Chapter Six. Identity theft issues are discussed below.

The abuser may also threaten to provide damaging information to a credit reporting agency. This type of threat is less serious because credit bureaus usually do not report comments or subjective opinions about an individual. Most information on a credit report is provided by creditors who subscribe to one of the credit bureaus and send monthly information on thousands of accounts by computer. A credit bureau will not even accept information from a non-subscriber.

Because credit reports are allowed to include information from publicly available court documents, one type of information that can potentially show up on a credit report is the fact that the survivor has obtained a protective order. Certain "tenant screening" companies, which are a form of credit reporting agency, will report to landlords that a prospective tenant has been involved in a domestic violence proceeding, sometimes without distinguishing between the abuser and the party seeking the protective order. The survivor could try to submit a written statement to the tenant screening company to explain that she was not the defendant in the protective order proceeding.

HELPING THE SURVIVOR WITH AN INADEQUATE CREDIT HISTORY

There are ways a survivor who lacks a credit history can begin to establish one. Some things can be done fairly quickly with the help of an advocate. Other methods require long-term efforts by the survivor.

Adding Information to a Credit History.

Using a Spouse's Joint Credit History If It Is Good. One way to improve credit history is to use positive information about joint accounts that had been primarily held in a spouse's name. There is a federal law that requires creditors who report information to credit bureaus to reflect the participation of both spouses, if they are both permitted to use or are contractually liable for an account. For example, a husband may have a credit card in his name, but the wife may be an authorized user. If that particular account has a good history, it is important to make sure that it is reflected in the survivor's credit history. The survivor can send a written dispute to the credit bureaus if the account is not—she should cite Equal Credit Opportunity Act, Regulation B, 12 C.F.R. § 202.10(a). The survivor should not hesitate to use the abuser's good credit history on joint accounts—after all, either her money or her labor supported the household enabling the abuser to make the payments on the joint account. Survivors should be advised to close all joint open lines of credit immediately. Even after a joint account is closed or paid off, the good credit history information will remain in a credit record.

Supplying Unreported Good Information. The survivor may have a good payment record with a landlord, a utility company, or another creditor, but the information does not appear on her credit report. The survivor can try to have the landlord, utility company or other creditor supply information to the credit bureau if they do not already do so. This is generally difficult to do because it requires convincing the creditor to become a subscriber to a credit bureau. A better strategy may be for the survivor to supply this information herself to the person from whom she is applying for credit, employment, etc. The federal fair lending laws require creditors to consider information an applicant presents to show that a credit history does not accurately reflect her creditworthiness.

Building a Credit History. A longer term approach for the survivor to deal with an insufficient credit history is to start building a new history on her own. The best way to do this is to start in small steps with necessary items only:

- A good payment history on rent, utilities, and student loans is the first step.
- Another step is to open a charge account with a local department store, buying only necessary items and paying off the balances right away.
- The survivor could try to get a small car loan, if it is affordable. She should beware of car dealers who prey on those with bad credit. Such dealers often charge over 20% interest and add extra fees and charges (for more on car issues, see Chapter Sixteen). The survivor should also avoid payday loans or car title loans. These lenders charge interest of

300% or higher. These short-term loans are a long-term debt trap from which it is very difficult to escape. These loans do not help to improve a survivor's credit history (see Chapter Twenty).

It is best if the survivor waits to take on new debt until she is in a stable situation and on her feet financially. A survivor attempting to build a credit history with new debt should beware of scam operators who advertise "easy credit" or "no credit history required." The survivor should also be cautioned against taking on more debt than she can handle. The end result will be delinquencies and defaults, trading no credit history for a bad credit history. If the survivor is unable to pay all her debts, Chapter Three has suggestions about which debts to prioritize.

There are of course special considerations for a survivor who lacks a credit history because she has changed her identity. She should not use any of the credit history from her prior identity, because the credit reporting agencies will merge the old and new identities together. Even listing debts from her old identity on a credit application form might result in cross-matching to the new identity. The lender will probably not ask the survivor for information about most of her unsecured debts, such as credit card debt. For some loans, however, especially mortgage loans, a potential lender is likely to request information about her debts, including unsecured debt. Until those debts have been resolved, it may be difficult for a survivor to obtain a mortgage loan or other secured loan without disclosing information that could result in cross-matching to the new identity.

UNDOING THE DAMAGE: FIXING A BAD CREDIT HISTORY

If a survivor has a bad credit history, whether or not as a result of her relationship with the abuser, there are ways to fix some of the damaging information. Consumers have a right under the federal Fair Credit Reporting Act, 15 U.S.C. §§ 1681–1681u, to delete certain information or to include their side of the story in their credit reports.

Old Information. Under the federal law, there are certain time limits that negative information can remain on a credit report. A credit bureau is not allowed to list the following information:

- Negative credit information older than seven (7) years
- Bankruptcy information older than ten (10) years
- Judgments older than seven (7) years or however long the time limit is for judgments under state law
- Criminal information older than seven (7) years, except that convictions can be reported indefinitely
- A tax lien more than seven (7) years after it was paid off (but the FTC says that unpaid tax liens can remain on a credit report indefinitely)

Correcting Errors. Consumers have a right under federal law to correct any erroneous information on their credit report. For example, a credit report may list a defaulted debt incorrectly as belonging to both the abuser and the survivor, when only the abuser is liable for the debt.

A survivor should send a written dispute letter to each credit bureau that has reported incorrect information. (A sample letter is included at the end of this section.) Federal law requires credit bureaus to reinvestigate the entry and correct erroneous information. In most circumstances, the agency is required to get back to the consumer within thirty days with the results of the investigation. Send the original of the letter to the credit bureau and a copy, with all the supporting documents, to the creditor that reported the incorrect information.

The creditor who initially supplied the information to the bureau also has a duty to correct and update the information. If a consumer can show that the information reported by a creditor is not accurate or complete, the creditor must provide the bureau with the information necessary to make the report correct or complete.

Advocates should advise the survivor to check her credit report periodically after the entry is corrected to make sure that the incorrect information has been deleted permanently. Inaccurate items have a habit of popping up again even after they are corrected.

Explaining Damaging Items. The survivor can try to send the credit bureaus an explanation of why she is delinquent. The credit bureaus are not required to include the explanation in her file, but they may agree to do so. In contrast, the credit bureaus are required to include in the survivor's report any explanation of why an entry is inaccurate. For example, the credit bureaus may not have to include a survivor's letter that explains she could not pay a debt because she had to leave her home due to abuse. However, they must include a letter that states she disputes owing the debt because it was actually incurred by the abuser and he forged her signature. The survivor's explanation may be limited to 100 words if the credit bureau helps her to write it, and, in any case, it is best to keep the explanation short.

If a survivor is comfortable, a better approach may be to explain the delinquency to prospective lenders, landlords, or employers. For lenders, federal law requires that they at least consider a consumer's explanation. Similarly, some mortgage lenders are required to review any letter a consumer provides to explain credit blemishes.

Finally, if a survivor has a negative credit report, it may not be as important as she thinks. For example, when a survivor is dealing with a utility company, her credit record will usually only impact the security deposit that she is required to pay to obtain utility service. It will not prevent her from getting service (unless the utility company discovers from the credit report that she owes a back debt that the company did not already know about). Credit history is also generally not an obstacle to obtaining student loans—the key issue for most student loans is whether she is in default on a *prior* student loan.

Avoiding the Abuser's Bad Credit History. If a survivor's own credit history is a good one, but her abuser's is bad, she still may be concerned that a creditor will see the abuser's bad credit history. The survivor does have some protections in such cases. If she is only applying for credit in her name, federal fair lending law prohibits a creditor from reviewing her spouse's or ex-spouse's credit history. Following are exceptions to this rule:

- If the survivor is relying on assets jointly owned with the abuser to establish creditworthiness
- If the survivor is taking a loan secured by a home or other property that she still owns jointly with the abuser (in that case, the creditor will probably want the abuser to co-sign the loan)
- If the survivor is still married to the abuser and resides in a community property state (Arizona, California, Idaho, Nevada, New Mexico, Texas, Washington, and Wisconsin have community property laws to at least some extent)

Take Steps to Avoid Identity Fraud and Identity Theft. The number of people victimized by identity theft continues to grow. Survivors of domestic violence are not immune. In fact, survivors may be more susceptible.

Abusers often have access to the survivor's personal information that would enable the abuser to commit acts of identity fraud. In addition to possible financial gain, abusers may be motivated by the desire to damage the survivor's credit. For information on steps survivors can take to protect themselves from identity theft or to repair the damage if they are the victim of identity fraud please see Chapter Nineteen of this guidebook.

Beware of Credit Repair Agencies. As discussed above, there are many things a survivor can do for free to "fix" her credit or rebuild it. Credit repair companies can not do anything more than the survivor can do herself. Sometimes they can make matters worse. They may suggest a technique that they call "file segregation," in which they try to confuse the credit bureaus about a consumer's identity so that a new, clean file is created for the consumer. If the intent is to defraud creditors, this is illegal. (Note that this is different from an abuse survivor who establishes a new identity with the intent to avoid her abuser, which is not illegal.)

Here are some common (and wrong) claims made by credit repair companies:

"We can erase bad credit"
The truth is that no one can erase bad credit information from a credit report *if it is accurate.*

"Only we can remove old or inaccurate information"
The truth is that, if there are legitimate errors on a credit report or information that is old, the consumer can correct the report herself without paying a lot of money to one of these companies.

"The information on your report is accurate but we will erase it anyway"
The truth is that if this means lying to the credit reporting agency, it is illegal.

Often there is no legitimate way for survivors to "clean up" their credit record by removing all of the negative information. These survivors should be advised to remove what they can on their own and focus on getting financially stable. They should avoid credit repair agencies during this vulnerable time. Finally, they should be reminded that a bad credit record is not permanent and that most negative information will be deleted in seven years.

SAMPLE LETTER OF DISPUTE

Your Address

Date

Address of Consumer Reporting Agency

Address of Creditor

Dear Agency and Creditor:

[YOUR IDENTIFICATION INFORMATION: Name, address, and Social Security number]

I am writing to dispute the following item in my credit report: [clearly describe the item you are disputing]. I dispute this information because [explain clearly WHY you are disputing the information.]

[Example: *I am writing to dispute item #1 in my credit report. This is information from an account with Big City Department Store. I dispute this information because the account does not belong to me. It belonged to my ex-husband. I was never listed on the account and I never had authorization to use the account.*]

I request that you delete [or if appropriate correct] this inaccurate information. Please send me a copy of the corrected credit report.

[If possible:] I have enclosed information to support this claim.

Sincerely,

[ATTACH COPIES OF SUPPORTING DOCUMENTS, IF ANY.]

13

Student Loans

Many survivors find themselves dealing with student loan debt. A survivor may be delinquent or in default on old student loans. She may want to go back to school, especially if she has been enrolled in a welfare-to-work program or otherwise needs to transition from public assistance. Unfortunately, shady practices by vocational and correspondence schools pose a very real threat. Trade school fraud causes not only frustration and financial loss but also a loss of opportunity. This is especially true for young, low-income survivors hoping to break out of poverty.

Although many of the worst schools are now closed, a survivor who attended those schools in the past may continue to suffer the consequences. Defaulted loans for a worthless education may prevent her from returning to school and can ruin her credit history. Although trade school fraud was most common in the 1980s and 1990s, new problems continue to surface. Even students who attended legitimate schools are likely to experience difficulty repaying loans during periods of financial distress.

Fortunately, many survivors can eliminate old debts or arrange payment plans that they can afford. By resolving old debt issues, they can avoid harassment and finance new schooling. If the survivor does return to school, she should be advised to shop around first. In many cases, she may be able to find free or low-cost public education programs.

For additional information on student loans, see *NCLC Guide to Surviving Debt* and National Consumer Law Center's *Student Loan Law: Collections, Intercepts, Deferments, Discharges, Repayment Plans, and Trade School Abuses* (3d ed. 2006).

TYPES OF STUDENT LOANS

The first step for a survivor and her advocate is to identify what kind of student loan she has. There are many different types of student loans and many different lenders to whom the survivor might owe repayment. Her rights and strategies will vary depending on what type of loan she has. This chapter covers only federal student loans. Most student loans fall into this category.

There are also private loans and state loans. If the survivor has a private loan, she may check her loan documents to find out the name of the company and then contact that company for more information about assistance if she is having trouble paying the loans. This is because these loans have different rules from the federal loans discussed in this chapter.

Stafford and PLUS Loans. Most federally guaranteed student loans fall into one of two categories. They are either Federal Family Education Loans (FFELs) or Direct Loans. FFELs are guaranteed by the government but given out by banks or other financial institutions. Direct Loans are loans directly from the federal government to borrowers with the assistance of the school. Lenders and guaranty agencies are cut out of the Direct Loan process.

Both FFELs and Direct Loans can be any of the following types:

- *Stafford Loans* (formerly called Guaranteed Student Loans or GSLs) can be either subsidized or unsubsidized. Subsidized loans are given out based on financial need. Borrowers are not charged interest before repayment begins. Unsubsidized loans, on the other hand, are not based on financial need. Interest is charged on unsubsidized loans from the time the loan is disbursed until it is paid off.
- *PLUS Loans* are loans for parents to help finance their children's education.
- *Consolidation Loans.* There are both FFEL and Direct consolidation loans. These programs will allow the survivor to combine one or more loans into a new loan that has different, and hopefully better, terms.

Perkins Loans. Perkins Loans, formerly called National Direct Student Loans or NDSLs, are made directly from the school attended by the consumer. The consumer repays the school. If the consumer stops paying, the loan is eventually turned over to the U.S. Department of Education.

A survivor can identify what type of loan she has by looking at the loan application and promissory note. She can also ask the lender or debt collector to identify the type of loan. Alternatively, she may use the Department of Education's National Student Loan Data System. To use this system, the survivor will need to get a Personal Identification Number on-line at www.nslds.ed.gov or call 1-800-4FED-AID, TDD: 1-800-730-8913.

FFEL loans can be complicated, and understanding them may be difficult. Even if the school helps the survivor fill out the loan papers, a FFEL loan is actually from a bank. The bank may then sell the loan to another lender, such as the Student Loan Marketing Association (Sallie Mae). Whoever is holding the loan might hire another company to "service" the loan. These loan servicers will receive payments and correspond with the survivor. If she stops making payments on the loan, it is then turned over to a guaranty agency. Certain older loans are eventually passed on to the U.S. Department of Education. Both the guaranty agency and the Department of Education may hire a debt collection agency to attempt to collect on the debt.

Direct Loans are simpler. The school, not the bank, arranges for a loan between the U.S. Department of Education and the student. Payments are made directly to the United States Department of Education.

WHAT MAY HAPPEN IF A SURVIVOR IS IN DEFAULT ON HER STUDENT LOANS

The government has a number of actions it can take to pursue student loan defaulters. These methods can be used many years after the loan was made because there is no time limit on the collection of student loans. The discussion below lists the various actions the government may take and ways to deal with them. The discussion later in this chapter, in the section entitled "Getting Out of Default on Student Loans," looks at the ways the survivor can stop the student loan collectors entirely by getting out of default.

If the survivor is in default, the government can deny her new student loans and grants. This can prove to be a terrible trap: the survivor wants to go back to school to obtain the training she needs to increase her income so that she can pay her debts, including her old student loan; but, because she has been unable to pay her student loans, she is in default and may not be eligible for new student loans. If her goal is to get new financial assistance in order to return to school, she should carefully review the discussion later in this chapter on getting out of default.

Most student loan defaults will also show up on a credit report. How long the information remains on the survivor's report depends on the type of loan. Most defaults will remain on a credit report for up to seven years. Perkins Loans, however, may be reported indefinitely. For more information on credit reports, see Chapter Twelve.

Tax Refund Intercepts. If the survivor is in default on a student loan, the government can take her tax refund, including any earned income tax credit she is owed (for more information on the Earned Income Tax Credit see Chapter Twenty-One). The only safe way to avoid this collection method is not to have a tax refund due. The survivor can decrease her withholding or lower any estimated tax payments she makes. She will then have little or no refund that can be seized.

She should receive a notice before any actual interception of her tax refund. The notice should inform her of her right to contest the interception. She should check whatever boxes are appropriate on the form (for example, "the school closed" or "the school defrauded her") and return it immediately, asking for a hearing. The form should be sent back with return receipt requested to prove it was received. The survivor will have to do this every year that she gets a notice unless she is able to resolve the default through the hearings appeals process.

She should also be notified after any seizure and should complain to the Department of Education if she did not have a chance to raise her defenses before her refund was seized.

Wage Garnishment. Student loan collectors have the right to garnish a certain amount of wages *without first obtaining a court judgment.* The amount that can be garnished is the lesser of 15% of the survivor's disposable pay or the amount of disposable pay over $154.50 per week. Disposable pay is close to take-home pay and includes gross pay minus taxes and other amounts that are deducted by law.

For example:

The survivor has weekly disposable pay of $200. Fifteen percent of her disposable pay is $30 (15% of $200 = $30).

The amount by which her weekly disposable pay exceeds $154.50 is $45.50 ($200 – 154.50 = $45.50).

The government can take the lesser of the two amounts. Since $30 is less than $45.50, this is the amount the collector can take each week from the survivor's wages.

There are a number of ways a survivor can stop garnishments to repay her student loan. She can ask for a repayment agreement instead of the garnishment. She can stop a wage seizure if she lost her old job involuntarily and has not been continuously employed in her new job for a full year. Generally she will have to appeal the garnishment in order to raise this unemployment issue.

The government is required to give the survivor notice of her right to a hearing. She can request a hearing and explain why she thinks she need not repay the loan. Among other reasons, garnishment may be halted if she can show that it would result in extreme financial hardship.

Federal Benefit Offsets. Because Social Security is considered so essential for survival, it has traditionally been protected from attachment by creditors. A 1996 law takes away some of this protection, but only when federal agencies are collecting debts owed to them.

Not all federal benefits may be taken. However, Social Security Retirement and Disability benefits can be offset.

Supplemental Security Income (SSI) cannot be taken under this law.

Even if the survivor receives benefits that the government can now seize, she does not have to worry that the government will take her entire check. The government cannot take any of the first $9000 ($750 per month) of benefits. In addition, no matter how much money the survivor gets, the government cannot take more than 15% of total benefits.

For example:
The survivor receives a monthly Social Security benefit of $850. The first $750 is completely protected from offset.
The government can only take the lesser of
(1) 15% of the total benefit (= $127.50) or
(2) the amount left above $750.
In this case, the amount left is $100. Since this is less than $127.50, the amount of the offset would be $100.

Other Consequences. The IRS can also take the survivor's Social Security benefits to collect tax debts, and the rules are different for this program.

If the survivor defaults on her loans, a large portion of anything she pays to a collection agency on the loan will go to collection agency fees and not to pay off her loan. The government can also sue her to try to collect on the loans. Although the government has become more aggressive in suing borrowers, the odds of the survivor being sued are still relatively low. If she is sued, she most likely will have a number of defenses (see Chapter Five for more information about dealing with collection lawsuits).

GETTING OUT OF DEFAULT ON STUDENT LOANS

The discussion above summarized the ways that the government can try to collect on the survivor's defaulted student loans. But she can avoid these problems by getting out of default, as described below. In addition, getting out of default means that she can get financial assistance to go back to school.

If the survivor is attempting to get out of default to avoid the government's aggressive collection tactics, she should first try to figure out whether she is truly in danger. It may be that she does not have sufficient wages to be garnished, no tax refunds to intercept, no special concern for her credit rating, and no interest in applying for new student loans and grants. In that case, she may decide to do nothing and instead use what income she has to pay her rent, mortgage, utility bills, or other priority debts. If she is not safe from collection or she wants to go back to school, the discussion below lists some strategies to help get out of default.

Discharges. Discharges are the most powerful remedies available to survivors with student loans. These remedies are available regardless of whether she is in default. If a survivor qualifies for a discharge, her loan will be cancelled. She will also get back all the money she has paid or that has been taken from her to pay the loan. In most cases, the government is also required to help remove negative information from credit reports related to the loan. Unfortunately, not everyone qualifies for these discharges. Each federal discharge and the requirements to receive the discharges are summarized below. Federal discharge forms can be downloaded from www.ed.gov/offices/OSFAP/DCS/forms/index.html.

1. *Closed School Discharge* (34 C.F.R. § 682.402(d)). The survivor may qualify for a closed school discharge if the school closed while she was enrolled or soon after she withdrew from the school. This type of discharge applies only to loans received at least in part on or after January 1, 1986. The survivor must have been enrolled at the time of school closure or, if she withdrew, the withdrawal must have occurred within

ninety days of the closure. The Department of Education maintains a list of official closure dates, available at www.ed.gov/offices/OSFAP/Students/closedschool/search.html.

2. *False Certification Discharge* (34 C.F.R. § 682.402(e)). The survivor may qualify for a false certification discharge if the school falsely certified that she had the ability to benefit from the program. This type of discharge applies only to loans received at least in part on or after January 1, 1986. Perkins Loans are not eligible.

   To qualify, the survivor must show that her eligibility to borrow was falsely certified by the school. In most cases, students with high school diplomas or GEDs at the time of admission are not eligible for the discharge. There are exceptions to the high-school-diploma requirement: the survivor may qualify if she was unable to meet minimum state employment requirements for the job for which she was being trained or if the school forged or altered the loan note or check endorsements. Beginning in July 2006, victims of identity theft are also eligible for a discharge if they can show that the loan was falsely certified due to a crime of identity theft.

   If the survivor thinks she might qualify for such a discharge she should ask whoever is holding the loan for the appropriate cancellation request form. These forms are also available on the Department of Education website at www.ed.gov. She should be prepared to meet resistance and delay. Because it usually takes a long time to process the application, it is a good idea to request a forbearance so that collection activities will stop while the application is pending.

3. *Unpaid Refund Discharge* (34 C.F.R. § 682.402(l)). The survivor can cancel all or a portion of a loan received after January 1, 1986, if she left school and the school failed to pay a refund owed to her. Perkins Loans are not eligible, but failure to pay a refund can be raised as a defense if the school sues to collect on the loan.

4. *Disability Discharge.* The survivor can discharge loans if she can document a permanent and total disability. Pre-existing conditions qualify only if her condition has deteriorated.

5. *Bankruptcy.* It is generally difficult, but not impossible, for a survivor to discharge a student loan in bankruptcy. Currently, the only way to discharge a student loan in bankruptcy is to show that repayment will "impose an undue hardship on the debtor and debtor's dependents." The discharge for loans more than seven years old was eliminated in 1998.

For more on bankruptcy and student loans, see NCLC's manual, *Student Loan Law: Collections, Intercepts, Deferments, Discharges, Repayment Plans, and Trade School Abuses.*

6. *State Discharges.* State tuition recovery funds (STRFs) can be a valuable source of relief for a student who cannot obtain a federal discharge but was defrauded by a school that has become insolvent. The majority of states have either a STRF or a bond program to reimburse defrauded students. For more information on these funds, see NCLC's manual, *Student Loan Law: Collections, Intercepts, Deferments, Discharges, Repayment Plans, and Trade School Abuses.*

Repayment Options. Student loan borrowers have many special repayment options. For a survivor who does not qualify for any of the student loan discharge programs discussed above, these plans can be particularly effective. Deferments may also be available for those not already in default. The primary types of deferments are: student deferments; unemployment deferments not to exceed three years; and economic hardship deferments, granted one year at a time for a maximum of three years.

Even if the survivor is in default, forbearances are available. Forbearances are less advantageous than deferments because interest continues to accrue while the loan payments are reduced or postponed.

Loan consolidation is another possibility, particularly if the survivor does not qualify for a discharge but wishes to get new loans and grants. She can consolidate her defaulted student loans into a Federal Direct Consolidation Loan with an Income Contingent Repayment Plan (ICRP). Monthly ICRP payments are calculated based on a formula that allows borrowers to pay very small payments (sometimes even no payments) when their incomes are very low. Applications can be obtained by calling 1-800-557-7392 or on-line at www.ed.gov/DirectLoan.

An on-line calculator can be used to figure out the monthly payment under various repayment plans. See www.ed.gov/DirectLoan/calc.html.

Another option is for the survivor to request a reasonable and affordable payment plan based on her total financial circumstances or for her to rehabilitate her loans. Generally, she will have to request these plans from her loan holders, usually a lender or guaranty agency.

ADDITIONAL RESOURCES

The National Consumer Law Center publishes a manual, *Student Loan Law: Collections, Intercepts, Deferments, Discharges, Repayment Plans, and Trade School Abuses* (3d ed. 2006).

The Department of Education has an ombudsman office that will assist student loan borrowers. The toll-free phone number is 877-557-2575; the website is at www.sfahelp.ed.gov. The survivor should first try to work out any problems on her own before contacting the ombudsman office.

The Department of Education has a helpful website, www.ed.gov. The "Student Guide" is available in English and Spanish on the website or by calling the Federal Student Aid Information Center at 1-800-4-FED-AID. This is an excellent resource for understanding the different types of loans and repayment options.

ADDITIONAL RESOURCES

14

Credit Discrimination

Survivors leaving relationships may find it difficult to obtain credit. Sometimes this is due to a poor or insufficient credit history. (For advice on dealing with a poor credit history, see Chapter Twelve.) However, some difficulties may be caused by illegal discrimination.

All creditors discriminate when making loans. They decide whether to extend credit or what the terms of the loan will be based on past payment history, income, employment, or assets. Such discrimination is generally permissible. Unfortunately, a large number of lenders also discriminate based on impermissible factors such as race, gender, age, and marital status among others. Women, especially women of color, face difficulties obtaining market-rate first and second mortgages. Creditors discriminate as to which customers they solicit for credit, to whom they grant credit, or how their credit customers are treated in subsequent stages of the credit transaction, such as in loan servicing and debt collection. Many consumers are not even sure if they are eligible for credit or do not understand why they are turned down for credit.

Illegal discrimination cuts off access to credit for those who need it most. This denial of access to credit affects many aspects of ordinary life. For example, the absence of credit or presence of "bad" credit may be the reason why a survivor is denied admission to rental housing or prevented from opening a bank account.

There is a direct and measurable cost of this discrimination. Predatory, high-interest-rate first- and second-mortgage lenders and others target the very groups discriminated against by traditional lenders. Another direct consequence of credit discrimination is lost opportunity for home ownership, lost opportunity for a college education, and denial of access to medical care and other essential services.

The key federal laws prohibiting credit discrimination are (1) the Equal Credit Opportunity Act (ECOA); (2) the Fair Housing Act (FHA); (3) other federal civil rights acts such as 42 U.S.C. §§ 1981 and 1982; and (4) state credit discrimination laws. For more information on these laws, see NCLC's manual *Credit Discrimination* (4th. ed. 2005 and Supp.).

Federal credit discrimination laws prohibit creditors from discriminating against racial and ethnic minorities, women, elders, the disabled (housing-related credit only), public assistance recipients, married women, and others. (The FHA also prohibits discrimination in rental housing, a subject beyond the scope of this guidebook.) For more information on this topic, contact a local fair housing center. A list of fair housing organizations is available at the website of the National Fair Housing Alliance, www.nationalfairhousing.org.

Creditors may not discriminate based on the following factors:

Gender. Federal lending laws prohibits gender discrimination. Federal regulations set out special rules for judging the credit history of women whose accounts have been subsumed under their husband's name (see Chapter Twelve).

Marital Status. Federal fair lending law prohibits discrimination on the basis of marital status, including discrimination against an individual because she is single, divorced, separated, married, or widowed. Thus, a creditor may not discriminate against an abuse survivor because she is separated or divorced from her abuser. Federal regulations set out specific prohibitions against:

Credit checks on spouses or ex-spouses—If a borrower is applying for credit only in her name, a creditor is prohibited from seeking to obtain a spouse's or ex-spouse's credit history. (For more information on this topic, see Chapter Twelve.)

Co-signature requirements—Similarly, a creditor cannot require a married borrower to have his or her spouse co-sign a loan if the borrower qualifies for the loan individually and is not seeking a joint account. However, a creditor can require a co-signature if the borrower is relying on joint assets to qualify for the loan or the borrowers lives in a community property state. For a list of states that have community property laws, see Chapter Six.

Families with Children. The FHA prohibits creditor discrimination because of familial status, defined basically as having children or foster children or being pregnant. This only applies to housing-related discrimination.

Discrimination Against Public Assistance Recipients. The ECOA prohibits creditors from discriminating against someone because she receives public assistance, such as TANF or Food Stamps.

Discrimination Based on Other Sources of Income. The ECOA prohibits creditors from discriminating against an applicant because her source of income is from part-time work, child support, alimony, or retirement benefits. This is because these types of income are often associated with protected categories such as gender, marital status, or age.

There is no specific federal statute prohibiting discrimination against domestic violence survivors. New York City does have an ordinance prohibiting discrimination against abuse survivors. Also, some states prohibit discrimination against abuse survivors in the area of insurance. Below are some examples of state laws that specifically prohibit insurance companies from discriminating against survivors of domestic violence.

EXAMPLES OF STATUTES PROHIBITING INSURANCE DISCRIMINATION

CALIFORNIA: Cal. Ins. Code §§ 679.9, 10144.2, 10144.3, 10198.9, 10705 (West)
FLORIDA: Fla. Stat. § 626.9541(g)(3)
GEORGIA: Ga. Code Ann. § 33-6-4(b)(15)
ILLINOIS: 215 Ill. Comp. Stat. Ann. § 5/155.22a
IOWA: Iowa Code § 507B.4(7)(c)
MARYLAND: Md. Code Ann., Ins. § 27-504 (West)
MONTANA: Mont. Code Ann. § 33-18-216
NEW HAMPSHIRE: N.H. Rev. Stat. Ann. § 417.4(VIII)(f)
NEW YORK: N.Y. Ins. Law § 2612 (McKinney)
NORTH DAKOTA: N.D. Cent. Code § 26.1-39-24
OHIO: Ohio Rev. Code Ann. § 3901.21(Y) (West)
OKLAHOMA: Okla. Stat. tit. 36, § 4502
OREGON: Or. Rev. Stat. § 746.015(4)
PENNSYLVANIA: 40 Pa. Stat. Ann. § 1171.5(a)(14) (West)

NOTE: *This is only a partial list. Be sure to review your own state statutes for similar laws.*

Despite the lack of specific federal protections, advocates and survivors could argue that discrimination against someone because she has suffered from abuse is encompassed by other types of discrimination that are prohibited, for example:

Gender discrimination—Discrimination against domestic violence survivors may be a form of gender discrimination. For example, if the survivor is a woman, the gender discrimination may be based upon stereotypes about women in abusive relationships (for example, denying a woman survivor a loan because "she'll just go back to the abuser anyway").

Discrimination against the disabled—If the survivor is suffering from post-traumatic stress syndrome, it may constitute discrimination against the disabled if the creditor fails to make reasonable accommodations for that condition.

A survivor who suspects she is the victim of credit discrimination should contact her state or local anti-discrimination agency or civil rights organization. A list of state civil rights commissions may be found at www.neoc.ne.gov.

15

Credit and Debit Card Basics

THE IMPORTANCE OF STARTING FRESH

Previous chapters have discussed how the survivor should immediately disentangle herself financially from the abuser—if she can do so without risking retaliation by the abuser. Starting fresh means closing or taking herself off any bank accounts, opening a new bank account only in her name, and making sure that any money directly deposited into her bank account (paychecks, government benefits, dividends, and the like) is sent to the *new* bank account. She may also want to close out joint credit card accounts, remove the abuser as an authorized user from her credit card accounts, and contact the card issuer and to remove herself as an authorized user. (See Chapter Six for more about what is an "authorized user.")

It is also important to make sure that any correspondence from a credit or debit card issuer or bank is not sent to an address where the abuser has access. Otherwise, the abuser might be able to gain unauthorized access to the bank account or make unauthorized use of the credit card. The survivor may be able to prove that the abuser was not an authorized user of the card, but it is much easier to stop unauthorized use before it happens.

Once these steps are taken, the survivor can apply for new credit cards and obtain ATM or debit cards with new bank accounts. To minimize the chance that the abuser will steal and use the card, it is also be important for the survivor to use new Personal Identification Numbers (PINs) for these cards that are different from the PINs that she has used in the past.

This chapter provides advice for the survivor about the differences between debit cards and credit cards and what to look for in choosing them. This chapter also discusses the rights that card holders have when disputing transactions and charges to those cards.

UNDERSTANDING DIFFERENT TYPES OF DEBIT AND CREDIT CARDS

The first thing the survivor needs to know is what kinds of debit and credit cards are available to her and which ones should be avoided.

Debit Cards and How They Differ from Credit Cards. A debit card may look like a credit card, but it is not. A debit card will allow the survivor to have money taken directly from her bank account to pay charges made with the card. Merchants accept debit cards, like credit cards, to pay for goods or services.

The survivor can also use the debit card to take money out of ATM machines, but she does not need a debit card to do so. While most banks will automatically give a debit card to a new account holder, a consumer (or the survivor) can usually request a card that is solely an ATM card instead. This type of ATM card can only be used to withdraw cash at an ATM machine and not to make purchases from merchants.

Although they often look the same, there are important differences between credit and debit cards. When the survivor uses a debit card, the money is almost immediately taken from her bank account. This is different than using a credit card. When a credit card is used, the company that issued the card pays the merchant for the item purchased. The survivor will then owe this amount to the issuer. The amount she owes changes with each purchase. Unlike purchases made with a credit card, the amount she can spend with a debit card is tied to the amount in her bank account.

Some debit cards come with a VISA or MasterCard logo on them, and the merchant will give the survivor the option of using the card as "credit" or "debit." The credit option is confusing because the card is still being used as a debit card. What this choice actually means is: does the consumer want to use her debit card like an ATM card and enter her PIN for identification or does she want to use the debit card like a credit card and sign her name on the receipt for identification. Either way, the money is taken out of her bank account within a short period of time.

Advantages and Disadvantages of Debit Cards As Compared to Credit Cards. There are advantages and disadvantages to both types of cards.

Running up a balance. A debit card automatically takes money from a bank account, so the survivor is less likely to run up a big unpaid balance. However, many banks now allow consumers to use debit cards to withdraw more than they have in their accounts. These "bounce loans" (often marketed as "overdraft protection") are extremely expensive, with interest rates in the 300% to 500% range or even higher. The survivor can avoid these charges by making it clear to the bank that she does not want overdraft protection with her ATM or debit card.

With a credit card, a survivor can quickly run up a large balance that will take years to repay. However, she may prefer a credit card's flexibility of slower repayment with interest, especially if she is on a tight budget and wants to be able to pay her most pressing debts are paid first.

Right to dispute charges. The survivor's right to dispute charges is more limited when a debit, rather than a credit, card is used. If she purchases a vacuum cleaner from a nearby store with her credit card, it breaks during the first week of use, and the merchant refuses to fix it, she may dispute the charge for the vacuum on her credit card bill. (See discussion below.) There are *no* similar rights available if she used her debit card.

Liability for unauthorized use. The survivor's responsibility for losses from a lost or stolen card is generally much greater for a debit card than for a credit card. Under federal law, her responsibility is limited to $50 for unauthorized *credit card* charges no matter when she reports the lost or stolen credit card.

If survivor's *debit card* is lost or stolen, federal law caps her liability at $50, but only if she reports the lost or stolen card within two business days. If she fails to do so, she can be held liable up to $500 for unauthorized charges incurred after that two-day period. If she fails to report an unauthorized transfer within sixty days after the bank statement is mailed to her showing that transfer, she can be held liable for all unauthorized charges incurred after that point. (However, both VISA and MasterCard have "zero liability" policies that limit a consumer's debit card losses in some situations to $50.)

Whether the survivor relies on these protections when using a credit or a debit card, she will need to show that the use or transfer was "unauthorized." This may become a disputed issue with the bank. For example, it may *not* be considered an unauthorized transfer if the money is withdrawn by someone a consumer knows (such as her abuser) to whom she had previously lent her debit card and provided her PIN, even if this person took her card and used it without her permission a second time.

Another difference between debit and credit cards is that, if the survivor's debit card is used in an unauthorized transaction, the consequences may be worse because the money to pay for the purchase comes directly out of her bank account. Even if the money is later restored to her account, the temporary loss of these funds may cause checks to bounce, prevent her from paying important bills, or take away money she had planned to use for other pressing needs.

Secured Versus Unsecured Credit Cards. Some credit cards are known as secured cards. If the survivor obtains a secured card, she puts up some of her property as collateral for the account. Most cards are unsecured, meaning there is no property acting as collateral for the debt. For a more complete discussion of secured and unsecured debts, see Chapter Three.

All things being equal, the survivor should use an unsecured card rather than a secured card. The interest rates on secured cards are typically just as high as those on unsecured cards, but, if the consumer is unable to make payments, the issuer may attempt to take the property acting as collateral.

There are several different types of secured cards to watch out for:

Credit Cards Secured by Purchases. Some credit card lenders, usually store creditors such as major department stores, claim that items purchased with their card are collateral for the debt. If the survivor has problems making payments, those lenders may threaten to repossess the items bought with the card. In addition, this collateral may affect the survivor's rights if she later needs to file bankruptcy. While most threats to repossess such personal property are not carried out, it is a good idea to use an unsecured card instead of a secured card whenever possible.

Credit Cards Secured by a Bank Account. Another type of secured credit card allows the survivor a credit limit up to the amount she has on deposit in a particular bank account. If she cannot make the payments, she loses the money in the account. These cards are usually marketed as a way to reestablish credit by showing that a consumer can make regular monthly payments on a credit card. Some secured credit cards may be useful if the survivor lacks any credit history at all. However, she needs to be careful in considering secured credit cards that are marketed to consumers with poor credit records as a way to "fix" their problems. These cards are often subprime credit cards with very high rates or fees or have other abusive features.

Credit Cards Secured by the Home. Some lenders offer credit cards in connection with a home equity line of credit. If the survivor uses this card, the balance is secured against her home each time she uses it. Home-secured credit cards are almost always a bad idea—the potential consequence of nonpayment is the loss of the survivor's shelter.

Cashed Check Loans. Another credit offer the survivor should avoid takes the form of a check mailed to her home, usually by her credit card company. If she cashes the check, she not only accepts high-interest-rate credit but will also be stuck with a large balance on a new account right from the start. It is better to find a reasonable credit card offer and use the new card carefully.

EIGHT THINGS TO THINK ABOUT BEFORE ACCEPTING A NEW CREDIT CARD

Consumer credit card spending has expanded greatly in recent years largely due to lenders' increased marketing efforts. More than five billion credit card offers are mailed to consumers each year. Most of us get several offers for new credit cards every week. In the past, consumers facing money problems rarely got new credit card offers, but times have changed. Lenders now buy huge mailing lists and offer credit to everyone on the list without further evaluation.

Credit cards are a mixed blessing. On one hand, they can help the survivor avoid even higher cost lenders (like the ones discussed in Chapter Twenty), establish or re-establish her credit history, and give her the ability to buy major items she may need for a new household (such as furniture or appliances). Sometimes it is difficult to get by in our society without a credit card. On the other hand, it is very easy for the survivor to become overextended using credit cards and to take on more debt than she can manage.

The terms offered by a credit card are often confusing, misleading, or deceptive. Many cards fail to provide understandable information concerning late payment fees, penalty interest rates for missed payments, the nature of "teaser" or variable interest rates, billing methods, and the consequences of making only minimum payments. Often the relevant information will be provided only after the survivor has applied for the card and then only in small print. Most lenders retain the right to change credit card terms, including the interest rate, at their discretion.

1. **Avoid Accepting Too Many Offers.** There is rarely a good reason to carry more than one or two credit cards. A survivor should be very selective about choosing cards that are best for her. Having too much credit can lead to bad decisions and unmanageable debts. Too many credit card accounts may also lower her credit rating.
2. **Beware Subprime Credit Cards.** If the survivor has bad credit, instead of turning her down, sometimes the lender will offer her a subprime credit card. These cards generally come with very high interest rates,

expensive fees, and low credit limits. She may also be charged for unnecessary products such as "credit protection." Some lenders will actually issue cards with a low credit limit, and then add so many fees that the survivor cannot charge any purchases to the card because it is already maxed out when she receives it! Other lenders use subprime credit cards as a trick to revive old debts from other credit card companies. They may buy up the survivor's old debts and then offer her a new credit card. When the account is opened, the new lender slaps the old debt onto the new credit card account.

3. **Watch Out for Bait-and-Switch Offers.** The survivor may receive offers from some credit card lenders for an attractive, low-interest credit card with a high limit, but include—in the fine print—the statement that the lender can substitute a less attractive, more expensive card if she does not qualify. This substituted card often has a higher interest rate, more expensive fees, and/or a lower credit limit.

4. **Look Carefully at the Interest Rate.** The survivor should always know the interest rate on her cards and try to keep the rate as low as possible. It is often hard to do this, because the terms are so confusing and sometimes misleading. Credit card lenders usually have several interest rates for a credit card. They also constantly change their rates. The following are some important terms to understand:

   - *APR.* This is the interest rate expressed as an annual figure. Most cards have different APRs for purchases versus cash advances versus balance transfers and other types of transactions.

   - *Variable Rates.* Most credit cards use variable rates, which change with the rise or fall of a common index rate (an example of a variable rate might be "U.S. Prime Rate plus 5%"). It is important for the survivor to understand when and how the variable rate may change. Variable interest rates can be very confusing. Even "fixed" rates can be variable—the credit card lender usually has the right to change the interest rate with just fifteen days' notice.

   - *"Teaser" Rates.* A teaser rate is an artificially low initial rate that lasts only for a limited time, such as six months or less. After that, the rate automatically goes up. If the survivor builds up a balance while a teaser rate is in effect, she will end up repaying the debt at a much higher permanent rate.

- *Penalty Rates.* The survivor should be aware that many credit card contracts, including those that advertise low permanent rates, provide in the small print that the interest rate increases if she makes even a single late payment. Some lenders will increase the rate even if she is never late on her credit card but is late with a payment to any other creditor or if her credit score drops too low. This is known as "universal default."

5. **Fees, Fees, Fees.** Other terms of credit may be just as important as interest rates. It is important for the survivor to know that credit card companies now impose a number of different fees—late payment fees, fees for exceeding a credit limit, annual fees, membership fees, cash advance fees, balance transfer fees, even fees for buying lottery tickets with a card—and keep raising these fees every year. These fees significantly increase the cost of a credit card so that a card that appears cheaper with a low APR could end up being much more expensive.

6. **Look for the Grace Period.** Most credit cards offer a "grace period" or "free ride period," the amount of time in which the consumer can pay off purchases without incurring finance charges (cash advances usually do not have a grace period). Without a grace period, finance charges begin accruing immediately, and a low rate may actually be higher than it looks. If the survivor intends to pay off the balance in full each month, the terms of the grace period are especially important. Many credit cards have reduced their grace period. They have also reduced the time between when they send a bill and when the payment is due, increasing the risk of going past the grace period and having to pay both interest charges and a late fee.

   The survivor should also look out for early posting periods. For example, some companies have used times as early as 9 or 10 a.m. as the cut-off time for crediting payments received that day. Even if a payment is received later that same day, the company will consider it to be late and will charge a late fee. It is important to get payments in as early as possible. If the survivor is running very close to the deadline, she might consider paying—at least for that month—over the phone.

7. **Always Read Both the Disclosures and the Credit Contract.** Disclosures about the terms of a credit card offer will appear in a box, usually on the reverse side of or accompanying the credit card application. The survivor should review these carefully and make a copy if the disclosure box is on

the reverse side of the application. She should also read the credit contract, which comes with the card, and call the lender for an explanation of any terms she does not understand.

8. **If the Survivor Takes a Credit Card and Discovers Terms She Does Not Like: Cancel!** She does not need to keep a credit card if she does not like the terms. Of course, if she has used the card, she will need to pay off the balance. She should also cancel the card if the lender changes the terms and she does not like the new terms. Otherwise she will be stuck with the new (and probably unfavorable) terms.

AVOIDING CREDIT CARD PROBLEMS

Credit card debts can spiral out of control. Here are some ways the survivor can protect herself from getting in over her head.

Do Not Use Credit Cards to Finance an Unaffordable Lifestyle. If the survivor is constantly using a card without the ability to pay the resulting bill in full each month, she should consider whether her budget plan is realistic. It may not be workable for more than the short term.

Try to Avoid Making Financial Trouble Worse by Using Credit Cards to Make Ends Meet. Finance charges and other fees will add to the survivor's debt burden. However, using a credit card in a period of financial difficulty is preferable to taking out a home equity loan and putting her home on the line.

Do Not Get Hooked on Minimum Payments. Many credit card lenders set their minimum payments so low that it may take decades to pay off the debt—even if the survivor makes no new charges to the card. Paying just the minimum balance is a long-term debt trap. Also, lenders reserve the right to increase the minimum payment at their option. This means that a survivor might budget for a $50 minimum payment, only to find out that a new minimum payment of $100 applies.

Do Not Run Up the Balance Based on a Temporary "Teaser" Interest Rate. Money borrowed during a temporary 6%-rate period is likely to be paid back at a much higher permanent rate of 15% or more.

Make Credit Card Payments on Time If You Can Afford to Do So Within Your Budget. The survivor should avoid late payment charges and penalty rates if she can do so without endangering her ability to keep up with higher priority debts. Bad problems can worsen quickly if she has a new higher-interest rate and late charge to pay during a time of financial difficulty.

Most lenders will waive a late payment charge or default rates of interest only once. The survivor can also ask for a waiver if she makes a late payment accidentally or has a good excuse.

Avoid the Special Services, Programs, and Goods That Credit Card Lenders Offer to Bill to Their Cards. Most of these special services—credit card fraud protection plans, credit record protection, travel clubs, life insurance, and other similar offers—are bad deals.

Beware of Unsolicited Increases by a Credit Card Lender to the Credit Limit. Some lenders increase consumers' credit limits even when they have not asked for more credit. The survivor should not assume that this means the lender thinks she can afford more credit. The lender is more likely to have increased the limit because it thinks she will carry a bigger balance and pay more interest.

Be Careful About Juggling Cards to Take Advantage of Teaser Rates and Balance Transfer Options. It takes a great deal of time and effort to juggle cards to take advantage of terms designed to be temporary. The survivor should remember that all teaser rate offers are designed to get her locked into the higher rate for the long term, because that is how the lender makes the most money. Even people who successfully juggle many cards complain that use of numerous cards has a long-term negative impact on their credit records.

Do Not Max Out. It is risky for the survivor to charge her credit card up to its limit, as she is likely to incur high over-limit fees. Plus, a credit card account close to its limit will cause a big drop in her credit score. This may even cause the lender to impose a penalty rate.

CREDIT CARD DISPUTES

Most credit card holders will have some problem with card charges at some point. Mysterious charges, double billing, and mail-order merchandise that never arrive are all frustrating problems often faced by cardholders. Federal law protects consumers in these situations. There are three separate protections that survivors should know about.

Unauthorized Use of a Credit Card. Unauthorized use occurs when someone steals, borrows, or otherwise uses the survivor's credit card or card number without her permission. Unauthorized use of credit cards has increased as many more businesses accept credit card transactions by telephone and on the Internet.

Federal law limits the survivor's liability for unauthorized use of a credit card to $50. If someone steals her card, for example, the credit card lender can charge her a maximum of $50 no matter how much the thief has charged.

The situation may be trickier if someone the survivor knows has used her card. In general, she should not be liable if she did not authorize this use. But if she gave her card to the abuser, for example, she may be liable for any charges he runs up even if she told him to use the card for emergencies only. If the abuser took the survivor's card without her knowledge, however, the law limits her liability in the same way as if her card was lost or stolen.

As soon as the survivor learns of the unauthorized use of her credit card, she should call the lender to make a report. If she calls before unauthorized charges are incurred, she cannot be charged even $50, since the lender can take steps to cancel her card and send her a new one. If a charge unexpectedly appears on her bill for something she did not authorize, she can also use her right to dispute the charge, as discussed below.

Billing Error Disputes. The second type of credit card protection involves disputes about the bill. For example, a merchant may have overcharged the survivor on her card, charged her for products or work she did not receive, or processed a transaction in error. A law called the Fair Credit Billing Act forces lenders to follow specific "billing error" procedures to resolve these disputes. (As discussed above, this protection does not apply to debit cards.)

Information about how to raise a dispute appears on the back of each bill, including the mailing address to use. The survivor must raise a dispute *in writing* to the credit card company, usually by sending a letter. The letter must be sent within sixty (60) days of the first bill with the improper charges. The letter must include the following information:

- name and account number;
- the dollar amount disputed; and

- a statement of the reason for the dispute.

If appropriate, backup documentation such as a cancellation letter or a letter explaining the problem to the merchant should be included in the dispute letter.

Once the survivor has raised a dispute, the credit card company must investigate and report back to her in writing within two complete billing cycles or within ninety days, whichever comes first. In many cases, the charge will be canceled. Often a merchant whose billing is challenged will back off rather than risk losing the privilege of accepting business by credit card. Interest charges associated with a successfully disputed debt must also be canceled.

Until the dispute is resolved, the survivor does not need to pay the disputed portion of her bill. However, she must make a payment to cover any undisputed amount. The credit card company cannot report her as delinquent with respect to the disputed amount but may do so if part of her debt is undisputed and she did not make necessary payments.

Withholding Payment for Charges on a Credit Card. Withholding payment for disputed credit card charges is a very powerful tool that the survivor can use if she is dissatisfied with some aspect of a credit card transaction with a merchant. She can use this power if she has a legitimate complaint with the merchant initiating the card charges *and* she first makes a good faith effort to resolve the problem with the merchant directly. In addition, she can only dispute a charge to the extent to which that amount is outstanding on the credit card account. For example, if she pays off all but $200 on a credit card bill, she can only dispute $200 with a merchant, even if the amount in dispute is $500.

There are two other important limits to the right to dispute charges:

- the goods or services the survivor bought must have cost more than $50; and
- she must have bought those goods or services in her home state or within 100 miles of her mailing address (telephone and Internet sales from the consumer's home are usually treated as within her home state).

However, these last two limits do not apply if the credit card was issued by the seller (such as a department store card) or if the card issuer participated in the transaction through a mail solicitation suggesting that the survivor purchase certain goods using the issuer's credit card.

After the survivor notifies her credit card company that she is withholding payment, it cannot report the disputed amount as delinquent to a credit bureau until the dispute is settled or a court judgment is issued against the survivor. The lender cannot treat the dispute as "settled" or take collection action against the survivor unless it has completed a reasonable investigation of her claim.

16

Used-Car Fraud

A survivor leaving an abusive relationship often finds that she needs a car. While in the abusive relationship, she may have been using a car that was titled in the abuser's name. Sometimes the abuser may have intentionally limited the survivor's access to a vehicle during the relationship in order to control her. When the survivor leaves the abusive relationship, she will likely reenter the workforce (if she is not already working) and also make greater use of childcare. In many communities, public transportation is limited and a car becomes a necessity. The survivor may seek possession of the vehicle as part of a protection order, but sometimes this will not be possible.

When a survivor looks for a car, she is faced with potential abuses by used-car dealers and high-rate lenders, as well as other car-related consumer problems. This is especially true for women because they are often seen as easier targets for unscrupulous tactics.

TYPES OF SCAMS

There are a number of common scams involving used cars, which are described below. Federal law prohibits many of these abuses. In addition, many states have laws that protect consumers in new-and used-car purchases.

Odometer Fraud. Odometer fraud is a common used car scam. One type of odometer fraud involves tampering with an odometer so that its reading is less than the car's actual mileage. Another type is failing to disclose that an odometer has exceeded its mechanical limits (for example, when a car has really traveled 150,000 miles, not the 50,000 shown on the odometer).

There is a federal law prohibiting odometer fraud, and most states have similar laws.

Salvage Fraud. A car is generally considered "salvaged" if it has been damaged because of collision, flooding, fire, or involvement in other serious accidents, and the damage exceeds a percentage of the car's value. Many unscrupulous dealers patch up these cars and sell them to unsuspecting customers without disclosing the salvage history. Millions of these cars are still on the road.

Lemon Laundering. Lemon laundering involves a manufacturer buying back a lemon car from a consumer, then passing on that car to another consumer without its lemon history being disclosed.

Misrepresentation of the Number of Prior Users or Nature of Prior Use. Car dealers may misrepresent the number of prior owners. A typical representation is that the car was traded in to the dealer by someone who bought it as a new car and took excellent care of it. In fact, the car may have had a number of consumer owners, been passed between a number of dealers and wholesalers, or gone through several auctions.

Related misrepresentations concern the nature of the prior use. Consumers would certainly want to know if a car had previously been a rental car, police car, taxi cab, or lease car and whether it had been repossessed. Unfortunately, many dealers fail to disclose or, worse, lie about the car's prior use.

Problems with the Vehicle's Title. A car sold to a consumer can have a defective title for any number of reasons. The car may be stolen, or the VIN number may be fictitious. Pre-existing liens may not be satisfied, or the title may never be properly transferred to the consumer.

"As Is" Car Sales. Often dealers will to sell a car "as is." Federal law and many state laws restrict a dealer's ability to sell a car "as is."

FEDERAL AND STATE LAWS PROTECTING USED-CAR BUYERS

There are a number of state and federal laws intended to protect car buyers and to provide them with valuable information when they buy or lease used motor vehicles. **However, there is no automatic right to cancel an agreement to buy or lease a motor vehicle within three (or any number of) days.** A survivor should read over all lease or sale documents carefully before deciding to lease or buy a used motor vehicle or signing any document presented by a car dealer.

Implied Warranty of Merchantability. The implied warranty of merchantability is provided by the Uniform Commercial Code, which is a model state law that every state except Louisiana has adopted. (Louisiana has a different law that provides somewhat similar protections.) It provides that a product purchased or leased should operate as intended for a "reasonable" amount of time. Factors that go into evaluating what is "reasonable" include the age and condition of the product when purchased and the use to which it is put.

In some states this warranty may be "disclaimed." This means that the dealer selling the vehicle informs the buyer that the vehicle is being sold without this warranty. In order to be effective, disclaimers generally must be conspicuous. In addition, dealers may not disclaim implied warranties if they provide written warranties under the contract.

FTC Used Car Rule. The Federal Trade Commission or "FTC" Used Car Rule requires disclosure of certain information in the sale of used cars in the form of a "Buyers Guide." The Buyers Guide includes the following information:

- The vehicle make, model, year and vehicle identification number
- Name and address of the dealer or party designated to accept complaints
- Clear disclosure of warranty coverage

When a sale is conducted in Spanish, the Buyers Guide and the contract language must be available in both Spanish and English.

TIPS FOR USED-CAR BUYERS

When shopping for a used car, there are a few simple steps survivors can take to increase the chances that they will get a good car at a fair price with good financing terms.

Use a Logical Approach to Finding and Purchasing a Car. Finding a safe and reliable used car takes time and effort. Plan to spend several days if not weeks searching for the right car. It may be best to begin by making a list of the things that are most important to the survivor. With a limited budget, it is unrealistic to expect to find a car with all the latest features that is sporty and also safe and economical. In order to decide what is really important, she may wish to ask herself what the car will be used for. If it will be used only for short trips, gas mileage may not be important. If the survivor has a large family, size may be a factor. Safety, price, and reliability should be important for everyone.

Next, she can research what types of vehicles will meet her needs. *Consumer Reports* provides good information about different car models. The U.S. Department of Transportation's Auto safety hotline (1-800-424-9393) can provide information about recalls for a particular model. She can also research what would be a fair price for the cars that interest her. National Automobile Dealers Association (NADA) Books or Kelley bluebooks can be helpful in determining a fair price. Researching provides an opportunity to decide what car she needs and wants as opposed to what a salesperson wants to sell.

Investigate Individual Cars. Once a survivor finds a car that might be right for her, whether it is for sale at a used-car lot or being sold by a private owner, she should have a mechanic or knowledgeable person look at and inspect the car. Remember, a mechanical inspection is different from a safety inspection required in some states. To find a good mechanic, ask friends and relatives. She may wish to find a mechanic who is certified by the National Institute for Automotive Service Excellence (ASE). She may also check with the local Better Business Bureau to see if any complaints have been filed against the mechanic or the dealer. Ask to see receipts for any repairs or maintenance the owner has had done.

In addition to investigating the condition of the car, she also needs to research the car's history. Ask to see the title to see if it lists the previous owners and how long the seller has had it. Federal law requires that an odometer disclosure be on the title, and so the survivor must see the title itself at some point in the buying process. If she has access to the Internet, she may also want to use car research firms such as Carfax (www.carfax.com) to see how many previous owners it has had, what states it has been titled in, and if it has ever been branded a flood or salvage vehicle.

Paying for the Car. If the car is at a dealer's lot, the dealer will probably offer financing for the car. Before the survivor signs anything, she should ask to see a copy of the Truth in Lending disclosures. These are disclosures required by federal law that provide the annual percentage rate, amount financed, finance charge, and total payments on a uniform and easy-to-read form. These terms are required to be defined on the form. Federal law requires that these disclosures be given to the buyer before she signs so that she may review the terms. She may want to take this document home to review before signing. It is best to approach other lenders—perhaps the survivor's bank or credit union—and obtain the same Truth in Lending disclosures for loans they might offer. She then has the information to compare the possible loans and make an informed decision.

Read and Understand Everything Before Signing Anything. As with all consumer purchases, it is important for the survivor to read and understand any purchase documents before she signs them. It is also important for her to know all the terms of the deal before signing. The following are some helpful guidelines:

- Carefully review and check that all the terms, such as the interest rate and sales price, are the same as what was offered orally by the dealer.
- Make sure any options that are checked, such as credit insurance or a service contract, are add-ons that the buyer wants. Such add-ons are very profitable to dealers, who often slip these in even though the buyer has not requested them. If the survivor wants and selects options, she should make sure to understand the terms of these options.
- Make sure that all promises are in writing. Unless there is a promise **in writing** to make a particular repair or warrant that the vehicle is in good condition and free from defects, the dealer will claim that the car is sold "as is."
- It is also important to check that all the information on the contract is true. For example, if the contract lists a trade-in or down payment that was not made, do not sign the contract.
- Do not sign a blank contract.

Make Sure the Seller Signs Over the Title. In most states ownership of a vehicle is determined by title. The seller should sign over the title to the survivor. If the seller does not sign over title, then the survivor does not own the car (this is true even if the seller is financing the vehicle). The survivor must also see the federally required odometer disclosure document and should sign the disclosure. If the car is being financed by another lender, the lender most likely will have a lien against the title—in this case, the survivor will not get to keep a physical copy of the title. Once the loan is paid off, the lender should have the lien removed. In all cases, the survivor should make sure that she is shown the title at the time of purchase.

CONCLUSION

Following these steps, and armed with the information in this chapter, a survivor can greatly increase the chance that the car-buying process, and the purchased car itself, will be trouble-free. The extra effort she puts in before buying the car will be worth it when she experiences fewer problems and greater peace of mind once the purchase is made.

17

Private Child Support Collection Agencies

Many survivors know the frustration of being owed child support by an abuser but not being able to collect it. These survivors may be tempted to turn to a private child support collection agency for help, especially when the agency says they will only take a fee after the survivor gets her money. In the 1990s, a number of private, for-profit companies began specializing in collecting child support arrearages (back support) for custodial parents. Many of these companies target their advertising to low-income parents, especially those families that have left welfare.

Many custodial parents discover that using private collectors is not to their advantage. Unfortunately they often come to this realization only after they have contracted with the private collection agency. Private collectors are not regulated in most states and are not subject to the federal fair debt collection law discussed in Chapter Four.

THE COSTS OF A PRIVATE CHILD SUPPORT COLLECTION AGENCY

Private collectors charge hefty fees, often as high as 30% to 50% of the amount collected. This is precious money that low-income families could use to provide for their children. Furthermore, these fees only cover collection services. If the custodial parent needs legal assistance in obtaining a support order or enforcing it in court, the lawyer's fee will be in addition to the collector's fee.

Even worse, many of these private collectors engage in the following deceptive or unfair practices:

- Taking fees for money that they had no part in collecting. Often, private collectors collect fees from payments that a state agency obtained, such as an IRS tax refund intercept. In essence, the collector gets paid for the work that someone else did, and the family ends up with less money.
- Collecting payments from the non-custodial parents but never sending the money to the family.
- Collecting more than the agreed-upon fees.
- Treating current support as arrearages, so that the collector takes its 30% to 50% fee from the entire payment the custodial parent receives (even though only part or even none of it is really arrearages). The collector will take fees from the current support the custodial parent was *already receiving*, leaving the custodial parent in a *worse* position than when she first contacted the collector.
- Altering court orders so that support payments go directly to the collector and not to the family.
- Refusing to provide adequate account information to the custodial parent, such as how much has been collected from the non-custodial parent and how much the collector has taken.
- Collecting application fees of $100 or more, then closing down business and disappearing with the money.
- Threatening to sue custodial parents who complain about high fees or poor service.
- Misleading custodial parents into thinking that they are dealing with a state government agency by using deceptive names, for example, "Office of Child Support Enforcement Services."
- Engaging in the unauthorized practice of law, that is, signing court documents on behalf of the custodial parent without having a properly licensed attorney on staff.
- Entering into low-ball lump-sum settlements over arrearages despite the custodial parent's objection, for example, settling $32,000 in back support for only $10,000 even though the custodial parent did not accept the settlement.
- Refusing to let a survivor of domestic violence out of the contract even when she is afraid that the aggressive collection efforts by the private company is putting her in danger by angering the abuser.

A survivor should be made aware that private collectors cannot be relied upon to keep her location and other sensitive information confidential.

AGGRESSIVE HARASSMENT BY PRIVATE CHILD SUPPORT COLLECTORS

Private child support collectors are also notorious for their overly aggressive tactics against non-custodial parents. This is due in part to the fact that they are not subject to the federal fair debt laws discussed in Chapter Four.

The following are examples of harassment by private child support collectors:

- Demanding payment from grandparents, including bullying them into disclosing credit card numbers.
- Threatening the non-custodial parent's employer with the revocation of its business license unless the employer sends money to the collector.
- Repeatedly calling to harass relatives and neighbors of the non-custodial parent.
- Double billing, for example, collecting money that a state government agency has already collected.
- Collecting large lump-sum amounts from non-custodial parents, then closing down business and disappearing with the money.
- Threatening non-custodial parents with jail if they do not pay lump-sum amounts, even when the non-custodial parents offered to pay over a period of time.
- Threatening to (and actually) putting liens on the non-custodial parent's home when the collector has no legal right to do so.

For domestic violence survivors, such practices only introduce more stress and tension in an already volatile relationship. Abusers might blame the survivor for the private collectors' actions, potentially putting the survivor at additional risk for further abusive conduct. Double billing and outright fraud result in the abuser having less money to pay the survivor for support. If an abuser loses his job over harassment, it may also mean less money for the survivor. The abuser may "go underground" to avoid the private collector and cease to pay whatever child support he was actually providing.

QUESTIONS TO ASK A PRIVATE CHILD SUPPORT COLLECTOR

If the survivor insists on hiring a private collector, advise her at least to ask the following questions about any company she is thinking of hiring:

1. Are there any complaints against the private collector? The survivor should check with the Attorney General's Office, the Better Business Bureau, and other state or local consumer protection agencies in her home state and in the collector's home state. If she is able to access the Internet, the survivor can determine whether the Federal Trade Commission has filed any complaints against the private collector by using the search feature on the Federal Trade Commission's website (www.ftc.gov).
2. Is there an initial application or filing fee? If so, how much?
3. Does the company receiving the application fee actually do the collection work itself, or is it just a marketing agent that makes referrals to a general collection agency?
4. Is there a refund policy for the application fee if the collector is unable to collect from the non-custodial parent?
5. Can the contract be canceled? If so, what are the cancellation requirements?
6. What percentage will be deducted from each child support payment and for how long?
7. Will the collector deduct its fee from the entire support payment or just from any amount over and above the current amount of support that is already being received?
8. Will the support payments go to the custodial parent (or a court or state agency) first, or will they first go to the collection agency?
9. Will the company obtain her consent before agreeing to any settlement?
10. What kind of accounting and records of collection efforts will she be entitled to from the collector?
11. What is the collector's process for resolving complaints?
12. Will the custodial parent need to pay for legal expenses incurred by the collector in addition to the collection fee?

The answers to these questions (except for number 1) should be reflected in the written contract. The survivor should be advised to read over the contract carefully and seek help if she does not understand the contract. She should never sign a contract she does not understand. If the collection company makes any assurances orally, the survivor should be sure to get them in writing.

Before considering contracting with a private child support collection company, a survivor should review the information on child support found in Chapter Eleven of this guidebook.

ADDITIONAL RESOURCES

For more information on private child support collectors or related issues, the survivor can contact the Center for Law and Social Policy, the National Women's Law Center, and the National Consumer Law Center. Contact information is available in Appendix A at the back of this guidebook.

18

Quickie Foreign Divorce Scams

A number of con artists operate "quickie divorce" scams that prey upon people who are eager to get a fast divorce. These quickie divorce scams typically promise that they can obtain divorces in a few days or even in twenty-four hours, usually from countries such as the Dominican Republic, Haiti, and Mexico. They charge anywhere from a few hundred to several thousand dollars. While these scams have existed for decades, their number has increased with the rise of the Internet. Their search for victims is made easier because most communities lack low-cost, legitimate family law services.

A survivor who is married to her abuser may be a prime target for such schemes. Desperate to break her ties permanently with the abuser and finalize custody arrangements, she may be tempted by promises from the operators of these scams that the abuser does not need to show up or even be notified of the divorce.

Quickie divorce scams sometimes target immigrant communities. Scam artists will partner with local ethnic businesses, such as travel agencies and grocery stores, to advertise and process the quickie divorces.

The basic problem with quickie foreign divorces is that they often are not valid or recognized in the United States. While such foreign divorces can be valid in some limited circumstances, many of these quickie divorces are not legally valid. It is important for the survivor to know the following:

- If she or the abuser did not establish legal residence in the country where the divorce is obtained, that divorce is generally not valid. Yet many quickie divorce scams will advertise "no travel required" or tell her that she can "fly in, fly out" in a few hours to get the divorce.
- If the survivor files for divorce using a quickie divorce scam, but the abuser is not properly notified about the filing, the divorce can be

challenged legally. Some of these scams will not notify the other spouse about the divorce filing. Other scams will notify the other spouse by publication, that is, by using a small newspaper announcement published in the foreign country. But notice by publication is only allowed under certain circumstances, and failing to give notice is never allowed.

- The survivor may be told, or may believe, that a foreign divorce decree will be able to grant her child custody. However, a custody order from a foreign country will *not* be honored in the United States if the child never lived in that foreign country.
- A quickie foreign divorce also will not be recognized when it comes to dividing the marital assets (that is, house, car, other property) and awarding child support or alimony.

Usually, operators of quickie divorce scams will not inform the survivor about the limitations of these divorces or will actively deceive her by claiming that the divorces are valid. The end result is that the survivor will pay several hundred dollars for a worthless piece of paper. Even worse, she may re-marry even though she was never really divorced.

Survivors should be advised to avoid quickie divorce scams. If the survivor has obtained such a divorce or finds out the abuser has obtained one, she should consult a family law attorney. In the long run, the best way to prevent these scams from exploiting survivors is to continue advocating for additional free or low-cost family law services.

19

Identity Theft by the Abuser

Identity theft occurs when someone obtains another person's personal information and uses it to commit fraud or theft. According to the federal government, identity theft is one of the fastest growing types of crime in the United States.

While most people think of identity theft as a stranger-on-stranger crime, it can also be a crime perpetrated by abusers, family members, or acquaintances. Abusers often have critical information about survivors that enable them to perpetrate identity theft. One common example is an abuser who applies for a credit card using the survivor's name, then runs up charges on the card.

Identity theft is a crime, whether committed by a stranger or someone the survivor knows. There is a federal law against identity theft that makes it a crime to use someone's personal identification to commit or aid in the commission of a felony, such as defrauding a creditor.

DEALING WITH THE AFTERMATH OF IDENTITY THEFT

Unfortunately, fixing problems caused by identity theft is often difficult and time-consuming. It becomes further complicated when the abuser is the identity thief. Typically the survivor will be advised to file a police report, as many special rights under federal law for identity theft victims require the filing of such a report. The survivor may be reluctant, and rightfully so, to file a report for fear of angering the abuser. Advocates should talk with survivors about how the abuser might react and to be prepared for possible retaliation if the survivor decides to file a report. Even if a survivor decides not file a re-

TIPS FOR AVOIDING IDENTITY THEFT
(from the Federal Trade Commission)

- Sign your credit cards immediately.
- Do not carry your Social Security card with you. Keep it in a safe place at home or in a safety deposit box.
- Do not attach a personal identification number (PIN) or Social Security number to any card you carry with you. Do not attach or write a PIN or Social Security number on anything you are going to throw away (such as an invoice or receipt).
- Shred any document that contains your credit card or Social Security number before throwing it away. Buying a shredder may be the best investment you can make to avoid identity theft.
- Check receipts to make sure you received your own receipt and not someone else's.
- Alert your card issuer if you do not receive your statement. Someone may be stealing your mail.
- Do not give personal information or account numbers to anyone until you have confirmed the identity of the person requesting the information and verified that you need to provide this information.
- Frequently check your credit report to look for warning signs. (See the discussion on ordering credit reports in Chapter Twelve.)
- Put passwords on your credit card, bank, and home accounts. Avoid using easily available information like your mother's maiden name or your birth date.

port, she should not be held liable for credit that she did not apply for or use. Unfortunately, creditors will be very difficult to deal with if the survivor does not file a police report.

The survivor should be persistent in disputing fraudulent accounts even without a police report. She may need assistance in assembling a packet of materials with a letter explaining the fraud and documentation to back up her dispute. The survivor may even want to consider hiring a lawyer specializing in credit reporting issues. A list of consumer lawyers is available at www.naca.net.

Some steps that a survivor victimized by identity theft can take are discussed below. For more information on identity theft, contact the Federal Trade Commission, the Privacy Rights Clearinghouse, or the Identity Theft Resource Center. Contact information is included in Appendix A at the back of this guidebook.

Contact the Fraud Department of One of the Three Major Credit Bureaus to Place a Fraud Alert on Her Account. The survivor should tell the credit bureaus that she is an identity theft victim. She should request that a "fraud alert" be placed in her file. This can help prevent the abuser from opening additional accounts in the survivor's name.

A fraud alert added to a report asks creditors to check with the consumer before issuing credit. Creditors must take steps to verify the identity of an applicant whose report contains such a fraud alert. Although this check does not always work, it is effective much of the time and is an important first step to take.

As soon as the survivor makes this initial report to one of the major credit bureaus, and the bureau confirms her report, the other major credit bureaus will automatically be notified to place fraud alerts on her report as well. The survivor will be entitled to receive free copies of all three of her credit reports.

The initial fraud alert lasts only ninety days. In order to get an extended alert, the survivor will have to provide additional information, including an identity theft report. This is a copy of an official report filed with an appropriate federal, state, or local law enforcement agency.

In addition to the fraud alert, the credit bureaus are required to block the reporting of any information in a survivor's file that resulted from identity theft. Once a survivor provides the bureaus with proof of identity, an identity theft report, a list of theft-related information on the report, and a statement that the information does not relate to any of the survivor's transactions, the bureaus must start blocking the identified information within four business days.

At the same time, the survivor should order copies of her credit reports from the credit bureaus and review them carefully to make sure no additional fraudulent accounts have been opened or unauthorized changes made. Also, she should check the section of the credit report that lists "inquiries." When "inquiries" appear from the company(ies) that opened the fraudulent account(s), the survivor should request that these "inquiries" be removed from her report. In a few months, the survivor should order new copies of her reports to verify that the corrections and changes have been made and to make sure no new fraudulent activity has occurred.

Contact Creditors for Any Accounts That Have Been Tampered With or Opened Fraudulently. The survivor should contact all creditors, including credit card companies, phone companies and other utilities, and banks and other lenders. She should ask to speak with someone in the security or fraud department of each creditor and follow up with a letter. It is particularly important to notify credit card companies in writing because it invokes certain rights under federal law, as discussed in Chapter Fifteen.

The survivor should immediately close accounts that have been tampered with. When she opens new accounts, she should ask that a password be used before any inquiries or changes can be made on the account. She should also avoid using information that her abuser would know or could easily find out, like her mother's maiden name, her birth date, the last four digits of her Social Security number, or a series of consecutive numbers.

File a Report with the Local Police or the Police in the Community Where the Identity Theft Took Place. The survivor should consider filing a police report about the abuser's identity theft. Having a copy of the police report will help her when dealing with creditors, and most identity theft victims are advised to file reports. Filing such a report also allows the survivor to obtain a fraud alert for an extended period as described above. However, before filing a police report, the survivor should consider any risk to her safety if the abuser is arrested and/or prosecuted.

Like domestic violence itself, some police may be reluctant to consider identity theft between spouses or intimate partners to be a crime. At a minimum, if she wants to, the survivor should insist on her right to file a police report. She should point out the definition of identity theft in the law. Even if the police do nothing, the survivor will need a copy of the police report itself to show the bank, credit card company, or others who want proof of the crime.

The survivor should also consider filing a complaint with the Federal Trade Commission (FTC). The FTC cannot bring criminal cases, but it can provide information about how to resolve problems. The FTC has a special Identity Theft Hotline (1-877-IDTHEFT), or a complaint can be filed online at www.consumer.gov/idtheft.

If the abuser is prosecuted for identity theft, he can be ordered to pay restitution to the survivor. Restitution may include reimbursing the survivor for the costs of correcting the credit history, any portion of the debt she was forced to pay, any lost wages she suffered if she had to attend civil or administrative proceedings associated with the debt, and attorney fees she incurred to defend against the claim of debt.

Close Bank Accounts That Have Been Tampered With. The survivor should use a Personal Identification Number (PIN) when opening any new accounts. In addition, if the abuser has stolen or misused the survivor's checks, the survivor should stop payment. Also, the survivor should contact the following major check verification companies to request that they notify retailers using their databases not to accept these checks:

- National Check Fraud Service: 1-843-571-2143
- SCAN: 1-800-262-7771
- TeleCheck: 1-800-710-9898 or 1-800-927-0188
- CrossCheck: 1-707-586-0551
- Equifax Check Systems: 1-800-437-5120
- International Check Services: 1-800-526-5380

If the survivor's ATM card has been lost, stolen, or otherwise compromised, she should cancel the card as soon as she can and get another with a new PIN.

Other Steps. There are other actions the survivor may wish to consider. If the abuser is using the survivor's Social Security number to apply for a job or is otherwise misusing it, the survivor should call the Social Security Administration, which will help to verify the accuracy of earnings reported on her number. If the survivor believes her mail was stolen, she should contact the post office.

The survivor may have additional protections if she lives in a state that has passed special laws to protect victims of identity theft. One of the most important protections, available in a number of states, is the right to put a freeze on a credit report. (If the survivor is able to access the Internet, she can go to the Consumers Union website at www.consumersunion.org/campaigns/learn_more/002355indiv.html for a list of states with security freeze laws.)

Freezes are more powerful than fraud alerts. If the survivor places a freeze on her credit report, potential users will be told that the report is unavailable. The survivor can allow only those creditors and others she chooses to see her report using a special password. She should ask the credit reporting agency if a freeze is available to her, or she can check with her state Attorney General or consumer protection office to find out more.

ADDITIONAL RESOURCES

For additional information on identity theft, contact the Federal Trade Commission, the Identity Theft Resource Center, or the Privacy Rights Clearinghouse. Contact information for each organization is included in Appendix A at the back of this guidebook.

20

High-Cost Credit

COMBATING HIGH-COST CREDIT

In the aftermath of domestic violence, the survivor often faces a need for cash. Due to the lack of affordable credit, she may be tempted to use high-cost lenders. These lenders bleed millions of dollars from the pockets of those least able to afford it.

A survivor and her advocate should use a multi-faceted approach to challenge such high-cost loans. The approach should include the following:

- *Education.* The survivor needs to know about the cost of credit and how much it impacts her budget. High-cost lenders make their products as convenient as possible. They also do their best to avoid clearly disclosing the cost of their products. It may be easier to determine the true cost of such services once the survivor's budget is reviewed.
- *Alternative Sources of Credit.* It is difficult for the survivor to avoid high-cost lending when there are few (or no) alternatives available. For this reason, she will need help in learning more about alternative, less expensive sources of credit in her community. The survivor should try to use low-cost checking and savings accounts (to the extent they are available in low-income neighborhoods) in order to avoid the costs of check cashers. Credit unions, including many community development institutions, can also be useful, as these institutions make small loans to their members that can be used to purchase appliances or pay medical and car-repair bills. In addition, the survivor should find out about the non-profits in her state that may make small business loans for those clients who wish to avoid high-cost lenders when starting up their own businesses. More information

about community development credit unions is available from the Coalition of Community Development Financial Institutions (703-294-6970, www.cdfi.org) and the National Federation of Community Development Credit Unions (212-809-1850, www.natfed.org).

- *Legal Challenges.* Individual and class-wide litigation is another critical strategy. For advocates, a number of NCLC publications are available to help with legal challenges against over-reaching creditors and lenders, including: *STOP Predatory Lending* (2002); *The Cost of Credit: Regulation, Preemption, and Industry Abuses* (3d ed. 2005 and Supp.), and *Truth in Lending* (5th ed. 2003 and Supp.). NCLC also publishes a consumer education brochure, *Borrower Beware* that summarizes high-cost lending issues (available in English, Spanish, Chinese, Korean, Vietnamese and Russian—see the order form in the back of this guidebook to order). For updates, see NCLC's website, www.consumerlaw.org.
- *Legislation.* Advocates should focus on strengthening existing state, federal, and local laws, fighting industry-backed proposals, and developing new protections.

THE HIGH COST OF DIFFERENT KINDS OF SMALL LOANS

Payday Loans. Payday loans go by a variety of names, including "deferred presentments," "cash advances," "deferred deposits," or "check loans," but they all work similarly. The survivor writes a check to the lender for the amount borrowed, plus a fee that is either a percentage or a flat dollar amount, or signs an agreement to debit her bank account automatically. The typical annual percentage rate (APR) is at least 390% and averages close to 500%, though advocates and credit code enforcement agencies have noted rates of 1300% to 7300%. The check (or debit agreement) is then held for up to a month, usually until the survivor's next payday or receipt of a government check. She redeems the check by paying the face amount, allows the check to be cashed, or pays another fee to extend the loan.

These loans are marketed as a quick and easy way to get cash until the next payday. To qualify, the survivor need only be employed for a period of time with her current employer or receive government benefits, maintain a personal checking account, and show a pay stub and bank statement. Credit reports are not routinely reviewed.

Abuses in making and collecting payday loans occur in a variety of ways. Cash-strapped consumers are rarely able to repay the entire loan when payday arrives because they need the new paycheck for current living expenses. Payday lenders encourage these consumers to roll over or refinance one payday loan with another; those who do so pay yet another round of charges and fees and obtain no additional cash in return. If the check is returned for insufficient funds or the loan otherwise goes unpaid, the lender may threaten to involve the criminal justice system, a tactic that is possible only because a check, rather than a mere promissory note, is involved.

There are many legal claims available to challenge these loans. These are discussed in detail in NCLC's manual, *The Cost of Credit: Regulation, Preemption, and Industry Abuses* and in other NCLC publications. Payday loans are generally illegal in some states. In other states, the laws allow these loans but may impose restrictions on them. Appendix G is a state-by-state summary showing whether payday loans are legal.

Pawnbrokers. Pawnbrokers are companies that allow consumers to trade something of value, such as jewelry or a stereo, in exchange for cash—usually only one-half of the value of the property—which must then be repaid within a certain period of time. Otherwise, the pawnbroker can sell the property and keep the money. If the survivor uses a pawnbroker to obtain cash, she will be charged fees and only receive at most half the value of the property in cash, which means that she may be paying up to 200% interest per year.

Almost every state has enacted laws that regulate pawnbrokers in some way. Most states set ceilings on interest rates and other fees that pawnshops can charge on loans.

Auto Title Pawns. Auto title pawn transactions are a relatively new phenomenon. In such a transaction, the survivor pawns title to her car in exchange for a sum of cash. The lender may then claim title to the car and lease it back to the survivor. Other title pawn lenders may hold onto the certificate of title without any attempt to transfer ownership. If the survivor fails to pay the cash advanced plus interest and fees when due, the lender repossesses her car. The effective interest rate of an auto pawn can be astronomical, with annual percentage rates of over 900%.

For example:

- The survivor gives her car title ($1000 value) and gets back half the value of the car = $500
- She is required to pay weekly installments of $103.30 for 10 weeks ($103 × 10 weeks) = $1033

  $1033 paid
– $ 500 received
= $ 533 (830% interest on an annual basis).

A few states have legalized auto pawn lending. In the remaining states, there are several legal theories to attack auto title pawn practices, including the argument that the auto title pawnbroker is not a true pawnbroker because it does not retain possession of the pledged car. More information can be found in NCLC's manuals, *The Cost of Credit: Regulation, Preemption, and Industry Abuses* and also in *Repossessions.*

Rent-to-Own Transactions. Rent-to-own (RTO) businesses are essentially appliance and furniture retailers that arrange lease agreements for people who cannot purchase goods with cash. They target primarily low-income consumers by advertising in ethnic and non-English media, public transportation, and in public housing projects. The lease agreements offered by RTOs contain purchase options that typically allow the lessees to obtain title to the goods by making a nominal payment at the end of a short term (for example, eighteen months). Since the leases are short term, the "rental payments" are due weekly or monthly.

The survivor may be drawn to RTO businesses by many features that appear attractive: no credit checks, quick delivery, weekly payments, no or small down payments, quick repair service, and no harm to one's credit rating if the transaction is canceled. However, she should be advised that many of these RTO "leases" are disguised sales made at astronomic and undisclosed effective interest rates.

For example:

- The survivor rents a 19-inch color TV ($300 value)
- She pays $16/week × 52 weeks = $832

  $832 paid
– $300 (value of the TV)
= $532 (254% interest on an annual basis)

In nearly every state, there are RTO statutes that insulate dealers from most consumer abuse claims. Nevertheless, legal handles still exist to catch some of the more egregious practices of RTO dealers. For more information, see NCLC's manuals, *The Cost of Credit: Regulation, Preemption, and Industry Abuses* and also *Repossessions.*

Tax Refund Anticipation Loans. Tax refund anticipation loans involve cash advanced against the consumer's expected tax refund. They are generally available through tax preparers. However, a used-car dealer or two and some retail merchants near tribal reservations have been known to engage in this practice. Most refund lending is now performed by banks through national tax preparation chains or local tax preparers.

A survivor can expect to pay three sets of fees for a tax refund anticipation loan: a fee to the tax preparer for filling out the federal and state tax forms, typically \$60 to \$300; a fee for the electronic filing, with the average fee being \$40; and a loan fee to the lender, typically set on a sliding scale based on the amount of the expected refund. Typical loan fees range from \$30 to \$100 but can be as high as half the refund. What the survivor will receive in hand is the refund minus the loan fee, the tax preparation fee, and the electronic filing fee. The total amount of the three fees can range from \$130 to \$440.

Tax refund loans speed up receipt of cash from tax refunds, but not by much. The refund anticipation loan puts cash into the survivor's hand in one or two days, accounting for its appeal as a quick and "painless" way to get cash. But, based upon the actual amount of time the money is lent—about ten days—the annual percentage rate for these tax refund loans is about 67% to 774%.

The survivor may not realize that electronic filing alone cuts the wait to about ten days if she has a bank account into which the refund can be direct deposited. Often, the lender will not explain this reduced wait or will include the information only in small print in a long loan document.

Aside from having her tax refund reduced by fees, a survivor who is entitled to an earned income tax credit will be hit especially hard since the purpose of the earned income tax credit is to augment the income of wage earners at the lowest end of the economic spectrum. More information on tax refund anticipation loans can be found in a report issued by NCLC and the Consumer Federation of America, entitled *Another Year of Losses: High-Priced Refund Anticipation Loans Continue to Take a Chunk Out of Americans' Tax Refunds* (February 2, 2006), available in full at www.consumerlaw.org.

21

Federal Tax Issues for Survivors

Survivors often face many tax issues after leaving an abusive relationship. If the survivor was married to the abuser, they may have filed joint returns. Both spouses are liable for taxes due if they filed a joint return. The survivor may have been coerced into signing an erroneous or even fraudulent joint return, she may have unwittingly signed it, or her signature may have been forged. This chapter will discuss some federal tax issues faced by survivors and will provide suggestions to help the survivor facing these situations, including how she can get help with her tax problems. A good source of information about taxes is the IRS website at www.irs.gov.

TAX TIPS FOR SURVIVORS

File the Return on Time Even If Unable to Pay the Taxes Owed. If the survivor is unable to pay her taxes, one of the worst things she can do is not to file a tax return. In general, all U.S. citizens and resident aliens must file income tax returns if their taxable income exceeds certain amounts. (For 2005 this amount is $8200 for individuals, $10,500 for heads of households, and $16,400 for joint filers. Different amounts apply to those over 65. Self-employed taxpayers must file an income tax return if they earned over $400. These dollar amounts go up each year.)

April 15th is the deadline for most people to file individual income tax returns and pay any taxes owed. Filing extensions are available, but this does not extend the time to pay any taxes owed.

If the survivor owes taxes and fails to file a tax return by April 15, she may be prosecuted for a misdemeanor crime (although usually this does not occur). More likely, the IRS will assess a penalty. The IRS may also prepare a "substitute for return," and base its collection activity on that return. If the survivor owes taxes and is late sixty days or less in filing, the combined *late-filing* and *late-payment* penalty is 5% of the taxes owed for each month or part of a month that the return is late, up to 25%. If the return is over sixty days late, the minimum penalty is the smaller of $100 or 100% of the tax owed.

The penalties will be *much* smaller if the survivor files a tax return even if she is unable to send in a tax payment. Failure to pay is not, by itself, a crime. Instead, the survivor will simply be behind on a debt. The penalty for late payment is only a fraction of the larger penalty for not filing a return—it starts at only one-half of 1% of the tax owed for each month late, up to a maximum of 25%. Interest will also be assessed on the amount owed.

Getting an extension to file may seem like a good solution, but it generally is not. The IRS will automatically grant a four-month extension if the survivor makes a request along with payment of the taxes likely owed. But she should keep in mind that this is only an extension of time to *file*. It does not provide more time to *pay* the taxes owed, and there will be a charge for both interest and probably a late-payment penalty during the time of the extension. As noted above, if the survivor cannot pay the taxes due, it is a better idea to file the return, pay as much as possible, if anything, and then consider negotiating with the IRS.

Earned Income Tax Credit. The Earned Income Tax Credit (EITC) can help a low-income survivor's budget by providing much-needed funds. In order to qualify for the EITC, the survivor must have worked and her income must be below a certain amount. The survivor must file a tax return to receive the EITC. Even a survivor whose earnings are so small that she does not owe any taxes can get cash back through an EITC if she meets these requirements.

The tax credit is larger and the income cut-off is higher if the survivor had a "qualifying child" living with her for over six months of the year. (The six months need not be consecutive.) A "qualifying child" is

- a son, daughter, stepchild, grandchild, or adopted child;
- a brother, sister, stepbrother, stepsister, or a descendent of one of these relatives; or
- a foster child who was placed with the survivor by an authorized government or a private placement agency.

The child must be under age 19, or under 24 if a full-time student, but children of any age who have total and permanent disabilities may qualify.

Even if the survivor has not qualified for this credit in the past, she may now qualify due to changed circumstances such as divorce or separation. The survivor can even get advance payments on part of the EITC, which could help her balance her budget, by giving an IRS Form W-5 to her employer. A fact sheet on the EITC, updated annually to reflect changes in the tax laws, is available from the Center for Budget and Policy Priorities, www.cbpp.org.

Sometimes when the survivor attempts to file her tax return to claim the EITC, she will be told that her return has been rejected. She may discover that her abuser has already claimed the children on his tax return even though he does not have custody. If this happens, the survivor should file a return claiming the EITC anyway. She may have to file a paper return in order to claim the credit. If she attempts to file electronically, the return will be rejected since the children have already been claimed.

When the survivor claims the children after the abuser has already done, so there is a good chance both will be audited. If the survivor can prove she is entitled to claim the children for the EITC (usually by showing that the children claimed lived with the survivor for more than six months in a given year), she should be able to get the credit from the IRS. The survivor must respond to IRS requests for information showing that she is entitled to claim the children by providing information like school records, leases, or other documentation showing that her children lived with her for the required amount of time. The survivor should be aware that the resolution of these issues may take months, or even longer.

Notifying the IRS of a Change in Address. If the survivor moves, she should notify the IRS using Form 8822. This way she will receive any refund or notices. Sometimes the abuser will not forward important mail to her. If she is attempting to keep the abuser unaware of her new location, she should request that the address not be disclosed to any third party, including anyone with whom she has filed a joint return. Alternatively she could have her mail sent to a post office box or in care of a trusted friend.

TAX COLLECTION ISSUES

Often a survivor may have filed a return either on her own or jointly with the abuser and simply not have the funds to pay the amount due. In these situations, the IRS may use methods to force payment that are not permitted by private creditors.

If the survivor does not file a tax return that includes a calculation of the amount due, the IRS will prepare and post a "substitute for return," which will become final after notice to her. The substitute for return will generally be the least favorable to the survivor and would not reflect such preferences as head of household filing status, dependency exemptions, and the EITC.

The IRS will then send several letters asking for payment of the amount it claims is due. The last letter is called a "Notice of Tax Due and Demand for Payment." If the survivor does not respond to this notice, the IRS will send a notice saying that it is placing a tax lien on all property owned by her, such as a house or car. This lien allows the IRS to claim property as security for the tax debt. It makes the tax debt a secured debt.

The IRS may also send a notice that it will seize or place a "levy" on the survivor's property. The IRS can take any or all of her property, such as bank accounts, paychecks, and even homes, with the exception of certain types of "exempt" income and possessions.

A portion of the survivor's wages is usually exempt from a levy—about $150 a week of the survivor's wages if the survivor is single (more for married filers and heads of household, with the amount depending on the number of exemptions). Also exempt are unemployment and workers' compensation, certain public assistance benefits, job training benefits, income needed to pay court-ordered child support, and certain pension benefits. Other exempt property can include certain amounts of clothing, furniture, personal effects, and job-related tools. A state homestead exemption (discussed in Chapter Five) will not protect a home from an IRS tax lien or seizure.

The IRS can also recover past-due taxes by seizing certain of the survivor's federal wages, benefits, and other federal payments, including Social Security (but not Supplemental Security Income). This is a different levy from the federal benefits offset discussed in Chapter Thirteen. If the government offsets Social Security benefits for a student loan debt owed by the survivor, the first $750 of monthly benefits is exempt, but this is not true for tax levies. The IRS can levy 15% of the entire Social Security benefit or even more, regardless of whether or not the remaining benefit is less than $750.

SUGGESTIONS FOR SURVIVORS WHO OWE FEDERAL INCOME TAX

The Options. When a survivor has filed a return but cannot afford to pay the taxes due, she will generally have four options. When investigating her options or attempting a solution, help from a tax professional is recommended. The four options are

1. pay the taxes using a credit card or some other source of funds;
2. enter into an installment plan with the IRS;
3. negotiate with the IRS by seeking an "offer-in-compromise;" or
4. request a temporary hardship determination, also called "currently not collectible" status.

All of these options except the first one require IRS approval. If IRS does not grant approval, the survivor has the right to seek an appeal or ask for a review of the case.

Finding Another Source of Funds to Pay the Taxes. The first option is to find another source of funds to pay the taxes. One way to do this is to put the tax obligation on a credit card. A credit card payment will need to be processed by a private company that will charge a "convenience" fee, generally about 2.5% of the payment. The credit card interest may be less than IRS interest and penalties, but this is not always true. However, charging the tax to a credit card provides time to develop a plan to pay down the credit card debt.

A survivor should only put amounts on a credit card that she believes she can repay. But, if circumstances change and she cannot repay the debt as soon as required, it may be easier to deal with the credit card company than the IRS. In addition, the credit card company does not have the extraordinary powers that the IRS does to force payment.

Installment Plans. The second option is to ask the IRS to allow payment of the amount due in monthly installments over a period of up to three years. The IRS will generally allow this but will impose interest, penalties, and a "user fee" of $43. The interest rate will be the federal short-term rate plus 3%, which is lower than most rates for unsecured loans. If an installment plan is approved, the penalty for late payment is only one-quarter of 1% for each month that the installment remains unpaid. Even with the penalties, an installment plan may cost less than putting the taxes on a credit card. Sometimes the IRS will even drop penalties. The IRS will only drop interest, however, if the IRS made an error that resulted in the tax liability.

The survivor may ask for an installment plan by attaching an IRS form 9465, "Installment Agreement Request," to her return. She may also call the

IRS at the phone number on the bill or notice. Taxpayers should always be sure that any installment plan is in writing. Note that, even if the survivor pays taxes under an installment plan, the IRS may still place a lien on her property until the final payment is made. However, the IRS cannot execute a levy while the installment plan is in effect. If the survivor has income or property that the IRS could seize, negotiating an installment payment plan with the IRS may be the best option.

Offer-in-Compromise. The third option is for the survivor to seek an offer-in-compromise. This is when the IRS settles and allows the payment of an amount less than what it claims was owed. An offer-in-compromise is generally granted only when a dispute exists as to what is owed or there is doubt that the past-due taxes could ever be collected in full. There are special IRS forms to fill out to request an "offer-in-compromise" (Forms 656 and 433-A or 433-B). If the survivor requests an offer-in-compromise, she must also pay a $150 application or "user" fee if her income is above the federal poverty guideline, as well as a partial up-front payment when making this request. Unless the offer is based on a dispute over whether and how much of the tax is owed, the amount the survivor offers must equal or exceed her net equity in assets, her ability to make installment payments from future income, and other amounts at her disposal.

Temporary Hardship Deferral. The fourth option is for the survivor to seek a temporary hardship determination from the IRS, called "currently not collectible" status. The IRS will only grant this status if she does not have any assets that could be used to pay the taxes and does not have any income left after "allowable expenses." Allowable expenses are those determined by the IRS as what is necessary for living expenses. IRS determinations are based on the information included in Forms 433-A, 433-B, or 433-F. The survivor should be aware that what she may consider to be an undue hardship may be viewed by the IRS as a mere inconvenience.

"Currently not collectible" status is not permanent and does not mean that the tax owed by the survivor is forgiven or reduced. This status can change if her financial circumstances improve, if she files another return with a balance due, or if she does not file a tax return. The IRS will monitor tax returns and remove the hardship status if her returns suggest an improvement. Also, interest will continue to accumulate during this time, but penalties will not. To apply for "currently not collectible" status, the survivor must fill out

Form 433-F, "Collection Information Statement," which can be obtained from the IRS. In some cases, IRS agents can collect the information for Form 433-F over the telephone and make the "currently not collectible" determination.

SEEKING A HEARING

If the survivor receives a notice that her property is being levied upon or that a lien is being placed on it, she can request a review of her case, called a "Collection Due Process" hearing, by submitting Form 12153. She has thirty days after receiving the notice to request a hearing. The hearing will result in a suspension of collection activities, including levies, during the appeals process. During the hearing, she can dispute that she owes the tax or request one of the payment options discussed previously, such as an installment plan, an offer-in-compromise, or a hardship determination. Even if she does not make the request within thirty days, she can request a hearing. While such a request will not necessarily delay collection, it often will, and this will allow the survivor to propose collection alternatives to an impartial IRS appeals officer.

BANKRUPTCY

Bankruptcy is not as effective a remedy when dealing with taxes as with other debts. In general, most taxes cannot be discharged in a chapter 7 bankruptcy. Some exceptions apply when the taxes are more than three years delinquent if the survivor properly filed her tax return for the year in question. Even then, existing tax liens are likely to remain on her property even after the bankruptcy. In a chapter 13 reorganization, the full amount of the taxes owed can be paid in installments over a period of up to five years. For more information about bankruptcy, see Chapter Eight.

RELIEF FROM LIABILITY FOR JOINT RETURNS

In certain limited cases, a survivor's responsibility to pay a tax may be cancelled when the tax is owed entirely by her spouse or ex-spouse. This is true even if she filed a joint return. Generally, a request for any of the types of relief outlined in this section must be made within two years after IRS starts collection activity against her. As with all the suggestions in this chapter, help from a tax professional is recommended.

A survivor may seek to avoid liability under a joint return in three ways:

1. Innocent spouse relief
2. Allocation of liability
3. Equitable relief

The first two are options only if the taxes owed on the face of the jointly filed return were paid but the IRS later determines additional taxes are owed. The third option, equitable relief, is available even if the taxes owed as shown by the joint return were not paid.

In addition, the survivor may be able to claim that she has no liability for a joint return if she was forced to sign the return. A signature made under duress (coercion or force) is not valid and should not create liability for the survivor.

Innocent Spouse Relief. Often abusers withhold important information from survivors as part of their abuse. The abuser may not allow the survivor access to financial information in an effort to control her. Sometimes she may have signed a joint return without knowing that the abuser was under-reporting income or that some other information on the return was wrong. When the IRS discovers the inaccuracy, it may begin collection activity. Innocent spouse relief is available when the survivor signs a joint return that contains misinformation if (1) she did not know and had no reason to know of the false information and (2) it would be unfair to hold her responsible.

Allocation of Liability. If the survivor finds that she owes the IRS money because the taxes owed were greater than what was reported on a joint return, she may seek relief from a portion of the taxes owed. She must show that she and her spouse have had separate households for twelve months or that they divorced or have obtained a legal separation. She must also show that she neither knew nor should have known of the erroneous information in the return.

Equitable Relief. Equitable relief may be available to the survivor in many circumstances that do not allow for innocent spouse relief or allocation of liability. It is available even if the joint return showed on its face that taxes were due and that amount was not paid. The survivor must show that it would be unfair to hold her liable for this debt to obtain this relief. She must not be eligible for innocent spouse relief or allocation of liability discussed above. When deciding to grant equitable relief, the IRS may look at the following factors:

- financial hardship;
- abuse during the relationship;
- the survivor's belief that the abuser would pay the taxes;
- a state court order that the abuser pay the taxes; and/or
- mental or physical disability of the survivor when she signed the return or when she requests relief.

AVOIDING REFUND ANTICIPATION LOANS

Tax refund anticipation loans are a form of very high-cost credit offered by commercial tax preparers and, occasionally, used car dealers and retail merchants. They can cost the survivor hundreds of dollars—translating into annual percentage rates as high as 700%—to get the tax refund just a week or two faster than from the IRS (if she uses electronic filing and direct deposit). If the survivor uses a commercial tax preparer, she should be careful not to agree to a refund anticipation loan she does not want. There are also free tax preparation services—called Volunteer Income Tax Assistance (VITA) programs—available in may cities for low-income taxpayers. More information about refund anticipation loans may be found in Chapter Twenty.

GETTING HELP

There are several resources available to survivors and others with tax problems. One resource is the Taxpayer Advocate Service, an independent group within the IRS that helps taxpayers. There is at least one Taxpayer Advocate in each state. These advocates have the power to issue "Taxpayer Assistance Orders" (TAOs).

The TAO can force the IRS to cease collection or audit actions, release liens or levies, or stop any other activity. The survivor can seek the assistance of the Taxpayer Advocate Service if she

- is suffering or about to suffer a significant hardship;
- is facing an immediate threat of adverse action;

- will incur significant costs, including fees for professional representation, if relief is not granted;
- will suffer irreparable injury or long-term adverse impact if relief is not granted;
- has experienced a delay of more than thirty days to resolve a problem or inquiry; or
- did not receive a response or resolution to her problem by the date promised.

Another resource is the Problem Resolution Program (PRP), a part of the IRS that handles complaints not resolved through normal procedures. Generally, before using the PRP, the survivor must show that she has been unable to resolve her problem using normal channels.

Yet another resource is the network of Low-Income Taxpayer Clinics (LITCs) in many states. LITCs can help the survivor if she has a dispute with the IRS and meets certain income eligibility requirements. A list of LITCs is available in IRS Publication 4134, available at www.irs.gov/pub/irs-pdf/p4134.pdf.

22

Driver's License Advocacy: Accessing Safety and Economic Independence

[*Endnotes can be found at the end of the chapter*]

Helping the survivor obtain a valid driver's license can be a crucial piece of comprehensive advocacy aimed at securing her safety and economic independence. Social science research indicates that, among other things, services that assist a survivor with transportation have a sizeable impact on her independence.[1] Survivors have specified that access to their own transportation is a high-priority need that can be very influential when it comes to deciding whether or not to return to an abusive partner.[2] Without access to transportation, survivors can feel trapped, powerless, and dependent on their abusers. Obtaining a valid driver's license can assist in eliminating some of the dependency and help a survivor work toward independence and safety.[3]

The need for a driver's license can be particularly strong if the survivor lives in a rural area. Physical isolation, limited accessible support services, and lack of public transportation can put a rural survivor in uniquely dangerous circumstances.[4] These added barriers can be used by batterers to engage in particular forms of abusive behavior.[5]

A valid driver's license can translate into greater mobility for a survivor. It can mean that a survivor has greater control over her own movement and is less dependent on her abuser.[6] A driver's license also can create the opportunity for a survivor to physically leave a dangerous situation. In particularly dangerous and lethal situations, a car can be a survivor's last safe place to hide. A driver's license also may mean an increased likelihood that a survivor will be able to access resources such as shelters, support networks of friends and family, and legal services. If a survivor has children, using public transportation to travel back and forth from childcare, school, and work can be extremely time consuming and often impossible without a driver's license. Finally, having a driver's license often is pivotal in her ability to obtain and maintain employment. Many jobs require applicants to have valid driver's licenses, while other jobs are located far from public transportation or the survivor's home.

ADVOCACY APPROACHES

A state may suspend the survivor's driver's license for several reasons. For example, federal law requires states to suspend the driver's licenses of individuals convicted of drug offenses or failure to pay child support.[7] States may also suspend or revoke an individual's driver's license for safety violations. Overwhelmingly, however, states suspend driver's licenses for failure to pay fines.[8] This chapter will focus on how to help the survivor overcome suspensions or revocations based on failure to pay fines.

Payment Plans. Many local and state courts will permit the survivor to enter into payment plans as a method for paying off unpaid fines. In smaller municipal courts, this may require her to appear before a judge to request and advocate for such a plan. In larger courts, court clerks often have a system in place for setting up payment plans.[9] Payment plans may require the survivor to pay a certain percentage of her fines as a down payment, followed by smaller monthly payments. If possible, she may want to commit to the smallest monthly payment that the court is willing to consider. This will make it less likely that she will default on the payment plan should she have unexpected higher expenses during certain months. If the survivor believes that she will be unable to make a payment, she can contact the court clerk's office to request additional time to make the payment.

Courts differ as to how a payment plan impacts the existing suspension or revocation. Some courts will lift the suspension once the court and the survivor have agreed to the terms of the payment plan. Other courts will not lift the suspension until the survivor pays the total amount in outstanding fines. The best practice is for the survivor to ask the court to lift the suspension once the payment plan is issued. This will allow her to apply for a valid license sooner rather than later.

Community Service. Unfortunately, a payment plan can impose a significant economic burden on the survivor. One alternative to cash payments is to perform community service as a down payment on a payment plan or for the entire amount of the outstanding fines. Typically, a court will credit her $10 for every hour of community service. The community service option, however, is not without its problems. For example, it may require a significant time commitment depending on the amount of fines outstanding.[10] Also, she may face transportation barriers that make it impossible for her to get back and forth to complete the community service hours. Finally, most courts will not lift the driver's license suspension until after she has completed all the community service hours needed to pay off the fines. This will prolong the time that she does not have a valid driver's license. To overcome this, the survivor can request that the court lift the suspension once she has completed enough community services hours for a down payment.

Reducing Tickets and Fines. The survivor and her advocate should consider appearing in court to challenge tickets and advocate for a reduction or dismissal in charges or fines. Courts are often willing to reduce the ticket to a lesser offense or to dismiss tickets outright to increase the likelihood that the individual will pay the fines on remaining tickets. This applies to both open and closed cases. The survivor and her advocate should not hesitate to try to reopen closed cases in an effort to adjust or dismiss tickets. Often the survivor will have her license suspended for unpaid parking tickets resulting from the abuser's use of her car. In these circumstances, the survivor and her advocate can present this information to the court as evidence of financial abuse and ask the court to dismiss the outstanding parking tickets.

OTHER POSSIBLE BARRIERS

REAL ID Act. In May 2005, the United States Congress passed the REAL ID Act. The law gave states three years to implement changes to their driver's license laws and procedures to meet minimum federal standards. These standards include biometric identifiers, information about each applicant's name, age, Social Security number, proof of identity, proof of state residency, and proof of legal presence in the United States. If a state fails to meet these standards, driver's licenses issued by that state cannot be used to board airplanes, to open bank accounts, or for other purposes yet to be determined. As of May 2006, Maine and Wisconsin were the only two states to have enacted legislation designed to comply with REAL ID.[11]

Fortunately, the Violence Against Women Act of 2005 (VAWA 2005) amended the REAL ID Act to allow exceptions for the protection of survivors of domestic violence and crime victims. Under VAWA 2005, the survivor may be able to have an alternative address (an address that is not her principal residence) printed on her driver's license and entered into the state's driver license database.[12]

Undocumented Immigrants and Accessing Driver's Licenses. Since September 11, 2001, several states have moved toward limiting undocumented immigrants' access to driver's licenses in the interest of national security. Some of these limitations became federal law when Congress passed the REAL ID Act in May 2005. Although Maine and Wisconsin are the only states at this time to have passed legislation complying with REAL ID, approximately twenty-five states have enacted other statutes that require an applicant for a driver's license to show proof of lawful presence in the United States.[13]

ADDITIONAL SAFETY CONSIDERATIONS

Although a valid driver's license and increased mobility can significantly increase the survivor's safety, there may be ways in which it decreases safety. It is important that the survivor bear in mind the particular risks of her situation. Federal law prohibits the release or use by any state Department of Motor Vehicles (DMV) of personal information about an individual obtained by the DMV in connection with a driver's license.[14] For additional safety, a survivor should consider using the VAWA 2005 REAL ID amendment described above that permits her to list an alternative address on her driver's license. In order for her to be eligible for such an exception, she may have to enroll in an address confidentiality program offered by her state. Also, she should be aware that, if she is issued a driving ticket or has her license suspended, a record of this may become publicly available and accessible through court computer and/or Internet-accessible case systems. The abuser may be able to access these systems to search for her name and find other information such as her date of birth and current address. To minimize this danger, when appearing in court, the survivor and her advocate should request that the court keep her address confidential.

ENDNOTES

1. Edward W. Gondolf & Ellen R. Fisher, Battered Women As Survivors: An Alternative to Treating Learned Helplessness 85–86 (1988); Margot Mendelson, *The Legal Production of Identities: A Narrative Analysis of Conversations with Battered Undocumented Women*, 19 Berkeley Women's L. J. 138 (2004).

2. Edward W. Gondolf & Ellen R. Fisher, Battered Women As Survivors: An Alternative to Treating Learned Helplessness 85–86 (1988); Nicole E. Allen, Deborah I. Bybee, & Cris M. Sullivan, *Battered Women's Multitude of Needs*, 10 Violence Against Women 1015, 1023 (2004).

3. *See* Margot Mendelson, *The Legal Production of Identities: A Narrative Analysis of Conversations with Battered Undocumented Women*, 19 Berkeley Women's L. J. 138, 196–197 (2004), for a discussion on how obtaining a driver's license can contribute to immigrant women's increased feelings of safety, entitlement, and belonging.

4. Neil Websdale, Rural Woman Battering and the Justice System: An Ethnography 5–8 (1998).

5. *Id.* at 83, 162.

6. Margot Mendelson, *The Legal Production of Identities: A Narrative Analysis of Conversations with Battered Undocumented Women*, 19 Berkeley Women's L. J. 138, 191 (2004).

7. Approximately twenty-seven states automatically suspend or revoke driver's licenses for some or all drug convictions unrelated to driving. Legal Action Center, After Prison: Roadblocks to Reentry 17 (2004). *See also* John B. Mitchell & Kelly Kunsch, *Access to Justice: Of Driver's Licenses and Debtor's Prison*, 4 Seattle J. Soc. Just. 439 (2005).

8. Barbara Corkrey, *Restoring Drivers' Licenses Removes a Common Legal Barrier to Employment*, 38 Clearinghouse Rev. J. of Poverty L. and Pol'y, 1, 523 (Jan.–Feb. 2004).

9. Prior to going to court, the survivor should be aware of any outstanding warrants for unpaid tickets or other charges. She may risk being taken into custody on outstanding warrants and should work with an advocate or attorney to arrange to have these warrants lifted by the court.

10. *See* John B. Mitchell & Kelly Kunsch, *Access to Justice: Of Driver's Licenses and Debtor's Prison*, 4 Seattle J. Soc. Just. 439, 465 (2005).

11. National Immigration Law Center, *2006 State Driver's License Legislation, available at* www.nilc.org/immspbs/DLs/state_dl_proposals_2006-5-8.pdf (2006).

12. Pub. L. No. 109-162, 119 Stat. 2960, 827 (2005).

13. National Immigration Law Center, State Driver's License Requirements, *available at* www.nilc.org/immspbs/DLs/state_dl_rqrmts_120504.pdf.

14. Drivers Privacy Protection Act, 18 U.S.C. § 2721.

APPENDIX A

Resource List

HELPFUL CONSUMER AND LEGAL RESOURCES

AARP
601 E St., NW
Washington, D.C. 20049
Phone: 202-434-2277
Website: www.aarp.org

American Bankruptcy Institute
44 Canal Center Plaza, Suite 404
Alexandria, VA 22314
Phone: 703-739-0800
Website: www.abiworld.org

American Bar Association
Commission on Domestic Violence
740 15th Street, N.W.
Washington, DC 20005-1019
Phone: 202-662-1000
Website: www.abanet.org/domviol/home.html

Battered Women's Justice Project
2104 4th Ave. South, Suite B
Minneapolis, MN 55404
Phone: 800-903-0111, ext. 1/612-824-8768
Website: www.bwjp.org

Center for Budget and Policy Priorities
820 1st Street, NE, #510
Washington, DC 20002
Phone: 202-408-1080
Website: www.cbpp.org

Center for Law and Social Policy

1015 15th Street, NW
Suite 400
Washington, DC 20005
Phone: 202-906-8000
Website: www.clasp.org

Consumer Action

717 Market Street, Suite 310
San Francisco, CA 94103
Phone: 415-777-9635/213-624-8327 (hotline)
Website: www.consumer-action.org

Consumer Federation of America (CFA)

1424 16th Street, NW
Suite 604
Washington, DC 20036
Phone: 202-387-6121
Website: www.consumerfed.org

Consumers Union

101 Truman Ave.
Yonkers, NY 10703-1057
Phone: 914-378-2000
Website: www.consumersunion.org

Health Care for All

30 Winter St., 10th Fl.
Boston, MA 02108
Phone: 617-350-7279
Hotline: 800-272-4232
Website: www.hcfama.org

Identity Theft Resource Center

PO Box 26833
San Diego CA 92196
Phone: 858-693-7935
Website: www.idtheftcenter.org

Legal Momentum

395 Hudson St.
New York, NY 10014
Phone: 212-925-6635
Website: www.legalmomentum.org (links to publications about state and local laws concerning employment discrimination against victims of domestic and sexual violence and time off from work for victims of domestic or sexual violence)

Lawyers Committee for Civil Rights Under the Law

1401 New York Avenue, NW
Suite 400
Washington, DC 20005
Phone: 202-662-8600
Website: www.lawyerscomm.org

The National Association of Attorneys General

750 First Street, NE, Suite 1100
Washington, DC, 20002
Website: www.naag.org (links to the each state's Attorney General's office)

National Coalition Against Domestic Violence

1120 Lincoln Street, Suite 1603
Denver, CO 80203
Phone: 303-839-1852
TTY: 303-839-1681
Website: www.ncadv.org

National Consumers League

1701 K Street, NW
Suite 1200
Washington, DC 20006
Phone: 202-835-3323
Website: www.natlconsumersleague.org

National Domestic Violence Hotline

PO Box 161810
Austin, TX 78716
Phone: 800-799-SAFE (7233) (Hotline)/512-453-8117 (Administrative—Materials Request)
TTY: 800-787-3224
Website: www.ndvh.org (24-hour, toll-free crisis intervention line, referrals to domestic violence and other emergency shelters and programs, and information about assistance networks and other domestic violence resources; informational materials on domestic violence and sexual assault, including national statistics)

National Online Resource Center on Violence Against Women

6400 Flank Drive, Suite 1300
Harrisburg, PA 17112-2778
Phone: 800-537-2238
TTY: 800-553-2508
Website: www.vawnet.org/index.php

National Women's Law Center
11 Dupont Circle, NW
Suite 800
Washington, DC 20036
Phone: 202-588-5180
Website: www.nwlc.org

Privacy Rights Clearinghouse
3100 5th Ave., Suite B
San Diego, CA 92103
Phone: 619-298-3396
Website: www.privacyrights.org

U.S. Public Interest Research Group
218 D Street, SE
Washington, DC 20003-1900
Phone: 202-546-9707
Website: www.uspirg.org

CREDIT BUREAUS

Equifax Credit Information Services, Inc.
P.O. Box 740241
Atlanta, GA 30374
Phone: 800-685-1111
Website: www.equifax.com

Experian National Consumer Assistance
Box 2002
Allen, TX 75013-2104
Phone: 888-397-3742
Website: www.experian.com

Trans Union L.L.C. Consumer Disclosure Center
P.O. Box 1000
Chester, PA 19022
Phone: 800-888-4213
Website: www.transunion.com

FEDERAL AGENCIES

Department of Housing and Urban Development (HUD)

451 7th Street S.W.
Washington, DC 20410
Phone: 202-708-1112
(A list of HUD-approved housing counseling agencies is available at website: www.hud.gov/offices/hsg/sfh/hcc/hccprof14.cfm or by calling 888-466-3487.)

Federal Trade Commission

Bureau of Consumer Protection
Washington, DC 20580
Phone: 877-FTC-HELP (382-4357)
Website: www.ftc.gov OR www.ftc.gov/bcp/menu-credit.htm (consumer credit rights)

Government Services Agency

Phone: 800-FED-INFO
Website: www.pueblo.gsa.gov (federal government's consumer information center containing direct links to federal indexes and agencies, consumer-help organizations, community nets and freenets and other sites providing helpful consumer information)

Internal Revenue Services

Phone: 800-829-1040 (telephone assistance)
Website: www.irs.gov
Taxpayer Advocate Service Information
Website: www.irs.gov/advocate (link to list of Low-Income Taxpayer Clinics at very end of page)

Volunteer Income Tax Assistance Program

Phone: 800-829-1040 (information about finding local tax preparation assistance for low- to moderate-income ($38,000 and below) people who cannot prepare their own tax returns)

United States Department of Justice

Executive Office for Immigration Review
Website: www.usdoj.gov/eoir/probono/states.htm (contact information for free immigration-related legal services throughout the states)

United States Department of Justice

Office on Violence Against Women
800 K Street, N.W., Suite 920
Washington, DC 20530
Phone: 202-307-6026
TTY: 202-307-2277
Website: www.usdoj.gov/ovw (links to a variety of helpful publications)

U.S. Department of Health & Human Services

Office of Child Support Services
National Domestic Violence Hotline
Phone: 800-799-SAFE (800-799-7233)
TDD: 800-787-3224

LEGAL SERVICES PROVIDERS

American Bar Association

Standing Committee on Pro Bono & Public Service
321 North Clark Street
Chicago, IL 60610
Phone: 312-988-5759
Website: www.abanet.org/legalservices/probono/volunteer.html (links to pro bono programs directory, state and local bar associations, and state and local legal aid and legal services offices)

LawHelp.org

Website: www.lawhelp.org (contact information for nonprofit legal services providers across the nation)

Legal Services Corporation

3333 K Street, NW, 3rd Floor
Washington, DC 20007-3522
Phone: 202-295-1500
Website: www.lsc.gov

National Association of Consumer Advocates

1730 Rhode Island NW, Ste 805
Washington, DC 20036
Phone: 202-452-1989
Website: www.naca.net

APPENDIX B

Visit SurvivingDebt.Org

Go to www.survivingdebt.org to find more information on how to get legal assistance. The website also has free consumer information, including consumer brochures on credit reports and credit scores, loans, banking, tax refunds, mortgages, home improvement scams, utility service, bankruptcy, and more. Click on the "Consumer Education Brochures" link at the bottom of the webpage to access the resources listed below. Be sure to check the website for future updates.

CONSUMER EDUCATION BROCHURES

- The Truth About Credit Reports & Credit Repair Companies (Available in English, Chinese, Korean, Russian, Spanish and Vietnamese)
- Don't Pay to Borrow Your Own Money: The Risks and Costs of Tax Refund Anticipation Loans (Available in English, Chinese, Spanish, Korean, Russian, and Vietnamese)
- High-Cost Home Loans: Don't Be a Target (Available in English, Chinese, and Spanish)
- Cashing Checks and Opening Bank Accounts: How to Save Money and Avoid Theft (Available in English, Chinese, Korean, Russian, Spanish, and Vietnamese)
- Beware of Dishonest Immigrant Consultants (Available in Chinese, English, Korean, Russian, Spanish, and Vietnamese)
- Shopping for Money Wire Transfer Services (Available in English, Chinese, Korean, Russian, Spanish, and Vietnamese)
- Borrower Beware: The High Cost of Small Loans, Pawn Brokers and Rent-to-Own Stores (Available in English, Chinese, Korean, Russian, Spanish, and Vietnamese)

EDUCATION BROCHURES FOR SENIORS (AND OTHER CONSUMERS)

- What You Should Know About Your Credit Report
- Tips for Consumers on Avoiding Foreclosure "Rescue" Scams
- Your Credit Card Rights

- Tips on Choosing a Reputable Credit Counseling Agency
- Dealing with Utility Companies Regarding Disputed Bills and Utility Deposits
- Protect Yourself from Identity Theft
- What You Should Know About Refinancing
- Tips for Seniors on Living Trusts
- Tips for Consumers on Reverse Mortgages
- What to Do If You've Become the Victim of Telemarketing Fraud
- When Your Social Security Benefits Are Taken to Pay Back Money to the Federal Government
- Answers to Common Bankruptcy Questions
- Using Credit Wisely After Bankruptcy
- Your Legal Rights During and After Bankruptcy

INFORMATION FOR ADVOCATES AND SERVICE PROVIDERS WORKING WITH SENIORS AND OTHER CONSUMERS

- Dreams Foreclosed: Saving Older Americans from Foreclosure Rescue Scams
- Understanding Credit Scores
- Credit Card Debt and Credit Counseling
- Avoiding Living Trust Scams: A Quick Guide for Advocates
- Medical Debt and Seniors: How Consumer Law Can Help
- When You Can't Go Home Again: Using Consumer Law to Protect Nursing Facility Residents
- Dealing with Utility Companies Regarding Disputed Bills and Utility Deposits
- Advice for Seniors About Credit Cards
- How to Help Older Americans Avoid Loss of Utility Services
- INTERNET RESOURCES: Helpful Consumer and Elder Law Web Sites
- Spending the House: A Quick Guide for Advocates on Reverse Mortgages
- What to Do When Utility Service Has Been Disconnected
- Protecting Older Americans from Telemarketing Scams: A Quick Guide for Advocates

APPENDIX C

Budget Forms

MONTHLY INCOME BUDGET			
	YOU	YOUR SPOUSE, PARTNER, OR OTHER CONTRIBUTING HOUSEHOLD MEMBER	TOTAL
Employment (1)	$	$	
Overtime			
Child Support/Alimony (2)			
Pension			
Interest			
Public Benefits (3)			
Dividends			
Trust Payments			
Royalties			
Rents Received			
Help from Friends or Relatives			
Other (List)			
TOTAL (MONTHLY)	$	$	$

We recommend that you make copies of this chart and use a new chart each month.

NOTES

(1) You can list either your take-home pay or your total employment income. If you use the total, remember to list all of your payroll deductions as expenses in the expense budget chart. If you use your take-home pay, remember to check your pay stub to make sure that there are no unnecessary deductions.

(2) Include only the amounts you are actually expecting to receive if any.

(3) This should include all money received from public benefits each month including food stamps, welfare, Social Security, disability, unemployment compensation, worker's compensation, etc. If you are receiving more than one type of income, then you may want to use the box labeled as "other" at the bottom of the income budget chart.

MONTHLY EXPENSE BUDGET	
TYPE OF EXPENSE (1)	**TOTAL**
Payroll Deductions (2)	
Income Tax Withheld	
Social Security	
FICA	
Wage Garnishments	
Credit Union	
Other	
Home Related Expenses	
Mortgage or Rent (3)	
Second Mortgage	
Third Mortgage	
Real Estate Taxes (4)	
Insurance (5)	
Condo Fees & Assessments	
Mobile Home Lot Rent	
Home Maintenance/Upkeep	
Other	
Utilities	
Gas	
Electric	
Oil	
Water/Sewer	
Telephone:	
Land Line	
Cell	
Cable TV	
Internet	
Other	
Food	
Eating Out	
Groceries	
Clothing	
Laundry and Cleaning	
SUBTOTAL PAGE 1	

MONTHLY EXPENSE BUDGET (cont.)	
TYPE OF EXPENSE (1)	**TOTAL**
Medical	
Current Needs	
Prescriptions	
Dental	
Insurance Co-Payments or Premiums	
Other	
Transportation	
Auto Payments	
Car Insurance	
Gas and Maintenance	
Public Transportation	
Life Insurance	
Alimony or Support Paid	
Student Loan Payments	
Entertainment	
Newspapers/Magazines	
Pet Expenses	
Amounts Owed on Debts (7)	
Credit Card	
Credit Card	
Credit Card	
Medical Bill (8)	
Medical Bill	
Other Back-Bills (List) (9)	
Cosigned Debts	
Business Debts (List)	
Other Expenses (List) (10)	
Miscellaneous (11)	
TOTAL	

We recommend that you make copies of this chart and use a new chart each month.

INCOME AND EXPENSE TOTALS	
A. Total Projected Monthly Income	______
B. Total Projected Monthly Expenses	– ______
Excess Income or Shortfall (A minus B)	= ______

NOTES

(1) Include the total expenses of everyone in your household who shares expenses.

(2) Do *not* fill out this section if you have used your take-home pay in your income budget. However, you should check your pay stub to make sure that there are no unnecessary deductions from your pay. *Do fill out this section if you used your gross employment income budget or if you are self employed.*

(3) Include amounts here only for your primary home. If you have a vacation home or a time share, include that below under "other expenses." This will help you determine whether you can make ends meet by giving up your second home or time share.

(4) Include your real estate taxes only if these amounts are not included with your escrow payment on your mortgage.

(5) Include your home insurance payments if these amounts are for renter's insurance or if they are not included with your escrow payment on your mortgage.

(6) This should not include your back bills. Back medical bills are unsecured debts which should be handled differently in your budget and listed below under "Amounts Owed on Debts."

(7) List here the monthly payments you plan to make on your unsecured debts like credit cards and medical bills.

(8) List your back bills here. Current anticipated medical expenses should be listed separately above as a higher priority expense. Old bills can generally be dealt with like other low priority unsecured debts.

(9) Some examples might include other debts owed to professionals such as lawyers or accountants, personal loans, bills owed to prior landlords, deficiency claims on prior foreclosures or repossessions and any other debt for which the creditor has no collateral.

(10) Everyone has a different situation. You should think about any other source of regular household expenses and list them here. Some frequently overlooked items include cigarettes, diapers, children's allowances, lay-away payments, rent-to-own, etc. Some of these items can be quite costly and will throw your budget out of whack if they are not accounted for.

(11) You may want to include a small sum here for the miscellaneous small expenses or for the emergencies which are unaccounted for elsewhere.

APPENDIX D

Crime Victim Compensation Programs

Alabama
Alabama Crime Victims Compensation Commission
2400 Presidents Dr., Ste., 300
Montgomery, AL 36116
P.O. Box 1548
Montgomery, AL 36102-1548
Phone: 334-290-4420
Phone: 800-541-9388 (victims only)
Fax: 334-290-4455
Website: www.acvcc.state.al.us

Alaska
Violent Crimes Compensation Board
P.O. Box 111200
Juneau, AK 99811-0230
Phone: 800-764-3040
Fax: 907-465-2379
Website: www.state.ak.us/Vccb

Arizona
Arizona Criminal Justice Commission
1110 W. Washington St., Suite 230
Phoenix, AZ 85007
Phone: 602-364-1146/877-668-2252
Fax: 602-364-1175
Website: www.acjc.state.az.us

Arkansas
Crime Victims Reparations Board
Office of the Attorney General
323 Center St., Suite 600
Little Rock, AR 72201
Phone: 501-682-1020
Phone: 800-448-3014 (in-state)
Fax: 501-682-5313/683-5569
Website: www.ag.state.ar.us

California
Victim Compensation and Government Claims Board
P.O. Box 3036
Sacramento, CA 95812-3036
Phone: 800-777-9229
Fax: 916-322-1487
Website: www.vcgcb.ca.gov

Colorado
Office for Victims Programs
Division of Criminal Justice
Department of Public Safety
700 Kipling St., Suite 1000
Denver, CO 80215
Phone: 303-239-5719
Fax: 303-239-4491
Website: www.dcj.state.co.us/ovp

Connecticut

Office of Victim Services
31 Cooke St.
Plainville, CT 06062
Phone: 860-747-4501
Phone: 888-286-7347 (in-state)
Fax: 860-747-6508
Website: www.jud.state.ct.us/faq/crime.html

Delaware

Violent Crimes Compensation Board
240 N. James St., Suite 203
Wilmington, DE 19804
Phone: 302-995-8383
Phone: 800-464-4357 (in-state)/800-273-9500
Fax: 302-995-8387
Website: http://courts.state.de.us/Vccb

District of Columbia

Crime Victims Compensation Program
D.C. Superior Court
515 5th St., N.W., #104
Washington, DC 20001
Phone: 202-879-4216
Fax: 202-879-4230

Florida

Division of Victim Services and Criminal Justice Programs
Office of the Attorney General
The Capitol PL-01
Tallahassee, FL 32399-1050
Phone: 850-414-3300
Phone: 800-226-6667 (victims only)
Fax: 850-487-1595/413-0633
Website: legal.firn.edu/victims/index.html

Georgia

Crime Victim Compensation Program
Criminal Justice Coordinating Council
503 Oak Place South, Suite 540
Atlanta, GA 30349
Phone: 404-559-4949
Phone: 800-547-0060 (victims only)
Fax: 404-559-4960
Website: www.state.ga.us/cjcc

Hawaii

Crime Victims Compensation Commission
333 Queen Street, #404
Honolulu, HI 96813
Phone: 808-587-1143
Fax: 808-587-1146
Website: www.ehawaiigov.org/psd/cvcc/html

Idaho

Crime Victims Compensation Program
Idaho Industrial Commission
317 Main St.
P.O. Box 83720
Boise, ID 83720-0041
Phone: 208-334-6080/800-950-2110
Fax: 208-334-5145
Website: www2.state.id.us/iic/crimevictims.htm

Illinois

Illinois Court of Claims
630 South College
Springfield, IL 62756
Phone: 217-782-7101
Fax: 217-524-8968

Crime Victim Services Division
Crime Victims Compensation Bureau
Office of the Attorney General
100 W. Randolph, 13th floor
Chicago, IL 60601
Phone: 312-814-2581/800-228-3368
Fax: 312-814-4231
Website: www.ag.state.il.us

Indiana

Violent Crime Victim Compensation Fund
Indiana Criminal Justice Institute
One North Capitol, Suite 1000
Indianapolis, IN 46204-2038
Phone: 317-232-1295/800-353-1484
Fax: 317-233-3912
Website: www.state.in.us/cji/victim/comp.htm

Iowa

Crime Victim Assistance Division, Dept. of Justice
Lucas Building, Ground Floor
321 E. 12th St., Room 018
Des Moines, IA 50319
Phone: 515-281-5044/800-373-5044
Fax: 515-281-8199
Website: www.state.ia.us/government/ag/cvad.html

Kansas

Crime Victims Compensation Board
Office of the Attorney General
120 S.W. 10th Ave., 2nd floor
Topeka, KS 66612-1597
Phone: 785-296-2359
Fax: 785-296-0652
Website: www.ink.org/public/ksag/contents/crime/cvcbrochure.htm

Kentucky

Crime Victims Compensation Board
130 Brighton Park Blvd.
Frankfort, KY 40601-3714
Phone: 502-573-2290/800-469-2120
Fax: 502-573-4817

Louisiana

Crime Victims Reparations Board
Commission on Law Enforcement
1885 Wooddale Blvd., Suite 708
Baton Rouge, LA 70806
Phone: 225-925-4437
Phone: 888-6-Victim (in-state)
Fax: 225-925-1998
Website: www.cole.state.la.us/cvr.htm

Maine

Victims' Compensation Program
Office of the Attorney General
State House Station #6
Augusta, ME 04333
Phone: 207-624-7882/800-903-7882 (in-state, victims only)
Fax: 207-624-7730
Website: www.maine.gov/ag/?r=crimeandvictims

Maryland

Criminal Injuries Compensation Board
Dept. of Public Safety and Correctional Services
Suite 206, Plaza Office Center
6776 Reisterstown Road
Baltimore, MD 21215-2340
Phone: 410-585-3010/888-679-9347
Fax: 410-764-3815
Website: www.dpscs.state.md.us/cicb

Massachusetts

Victim Compensation and Assistance Division
Office of the Attorney General
One Ashburton Place
Boston, MA 02108
Phone: 617-727-2200
Fax: 617-367-3906
Website: www.ago.state.ma.us

Michigan
Crime Victims Services Commission
320 S. Walnut St.
Lansing, MI 48913
Phone: 517-373-7373
Fax: 517-334-9942
Website: www.michigan.gov/mdch/0,1607,7-132-2940_3184---,00.html

Minnesota
Crime Victims Reparations Board
Office of Justice Programs
Department of Public Safety
445 Minnesota St., Suite 2300
St. Paul, MN 55101
Phone: 651-282-6256/888-622-8799
Fax: 651-296-5787
Website: www.ojp.state.mn.us

Mississippi
Crime Victim Compensation Program
Office of the Attorney General
P.O. Box 220
Jackson, MS 39205
Phone: 601-359-6766/800-829-6766
Fax: 601-576-4445
Website: www.ago.state.ms.us/divisions/crime_victim/cvcp.php

Missouri
Crime Victims' Compensation Unit
Dept. of Labor and Industrial Relations
P.O. Box 3001
Jefferson City, MO 65102
Phone: 573-526-6006
Phone: 800-347-6681 (victims only)
Fax: 573-526-4940
Website: www.dolir.state.mo.us/wc/forms/cv-1-3-ai.pdf

Montana
Crime Victims Compensation Program
Office of Victim Services and Restorative Justice
P.O. Box 201410
Helena, MT 59620-1410
Phone: 406-444-3653
Phone: 800-498-6455 (in-state)
Fax: 406-444-4303
Website: www.doj.state.mt.us/ago/victimservices/cvindex.htm

Nebraska
Crime Victims Reparations Program
Commission on Law Enforcement
P.O. Box 94946
Lincoln, NE 68509
Phone: 402-471-2194
Fax: 402-471-2837
Website: www.ncc.state.ne.us

Nevada
Victims of Crime Program
Department of Administration
2200 S. Rancho, Suite 130
Las Vegas, NV 89102
Phone: 702-486-2740
Fax: 702-486-2825

4600 Kietzke, Building I, Suite 205
Reno, NV 89502
Phone: 775-688-2900
Fax: 775-688-2912

New Hampshire
Victims' Assistance Commission
33 Capitol St.
Concord, NH 03301-6397
Phone: 603-271-1284
Phone: 800-300-4500 (in-state)
Fax: 603-271-2110
Website: www.statenh.us/nhdoj/victimwitness/victserviceindex.html

New Jersey

Victims of Crime Compensation Board
Department of Law and Public Safety
50 Park Place, 6th fl.
Newark, NJ 07102
Phone: 973-648-2107/800-242-0804
Fax: 973-648-3937/7031
Website: www.nj.gov/victims

New Mexico

Crime Victims Reparation Commission
8100 Mountain Road, N.E., Suite 106
Albuquerque, NM 87110-7822
Phone: 505-841-9432
Phone: 800-306-6262 (victims only)
Fax: 505-841-9437
Website: www.state.nm.us/cvrc

New York

Crime Victims Board
55 Hanson Pl., 10th floor
Brooklyn, NY 11217
Phone: 718-923-4325/800-247-8035
Fax: 718-923-4373

845 Central Ave.
Albany, NY 12206
Phone: 518-457-8727
Fax: 518-457-8658

65 Court St., Room 308
Buffalo, NY 14202
Phone: 716-847-7948
Fax: 716-847-7995

Website: www.cvb.state.ny.us

North Carolina

Crime Victims Compensation Commission
Victim's Compensation Services
Dept. of Crime Control and Public Safety
4703 Mail Service Center
Raleigh, NC 27699-4703
Phone: 919-733-7974
Phone: 800-826-6200 (in-state only, victims only)
Fax: 919-715-4209
Website: www.nccrimecontrol.org/vjs/cvcp0.htm

North Dakota

Crime Victims Compensation Program
Division of Parole and Probation
Box 5521
Bismarck, ND 58506-5521
Phone: 701-328-6195
Phone: 800-445-2322 (in-state)
Fax: 701-328-6186
Website: www.state.nd.us/docr

Ohio

Victims of Crime Compensation Program
Crime Victim Services Division
Office of the Attorney General
125 East Gay St., 25th fl.
Columbus, OH 43215
Phone: 614-466-5610/877-584-2846
Fax: 614-752-2732
Website: www.ag.state.oh.us/sections/crime_victims_services/index.htm

Oklahoma

Crime Victims Compensation Board
District Attorneys Council
421 N.W. 13th, Suite 290
Oklahoma City, OK 73103
Phone: 405-264-5006/800-745-6098
Fax: 405-264-5097
Website: www.dac.state.ok.us

Oregon
Crime Victims Assistance Section
Department of Justice
1162 Court St., N.E.
Salem, OR 97301-4096
Phone: 503-378-5348
Fax: 503-378-5738
Website: www.doj.state.or.us/CrimeV/comp.htm

Pennsylvania
Victims Compensation Assistance Program
Office of Victim's Services
Pennsylvania Commission on Crime and Delinquency
P.O. Box 1167
Harrisburg, PA 17108-1167
Phone: 717-783-5153/800-233-2339
Fax: 717-787-4306
Website: www.pccd.state.pa.us

Puerto Rico
Office for Crime Victims Compensation
Department of Justice
P.O. Box 9020192
San Juan, PR 00902-0192
Phone: 787-641-7480, 310-4515
Fax: 787-641-7477
Website: www.justicia.gobierno.pr

Rhode Island
Crime Victim Compensation Program
Office of General Treasurer
40 Fountain St., 1st floor
Providence, RI 02903-1856
Phone: 401-222-8590
Fax: 401-222-4577
Website: www.treasury.state.ri.us

South Carolina
State Office of Victim Assistance
Office of the Governor
1205 Pendleton St., Room 401
Columbia, SC 29201
Phone: 803-734-1900
Phone: 800-220-5370 (in-state, victims only)
Fax: 803-734-1708
Website: www.govoepp.state.sc.us/sova/index.htm

South Dakota
Crime Victims' Compensation Program
Department of Social Services
700 Governor's Drive
Pierre, SD 57501-2291
Phone: 605-773-6317
Phone: 800-696-9476 (in-state only)
Fax: 605-773-6834
Website: www.sdvictims.com

Tennessee
Criminal Injuries Compensation Program
Division of Claims Administration
Andrew Jackson Building, 9th floor
Nashville, TN 37243-0243
Phone: 615-741-2734
Fax: 615-532-4979
Website: www.treasury.state.tn.us/injury/index.htm

Texas
Crime Victim Compensation Program
Victim Services Division
Office of the Attorney General
P.O. Box 12548, Capitol Station
Austin, TX 78711-2548
Phone: 512-936-1200/800-983-9933
Fax: 512-320-8270
Website: www.oag.state.tx.us/victims/cvc.html

Utah
Office of Crime Victim Reparations
Commission on Criminal and Juvenile Justice
350 East 500 South, Suite 200
Salt Lake City, UT 84111
Phone: 801-238-2360/800-621-7444
Fax: 801-533-4127
Website: www.crimevictim.utah.gov

Vermont
Vermont Center for Crime Victim Services
Victims Compensation Program
58 South Main St., Suite 1
Waterbury, VT 05676-1599
Phone: 802-241-1250
Phone: 800-750-1213 (in-state only)
TTY: 800-845-4874 (in-state only)
Fax: 802-241-1253
Website: www.ccvs.state.vt.us

Virginia
Criminal Injuries Compensation Fund
Workers' Compensation Commission
11513 Allecingie Pkwy.
Richmond, VA 23235
Phone: 804-378-3434/800-552-4007
Fax: 804-378-4390
Website: www.cicf.state.va.us

Virgin Islands
Criminal Victims Compensation Commission
Department of Human Services
Knud Hansen Complex, Building A
1303 Hospital Ground
Charlotte Amalie, VI 00802
Phone: 340-774-0930, ext. 4104
Fax: 340-774-3466

Washington
Crime Victim Compensation Program
Department of Labor and Industry
P.O. Box 44520
Olympia, WA 98504-4520
Phone: 360-902-5355/800-762-3716
Fax: 360-902-5333
Website: www.lni.wa.gov/insurance/CVC.htm

West Virginia
Crime Victims Compensation Fund
West Virginia Court of Claims
1900 Kanawha Blvd., East. Room W-334
Charleston, WV 25305-0610
Phone: 304-347-4850/800-562-6878
Fax: 304-347-4915
Website: www.legis.state.wv.us/joint/court/victims/main.cfm

Wisconsin
Office of Crime Victims Services
Department of Justice
P.O. Box 7951
Madison, WI 53707-7951
Phone: 800-446-6564
Fax: 608-264-6368
Website: www.doj.state.wi.us/cvs/programs/cvc.asp

Wyoming
Division of Victim Services
Office of the Attorney General
122 West 25th St., Herschler Bldg., 1st floor
Cheyenne, WY 82002
Phone: 307-777-7200
Fax: 307-777-6683
Website: vssi.state.wy.us

APPENDIX E

Summaries of State Exemption Laws

This appendix summarizes provisions from the states' general exemption statutes, specifically those dealing with wages, homesteads and tangible personal property. This summary is intended to give advocates a snapshot of whether an individual is judgment proof, but is not comprehensive. More detailed summaries may be found in Appendix F of NCLC's *Fair Debt Collection* (6th ed. 2005 and Supp.). Advocates advising clients should consult their states' exemption laws for the most up-to-date exemption information and for additional, potentially relevant details not reflected here.

Statutes that provide special exemption rules for child support or other family support collections, or for other special types of debts, such as reimbursements to the state, are not summarized here and should be consulted separately where necessary. For example, statutes that create or regulate specific assets, like public or private pensions, workers' compensation, educational savings accounts, insurance, or crime victims compensation, often contain their own exemption language.

ALABAMA

Has state opted out of federal bankruptcy exemptions? Yes. Ala. Code § 6-10-11.

Wages: **Ala. Code §§ 5-19-15, 6-10-7, -120.**

Scope: Wages, salaries, or other compensation of laborers or employees, residents of Alabama, for personal services.

Amount: For consumer loans, consumer credit sales and consumer leases, similar to federal exemptions; for all other debts 75% of weekly disposable income is exempt. For consumer loans, disposable earnings are those left after legally required deductions. Disposable earnings do not include voluntary "periodic payments pursuant to a pension, retirement or disability program."

Homestead: **Ala. Const. art. X, §§ 205, 206; Ala. Code §§ 6-10-2, -4, -20, -41, -120, and -122.**

Amount: $5000 per individual not exceeding 160 acres is exempt, subject to certain liens. Mobile home explicitly included. If husband and wife own homestead jointly, each may claim the exemption separately "to the same extent and value as an unmarried individual." Exemption available whether debtor owns a fee or less estate, whether in common or in severalty.

Procedural requirements: Any resident may file sworn declaration with office of probate judge in county where property located. (This is not essential to claim of exemption; other procedure exists to claim exemptions after levy.)

Tangible personal property: **Ala. Const. art. X, § 204; Ala. Code §§ 6-10-5, -6, -120, -121, and -126.**

Household goods: $3000. All personal property, except for wages.

Clothing and jewelry: All necessary and proper wearing apparel of debtor and family; not covered by $3000 cap.

Miscellaneous and wildcard: Burial place and church pew; family portraits and books; not covered by $3000 cap.

ALASKA

Has state opted out of federal bankruptcy exemptions? Yes. Alaska Stat. § 9.38.055.

Wages: **Alaska Stat. §§ 09.38.030, .050, .065, .105, .115, .500; Alaska Admin. Code tit. 8, § 95.030.**

Scope: Money received by an individual for personal services, whether denominated wages, salary, commission or otherwise. For debtor who does not receive earnings weekly, semi-monthly or monthly, aggregate cash or other liquid assets available.

Amount: $438 of weekly net earnings is exempt, increases to $688 if individual's wages are sole support of household. Net earnings are gross earnings less sums required by law or court order to be withheld. Dollar amounts under this chapter are adjusted on October 1 of even-numbered years, in accordance with the Consumer Price Index. For debtor who does not receive income weekly, semi-monthly or monthly, cash and liquid assets up to $2750 per month.

Homestead: **Alaska Stat. §§ 09.38.010, .060, .065, .105, .115; Alaska Admin. Code tit. 8, § 95.030.**

Amount: $67,500 in a principal residence; multiple owners of single homestead may claim only their *pro rata* share of this amount (i.e., only one exemption per homestead); homestead is subject to certain liens. Amount adjusted for Consumer Price Index.

Procedural requirements: Not specified.

Tangible personal property: **Alaska Stat. §§ 9.38, .015, .020, .025, .115; Alaska Admin. Code tit. 8, § 95.030 (reports new amounts adjusted for CPI).**

Household goods: $3750, including household goods, clothing, and family pictures and heirlooms.

Motor vehicles: $3750 in car worth not more than $25,000.

Tools of Trade: $3500.

Jewelry: $1250.

Miscellaneous and wildcard: Pets: $1250. Health aids, burial plot, no cap.

ARIZONA

Has state opted out of federal bankruptcy exemptions? Yes. Ariz. Rev. Stat. Ann. § 33-1133.

Wages: **Ariz. Rev. Stat. Ann. §§ 33-1131, -1132, 12-1598.10(B)(5) and (F).**

Scope: Wages, salary or compensation for personal services, including bonuses and commissions or otherwise, including payments pursuant to a pension or retirement program or a deferred compensation plan.

Amount: Similar to federal. May be reduced to 15% in case of "extreme economic hardship" to debtor or family. Disposable income is calculated by subtracting those amounts required by law to be withheld. Garnishment forbidden if the debt was, at the time of service of the writ, subject to an effective agreement for debt scheduling between the judgment debtor and a qualified debt counseling organization.

Homestead: **Ariz. Rev. Stat. Ann. §§ 33-1101 through -1104.**

Amount: $150,000; Condos, co-ops, and mobile homes (with or without land) explicitly included. Married couple may claim only one exemption. Homestead is subject to certain liens. Debtor who does not claim homestead may exempt pre-paid rent or security deposit up to lesser of $1000 or 1? months rent.

Procedural requirements: No written claim or recording required. (But if debtor owns multiple properties, creditor may require debtor to designate one as homestead.)

Tangible personal property: **Ariz. Rev. Stat. Ann. §§ 33-1121.01, -1123 through -1125, -1127 through -1130, -1132.**

Household goods: $4000 furniture and appliances.

Motor vehicles: $5000 in one vehicle (up to $10,000 if debtor is physically disabled).

Tools of trade: $2500 (does not cover motor vehicle used only for commuting); $2500 farm equipment.

Clothing and jewelry: $500 clothing. $1000 wedding and engagement rings.

Bank accounts: $150 in one bank account.

Miscellaneous and wildcard: $250 musical instruments; $500 animals; $250 books; a burial plot; miscellaneous items worth $500; materials used for instruction of youth; health aids. *Note*: Husband or wife may each claim personal property exemption, which may be stacked.

ARKANSAS

Has state opted out of federal bankruptcy exemptions? No. Ark. Code Ann. § 16-66-217.

Wages: **Ark. Code Ann. § 16-66-208.**

Scope: Wages of all laborers and mechanics.

Amount: $25 per week is absolutely exempt; sixty days wages are exempt if debtor's property plus the wages do not exceed the amount exempt under the state constitution (*see* summary of art. 9 of the state constitution under Tangible Personal Property, *infra*).

Homestead: **Ark. Const. art. 9, §§ 3, 4, 5; Ark. Code Ann. §§ 16-66-210, -212, -218.**

Amount: Bankruptcy only: $800 for unmarried debtor, $1250 for married. Non-bankruptcy, married or head of household only: 80 acres rural or 1/4 acre urban, or if this land is not worth $2500, then up to 160 acres rural or one acre urban, up to a value of $2500.

Procedural requirements: None stated. Right not lost by failure to schedule. Non-debtor spouse may claim if debtor fails to do so.

Tangible personal property: **Ark. Const. art. 9, §§ 1, 2; Ark. Code Ann. §§ 16-66-218, -219, -220.**

Household goods: Bankruptcy only: Personal property used as residence or burial plot, if real property not claimed: $800 unmarried or $1250 married. Note: A federal decision, *In re* Holt, 894 F.2d 1005 (8th Cir. 1990), holds the personal property, motor vehicle and tools of the trade exemptions to be contrary to, and therefore limited by, the lower ceilings in the Arkansas Constitution.

Motor vehicles: Bankruptcy only: $1200.

Tools of trade: Bankruptcy only: $750.

Clothing and jewelry: Wedding bands, necessary wearing apparel.

Miscellaneous and wildcard: Any personal property: $500 married; $200 unmarried.

CALIFORNIA

Has state opted out of federal bankruptcy exemptions? Yes. Cal. Civ. Proc. Code § 703.130.

Wages: **Cal. Civ. Proc. Code §§ 706.050, .051, 052, 704.070.**

Scope: Compensation payable by an employer to an employee for personal services whether denominated as wages, salary, commission, bonus or otherwise. Employee is defined as a public officer or any individual who performs services subject to the right of the employer to control both what shall be done and how it shall be done.

Amount: Same as federal. Larger exemption if debtor can prove need: "the portion of the judgment debtor's earnings which the judgment debtor proves is necessary for the support of the judgment debtor or the judgment debtor's family supported in whole or in part by the judgment debtor is exempt from levy under this chapter."

Homestead: **Cal. Civ. Proc. Code §§ 487.025, 703.110, .040, 704.710 through .730.**

Amount: $50,000. Increases to $75,000 if debtor is family member and if at least one other family member owns no interest in homestead or only a community property interest. $125,000 for debtors over age 55 if income is under $15,000 (without joint income) or $20,000 (married debtors, joint income) and if sale is involuntary. $150,000 if over 65 or disabled; may include house, mobile home, boat or condominium. In bankruptcy, the debtor has the option of selecting the $17,425 exemption set forth at Cal. Civ. Proc. Code § 703.140.

Procedural requirements: Yes. *See* Cal. Civ. Proc. Code §§ 704.910 through 704.995 for declaration of homestead procedure.

Tangible personal property: **Cal. Civ. Proc. Code §§ 703.110, and .040, 704.010 through .070; Cal. Civ. Code § 703.150.** (In bankruptcy, the debtor has the option of selecting the exemptions set forth at Cal. Civ. Proc. Code § 703.140, which are similar to the federal exemptions.) Some personal property exemptions are adjusted every three years for the cost of living.

Household goods: Ordinary and necessary household furnishings, appliances, wearing apparel and other personal effects. Proceeds from execution sale of items of extra-ordinary value are exempt in the amount determined by the court to be sufficient to purchase ordinary and necessary replacement. No doubling of exemptions.

Motor vehicles: $2300 aggregate equity in motor vehicle(s); insurance or other compensation for loss or destruction of vehicle exempt for 90 days after receipt.

Tools of trade: $6075. Married couple engaged in same business may stack their exemptions. (Not more than $4850 of this amount for commercial motor vehicle.)

Clothing and jewelry: Ordinary and necessary wearing apparel; $6075 jewelry, heirlooms and works of art.

Miscellaneous and wildcard: Health aids. Family or cemetery plots.

COLORADO

Has state opted out of federal bankruptcy exemptions? Yes. Colo. Rev. Stat. § 13-54-107.

Wages: **Colo. Rev. Stat. § 13-54-104.**

Scope: Compensation for personal services; payments to independent contractors are protected. Also includes various insurance, disability, etc., benefits.

Amount: Similar to federal. Disposable earnings are defined as those left after certain voluntary health insurance deductions, as well as legally required taxes, etc. A higher percentage of earnings may be garnished to recover overpayments of certain state benefits.

Homestead: **Colo. Rev. Stat. §§ 38-41-201, -201.6, -202, -207, -208.**

Amount: $45,000 in a residence. Mobile or manufactured homes explicitly included.

Procedural requirements: Filing of homestead declaration permitted but not required. If filed, spouse's signature will be required for sale or encumbrance of property.

Tangible personal property: **Colo. Rev. Stat. §§ 13-54-101 to -103.**

Household goods: $3000 in household goods; $600 in food and fuel. Non-exclusive list of household goods includes computers, sound systems, cameras, bicycles, fax machines and toys, as well as the usual furniture, dishes, etc.

Motor vehicles: $3000 in vehicles or bicycles ($6000 if elderly or disabled).

Tools of trade: $10,000 in tools of trade; $25,000 in farm tools, equipment, and animals; married couple engaged in farming may claim only one farm equipment exemption.

Clothing and jewelry: $1500 in clothing; $1000 in jewelry.

Miscellaneous and wildcard: $1500 in books and family pictures; one burial site for debtor and each dependent; health aids.

CONNECTICUT

Has state opted out of federal bankruptcy exemptions? No.

Wages: **Conn. Gen. Stat. Ann. §§ 52-352b(d), 52-361a.**

Scope: Earnings by reason of personal services, including any compensation payable by an employer to an employee, whether called wages, salary, commission, bonus or otherwise.

Amount: Garnishment is limited to lesser of 75% of debtor's weekly disposable income or amount by which weekly disposable income exceeds forty times the federal or state minimum wage. Disposable income is that left after deductions of taxes, normal retirement contributions, union dues and fees, and health or group life insurance premiums. All wages earned by a public assistance recipient under an incentive earnings program are exempt. No garnishment unless judgment debtor has failed to comply with an installment payment order. Garnishment will be for the statutory maximum, unless the court provides otherwise pursuant to motion for modification. No more than one garnishment at a time. Employer may not discharge or discipline employee for garnishment unless there are more than seven wage executions in one calendar year.

Homestead: **Conn. Gen. Stat. Ann. § 52-352b(t).**

Amount: $75,000 excluding consensual or statutory liens; $125,000 for money judgment arising out of services provided at a hospital.

Procedural requirements: Not specified in exemption statute.

Tangible personal property: **Conn. Gen. Stat. Ann. § 52-352b.**
Household goods: Necessary food, furniture, bedding, and appliances.
Motor vehicles: $1500 (fair market value, less any liens and encumbrances).
Tools of trade: Tools, books, instruments, livestock, and feed, necessary for debtor's occupation, profession or farming.
Clothing and jewelry: Necessary clothing. Wedding and engagement rings.
Miscellaneous and wildcard: Wildcard $1000 in any property. Health aids, burial plot, certain military items, residential security deposit and utility security deposits.

DELAWARE

Has state opted out of federal bankruptcy exemptions? Yes. Del. Code tit. 10, § 4914.
Wages: **Del. Code Ann. tit. 6, § 4345, and tit. 10, § 4913.**
Scope: Salaries, commissions and every other form of remuneration paid to an employee for labor or services; does not include payment made for services rendered by self-employed person.
Amount: 85% exempt. For debts arising from retail installment sale, totally exempt for sixty days after default on the contract or installment account. Only one garnishment at a time.
Homestead: None.
Tangible personal property: **Del. Code Ann. tit. 10, §§ 4902, 4903, 4914 and 7323.**
Household goods: $5000 any personal property. Sewing machine held for use, not for sale.
Tools of trade: $50 or $75, depending on location.
Clothing and jewelry: Necessary wearing apparel, no cap.
Miscellaneous and wildcard: See above. Also family bible, books and pictures, church pew, burial place, no cap. Additional $500 wildcard for head of family.
Waiver: Allowed; both spouses' signatures required.

DISTRICT OF COLUMBIA

Has state opted out of federal bankruptcy exemptions? No.
Wages: **D.C. Code Ann. § 16-572.**
Scope: Compensation paid or payable for personal services, whether called wages, salary, commission, bonus or otherwise; includes periodic payments pursuant to a pension or retirement program.
Amount: Similar to federal. Only one garnishment at a time.
Homestead: **D.C. Code Ann. § 15-501(a)(14).**
Amount: Head of family or householder only: Debtor's aggregate interest in real property used as the residence of the debtor or property of the debtor or debtor's dependent in a cooperative that owns property that debtor or dependant uses as a residence.
Procedural requirements: Not specified in exemption statute.
Tangible personal property: **D.C. Code Ann. § 15-501 to -503.** (All tangible and intangible personal property exemptions are for householder or head of family only.)
Household goods: $8075 aggregate, single item $425: Household goods, furnishings, wearing apparel, books, animals, crops, musical instruments.
Motor vehicles: $2575 in one vehicle, if used in debtor's business.
Tools of trade: $1625; library and office furniture of professional person, $300.

Miscellaneous and wildcard: $850 any property; unused homestead exemption up to $8075; health aids; family pictures and library, $400.

FLORIDA

Has state opted out of federal bankruptcy exemptions? Yes, except as to exemptions provided by § 522(d)(10) of the bankruptcy act. Fla. Stat. §§ 222.20 and .201.

Wages: **Fla. Stat. Ann. § 222.11.**

Scope: Earnings, defined as compensation paid or payable in money of sum certain for personal services or labor whether called wages, salary, commission or bonus, of a head of family, defined as one who provides more than 50% of the support of a child or dependant.

Amount: Head of family: $500 per week of disposable earnings exempt, unless debtor has agreed otherwise in writing. Amount garnished may not exceed that allowed by federal law. Disposable earnings are those left over after all deductions required by law. Others: same as federal.

Homestead: **Fla. Const. art. X, § 4(a)(1); Fla. Stat. Ann. §§ 222.01, .02, .03, and .05.**

Amount: Up to 1/2 acre inside a municipality or 160 acres outside a municipality is exempt under the Florida Constitution regardless of value, with exceptions for four types of debts (taxes, purchase money debts, services or labor for home repair or improvement, and other labor performed on real property). By statute, a mobile home or modular home may be a homestead, whether or not the homeowner owns the land. In addition, if the homestead is outside a municipality and includes less than 160 acres, the debtor may exempt non-homestead land to bring the total up to 160 acres.

Procedural requirements: Permitted but not required to file declaration of homestead, may do so after levy.

Special provisions: None specified in exemption statute.

Waiver: Not specified in exemption statute.

Tangible personal property: **Fla. Const. art. X, § 4; Fla. Stat. Ann. §§ 222.061, and .07.**

Household goods: $1000 in any personal property.

Motor vehicles: Up to $1000 in any one motor vehicle.

Miscellaneous and wildcard: Professionally prescribed health aids.

GEORGIA

Has state opted out of federal bankruptcy exemptions? Yes. Ga. Code Ann. § 44-13-100(b).

Wages: **Ga. Code Ann. § 18-4-20(d)–(f)**

Scope: Compensation paid or payable for personal services, whether called wages, salary, commission, bonus or otherwise, including periodic payments pursuant to a pension or retirement program.

Amount: Similar to federal.

Homestead: **Ga. Code Ann. §§ 44-13-1, -40, and -100(a)(1).**

Amount: Bankruptcy only: $10,000, or if title to property is in one of two spouses who is a debtor, $20,000 per debtor in any property used as residence or burial plot. Non-bankruptcy: Aggregate of $5000, in real and personal property. May be waived except as to certain essential personal property.

Procedural requirements: None stated. Exemptions may be claimed after judgment.

Tangible personal property: **Ga. Code Ann. §§ 44-13-1, and -40.**

Household goods: Any real or personal property in the amount of $5000. Bankruptcy only: up to $300 per item, $5000 total in household goods, clothing, appliances, animals, books, crops or musical instruments.

Motor vehicles: Bankruptcy only: $3500.

Tools of trade: Bankruptcy only: $1500.

Clothing and jewelry: Bankruptcy only: $500 jewelry.

Miscellaneous and wildcard: Bankruptcy only: $600 plus unused amount of $5000 exemption; health aids.

HAWAII

Has state opted out of federal bankruptcy exemptions? No.

Wages: **Haw. Rev. Stat. §§ 652-1(a), (b), 651-121, 653-3.**

Scope: Wages, salary, stipend, commissions, annuity or net income under a trust.

Amount: 95% of first $100 earned per month, 90% of the next $100, and 80% of all sums in excess of $200 per month.

Homestead: **Haw. Rev. Stat. §§ 651-91, -92, -93, and -96.**

Amount: $30,000 for married person, head of family or person over 65 and $20,000 for all others; a co-op or long-term lease covered; subject to certain liens. Married couple may claim only one homestead; after decree of separate maintenance or interlocutory decree of divorce, each may claim individual exemption.

Procedural requirements: None stated. May be claimed at time of levy.

Tangible personal property: **Haw. Rev. Stat. §§ 651-121, and -122.**

Household goods: Necessary furniture, appliances and books.

Motor vehicles: $2575 (fair market value less liens and encumbrances).

Tools of trade: Tools, implements, one commercial fishing boat, motor vehicle reasonably necessary to, and used by the debtor in his or her trade, business or profession.

Clothing and jewelry: Necessary clothing; $1000 jewelry and watches.

Miscellaneous and wildcard: Burial place. Sales and insurance proceeds of exempt property exempt for six months after receipt.

IDAHO

Has state opted out of federal bankruptcy exemptions? Yes. Idaho Code § 11-609.

Wages: **Idaho Code §§ 11-206 through 11-207.**

Scope: Compensation paid or payable for personal services, whether called wages, salary, commission, bonus or otherwise, including periodic payments from pension or retirement program.

Amount: Similar to federal.

Homestead: **Idaho Code §§ 55-1001 through -1008.**

Amount: Lesser of $50,000 or net value of debtor's residence (includes mobile home or unimproved lands on which a residence will be built).

Procedural requirements: If land occupied as residence, homestead exemption is automatic; if owner wishes to claim homestead in land not yet so occupied, must record a declaration of homestead (as well as a declaration of abandonment of any previous homestead). Owner who plans to be away from homestead for more than six months must record declaration of homestead.

Tangible personal property: **Idaho Code §§ 11-603 through -607.**

Household goods: $500 single item, $5000 aggregate: furniture and appliances reasonably necessary for one household including one firearm, clothing, animals, books and musical instruments.

Motor vehicles: $3000 in one vehicle.

Tools of trade: $1500; a 160-inch water right for irrigation of lands the debtor cultivates.

Jewelry: $1000.

Miscellaneous and wildcard: $800 wildcard; health aids; $1000 in crops from 50 acres of land that the debtor cultivates; up to $500 per item portraits and heirlooms; military items; burial plot.

ILLINOIS

Has state opted out of federal bankruptcy exemptions? Yes. 735 Ill. Comp. Stat. Ann. § 5/12-1201.

Wages: **735 Ill. Comp. Stat. Ann. § 5/12-803 and -813; 740 Ill. Comp. Stat. Ann. § 170/4.**

Scope: Wages, salary, commission or bonus.

Amount: The greater of 85% of disposable income, or 45 times the greater of the federal minimum wage, or, for wage summonses served after 1/1/06, the wage prescribed by section 4 of the minimum wage law, is exempt. Disposable earnings are those left after all legally required withholding.

Homestead: **735 Ill. Comp. Stat. Ann. §§ 5/12-901, -902, -903.5, -906, -907.**

Amount: $15,000; if property is owned by two or more persons, each may exempt proportionate share of $30,000.

Procedural requirements: Not specified in exemption statute.

Tangible personal property: **625 Ill. Comp. Stat. § 45/3A-7; 735 Ill. Comp. Stat. § 5/12-1001.**

Household goods: $4000 in any other property. Right to receive certain benefits (insurance, crime victim reparations, personal injury or wrongful death award) remains exempt for two years after award "accrues"; proceeds of award remain exempt for five years, if traceable. Proceeds of sale of exempt property remain exempt to same extent as property is exempt.

Motor vehicles: $2400 in one motor vehicle.

Tools of trade: $1500

Clothing and jewelry: Necessary clothing.

Miscellaneous and wildcard: Bible, school books and family pictures and health aids; certificate of title to watercraft over 12 feet in length is exempt although the watercraft itself is not exempt.

Waiver: Not specified in exemption statute.

INDIANA

Has state opted out of federal bankruptcy exemptions? Yes. Ind. Code Ann. § 34-55-10-1.

Wages: **Ind. Code Ann. § 24-4.5-5-105.**

Scope: Earnings of an individual, including wages, commissions, income, rents or profits.
Amount: Similar to federal.
***Homestead:* Ind. Code Ann. §§ 34-55-10-2(b)(1) and -14.**
Amount: $15,000 subject to certain liens. The exemption is individually available to joint judgment debtors if property held by them as tenants by entireties. Additional exemption for "real estate or tangible personal property" of $8000.
Procedural requirements: None stated. May claim after judgment.
***Tangible personal property:* Ind. Code Ann. § 34-55-10-2.**
Household goods: $8000 in any tangible personal property or non-residential real property and $300 of intangible personal property, including bank accounts and cash; exemptions are subject to certain liens.
Miscellaneous and wildcard: Health aids (no cap).
Waiver: Not specified in exemption statute.

IOWA

Has state opted out of federal bankruptcy exemptions? Yes. Iowa Code Ann. § 627.10.
***Wages:* Iowa Code Ann. §§ 627.6, 642.21, and 537.5105.**
Scope: Compensation paid or payable for personal services, whether called wages, salary, commission, bonus or otherwise, including periodic payments from pension or retirement program.
Amount: Maximum garnishment ranges from $250 a year when expected earnings do not exceed $12,000 to 10% of annual earnings when such earnings exceed $50,000. Tax refund is exempt in bankruptcy only. In addition, if the debt arises from a consumer credit contract, greater of 75% or 40 times the minimum wage is exempt.
***Homestead:* Iowa Code Ann. §§ 561.1 through .3, 561.20 through .22, and 627.9.**
Amount: Up to 1/2 acre in city or town, otherwise 40 acres; also acreage up to $500 in value; building on the property used for business purposes is exempt up to $300. Only one homestead per household unit (defined as persons who reside together, whether or not related). Homestead purchased with pension money is fully exempt.
Procedural requirements: May select homestead and cause it to be platted, but failure to do so will not destroy exemption.
***Tangible personal property:* Iowa Code Ann. §§ 627.6, .6A.**
Household goods: $2000.
Motor vehicles: $5000 in the aggregate of: one motor vehicle, musical instruments, and up to $1000 in accrued wages and tax refunds. Exemption for accrued wages available in bankruptcy only. Motor vehicle not exempt as to claim for damages resulting from use of the vehicle.
Tools of trade: $10,000. Farming implements and livestock included, but may not be exempted for deficiency judgment upon foreclosure on agricultural land if debtor exercises the delay of enforcement provisions of § 654.6.
Clothing and jewelry: $1000 in clothing and storage trunks; any engagement or wedding ring.
Bank accounts: $100.
Miscellaneous and wildcard: One shotgun and either a rifle or a musket; $1000 in books and paintings; professionally prescribed health aids; burial space. Up to $500 aggregate in prepaid rent or security deposits, or utility security deposits.

KANSAS

Has state opted out of federal bankruptcy exemptions? Yes, except as to § 522(d)(10) (benefits, alimony, support, maintenance, certain pensions and similar payments). Kan. Stat. Ann. § 60-2312.

***Wages:* Kan. Stat. Ann. §§ 60-2310 and -2311.**

Scope: Compensation paid or payable for personal services, whether called wages, salary, commission, bonus or otherwise.

Amount: Similar to federal. If a debtor is prevented from working at his or her usual employment for two weeks, because of illness of the debtor or a family member, garnishment is forbidden until the expiration of two months after recovery from the illness. No employee may be discharged or disciplined because of wage garnishment. If a debt is assigned to a person or collection agency, the assignee may not use wage garnishment (except for certain child support, tax or court restitution collections).

***Homestead:* Kan. Stat. Ann. §§ 60-2301 and -2302.**

Amount: 160 acres of farm land or one acre in a town or city, subject to certain liens. Mobile or manufactured home explicitly included.

Procedural requirements: None stated. May be claimed at time of levy.

***Tangible personal property:* Kan. Stat. Ann. § 60-2304.**

Household goods: Household goods, fuel, food and clothing reasonably necessary at principal residence for one year.

Motor vehicles: $20,000, if used regularly to commute to work; disabled (definition at Kan. Stat. Ann. § 8-1124) no limitations.

Tools of trade: $7500.

Jewelry: $1000.

Miscellaneous and wildcard: Burial space; national guard uniforms and equipment.

Waiver: Not specified in exemption statute.

KENTUCKY

Has state opted out of federal bankruptcy exemptions? Yes. Ky. Rev. Stat. Ann. § 427.170.

***Wages:* Ky. Rev. Stat. Ann. §§ 427.005 and .010(2).**

Scope: Compensation paid or payable for personal services, whether called wages, salary, commission, bonus or otherwise, including periodic payments pursuant to pension or retirement program.

Amount: Similar to federal exemptions.

***Homestead:* Ky. Rev. Stat. Ann. §§ 427.060, .070, .100, and .160.**

Amount: $5000 in real or personal property used as a residence. In bankruptcy, an additional $1000 in real property may be exempted if this sum is not applied to exempt personal property.

Procedural requirements: None stated. May be claimed after judgment.

***Tangible personal property:* Ky. Rev. Stat. Ann. §§ 427.010(1), .030, .040, .150, and .160.**

Household goods: $3000 in household goods, clothing and jewelry. Explicitly excludes antiques, works of art, jewelry other than wedding rings, and electronic equipment except for one TV and one radio.

Motor vehicles: $2500.

Tools of trade: $300 tools of trade. $3000 farm implements and livestock. $1000 office, library and instruments and $2500 motor vehicle used by professional (i.e., clergy, doctor, dentist, attorney, chiropractor, veterinarian); $2500 motor vehicle if used by person who services essential mechanical, electrical or other equipment in general use.

Miscellaneous and wildcard: Health aids. Bankruptcy only: $1000 in any real or personal property.

LOUISIANA

Has state opted out of federal bankruptcy exemptions? Yes. La. Rev. Stat. Ann. § 13:3881(B)(1).

Wages: **La. Rev. Stat. Ann. § 13:3881.**

Scope: Earnings of any individual. Disposable earnings are those left after legally required deductions, and deductions in usual course of business for retirement, health insurance and life insurance.

Amount: Similar to federal exemptions.

Homestead: **La. Rev. Stat. Ann. § 20:1. *See* La. Const. art. 12, § 9.**

Amount: Residence and land, building and appurtenances on contiguous tracts of up to five acres if within a municipality, two hundred acres if not. Up to $25,000, except that for expenses resulting from catastrophic or terminal illness or injury, homestead is exempt up to full value. Some exceptions, including taxes, mortgage, certain criminal restitution.

Procedural requirements: Not specified.

Tangible personal property: **La. Rev. Stat. Ann. § 13:3881.**

Household goods: Clothing, household goods, non-sterling silverware, certain retirement plans; poultry, fowl and one cow for family use; a right of personal servitude of habitation and the usufruct under Article 223 of the Civil Code.

Motor vehicles: $7500 in one vehicle, must be used for work or commuting to work.

Tools of trade: Tools, instruments, books, and one utility trailer used for trade, calling or profession by which debtor earns living. Certain livestock.

Clothing and jewelry: Clothing; $5000 wedding and engagement rings.

Miscellaneous and wildcard: Household pets, family portraits, arms and military accoutrements, musical instruments.

MAINE

Has state opted out of federal bankruptcy exemptions? Yes. Me. Rev. Stat. Ann. tit. 14, § 4426.

Wages: **Me. Rev. Stat. Ann. tit. 9-A, §§ 5-105, 5-106 and tit. 19A, § 2356.**

Scope: Earnings of an individual.

Amount: For consumer credit transaction, maximum garnishment is lesser of 25% of weekly wages, or the amount by which wages exceed 40 times the federal minimum hourly wage. Disposable earnings are those left after legally required deductions.

Homestead: **Me. Rev. Stat. Ann. tit. 14, § 4422(1).**

Amount: $35,000 in real or personal property used as residence or burial plot, subject to certain exceptions; $70,000 if debtor over 60 or has mental or physical disability that prevents him or her from working and lasts at least twelve months or results in death;

$70,000 if minor dependent(s) of debtor have a principal place of residence with debtor. If debtor's interest in the property is held jointly with other person or persons, then the lesser of $35,000 or the debtor's fractional share of $70,000, or if debtor is over 60 or disabled, debtor's fractional share of $140,000. Increased exemptions for elderly or disabled do not apply to liens obtained prior to that provision's effective date, nor to tort judgments involving "other than ordinary negligence on the part of the debtor." Exemption does not protect property that has been fraudulently conveyed.

Procedural requirements: Not specified in exemption statute.

Tangible personal property: **Me. Rev. Stat. Ann. tit. 14, §§ 4422(2) through (9), (11), (15), and (16).** (Note that Maine's Domestic Relations Code, Me. Rev. Stat. tit. 19-A, § 2203, which allows seizure and sale of property for family support debts, has its own list of exemptions. It was originally scheduled to sunset on October 1, 1998, but the sunset provision was repealed in 1997 by 1997 Me. Laws ch. 669, § 4.)

Household goods: Household goods, not more than $200 per item; a cook stove, all heating equipment and various fuels; food and provisions for six months, all equipment necessary for harvesting food and material necessary to raise food for one growing season.

Motor vehicles: $5000.

Tools of trade: $5000; one fishing boat, not more than five tons. Farm equipment.

Clothing and jewelry: Clothing, not more than $200 per item; $750 in jewelry and a wedding and engagement ring.

Miscellaneous and wildcard: Books, animals, crops and musical instruments held for personal use but no more than $200 per individual item; health aids.

MARYLAND

Has state opted out of federal bankruptcy exemptions? Yes. Md. Code Ann., Cts. & Jud. Proc. § 11-504.

Wages: **Md. Code Ann., Com. Law § 15-601.1.**

Scope: All monetary remuneration paid to any employee for his or her employment.

Amount: Caroline, Kent, Queen Anne's and Worcester counties follow the federal scheme; in all other counties, the greater of $145 times the number of weeks in which wages earned or 75% of disposable wages is exempt; any medical insurance payment deducted from wages is exempt.

Homestead: **Md. Code Ann., Cts. & Jud. Proc. §§ 11-504 and -507.**

Amount: No explicit homestead exemption. $6000 wild card exemption, which may be applied to any type of property. In bankruptcy, additional $5000 in real or personal property. Both these exemptions are subject to certain liens.

Procedural requirements: None stated.

Tangible personal property: **Md. Code Ann., Cts. & Jud. Proc. § 11-504.**

Household goods: $1000 in goods held for family or household use. Additional $5000 in bankruptcy.

Motor vehicles: See wildcard.

Tools of trade: $5000.

Miscellaneous and wildcard: $6000 in money or property of any kind; health aids.

MASSACHUSETTS

Has state opted out of federal bankruptcy exemptions? No.

Wages: **Mass. Gen. Laws Ann. ch. 246, § 28.**

Scope: Wages for personal labor or personal services.

Amount: $125 per week is exempt.

Homestead: **Mass. Gen. Laws Ann. ch. 188, §§ 1 and 1A.**

Amount: $500,000 in principal family residence; the exemption is not available for debts for taxes, debts arising prior to purchase of the homestead, judgment debts for support of spouse or children. Each debtor who is 62 or older, or disabled, may exempt $300,000 per individual, whether property is owned individually or jointly. These increased figures do not take priority over any lien, right, or interest recorded or filed prior to Nov. 2, 2000.

Procedural requirements: Yes. Must file declaration of homestead. Does not protect against debts incurred before filing. Disabled debtor must file copy of SSI award letter, or physician's certificate stating that debtor meets SSI eligibility requirements, at time of filing homestead declaration.

Tangible personal property: **Mass. Gen. Laws Ann. ch. 235, § 34 and ch. 246, § 28.**

Household goods: Necessary clothes and beds, one heating unit, and up to $75 per month for utilities; $3000 in additional necessary household furniture.

Motor vehicles: One motor vehicle, worth up to $700, needed to maintain employment.

Tools of trade: $500.

Bank accounts: $125 in cash and bank deposits on wages due plus an additional $500 in a bank deposit.

Miscellaneous and wildcard: $200 books; various specified livestock, four tons of hay, $300 in provisions, one pew, military uniforms, one sewing machine not exceeding $200 in value.

MICHIGAN

Has state opted out of federal bankruptcy exemptions? No.

Wages: **Mich. Comp. Laws Ann. § 600.5311 (Mich. Stat. Ann. § 27A.5311).**

Scope: Wages.

Amount: Householders may exempt 60% of weekly wages, but not less than $15 per week, and an extra $2.00 per week per dependent other than a spouse. Other debtors may exempt 40% of weekly wages but not less than $10 per week.

Homestead: **Mich. Const. art. X, § 3; Mich. Comp. Laws Ann. §§ 559.214, 600.6022, .6023, .6024, and .6027 (Mich. Stat. Ann. §§ 26.50(214), 27A.6022, .6023, .6024, and .6027).**

Amount: $3500 not exceeding 40 acres rural or one lot inside city, town, or village, subject to certain liens; an equity of redemption as described in § 600.6060. Condos occupied as residence explicitly included.

Procedural requirements: If homestead has not been platted and set apart, debtor may designate at time of levy.

Tangible personal property: **Mich. Const. art. X, § 3; Mich. Comp. Laws Ann. § 600.6023 (Mich. Stat. Ann. § 27A.6023).**

Household goods: $1000 household furniture, utensils, books and appliances; six months of provisions and fuel; certain farm animals; six months supply of feed; tools of trade; certain disability benefits and retirement accounts.
Motor vehicles: Not specified.
Tools of trade: $1000 tools, materials, stock, vehicle for principal business or profession; for householder, certain livestock and feed.
Clothing and jewelry: All clothing.
Bank accounts: Householder may claim $1000 in savings and loan, if no homestead claimed.
Miscellaneous and wildcard: All family pictures; all arms required by law to be kept; a pew.

MINNESOTA

Has state opted out of federal bankruptcy exemptions? No.
Wages: **Minn. Stat. Ann. §§ 550.37(13), (14), (25), 550.136, and 571.922.**
Scope: Compensation paid to an employee, who performs personal services for employer who may control both what is done and how it is done, whether called wages, salary, commission, bonus or otherwise, including periodic payments pursuant to pension or retirement plan; compensation for the sale of certain agricultural products from family farm; maintenance as defined in the domestic relations statutes.
Amount: Garnishment limited to lesser of 25% of disposable earnings or amount by which disposable earnings exceed 40 times federal minimum wage. Disposable earnings are those left after all deductions required by law. If the debtor has been a recipient of needs-based assistance, or an inmate of a correctional institution, no garnishment is permitted for six months after return to employment and termination of all public assistance. A separate provision completely exempts proceeds of payments received by a person for labor, skill, material, or machinery contributing to an improvement in real estate. Private right of action for employee terminated because of wage garnishment.
Homestead: **Minn. Stat. Ann. §§ 510.01, .02, .06, .07, and 550.37(12).**
Amount: $500,000 for a farm, otherwise $200,000; home or house owned and occupied by debtor and land on which such house is situated but only a total of 160 acres outside a platted portion of a city or 1/2 acre inside a city. Manufactured homes specifically included.
Procedural requirements: None stated. If homestead has not been set apart, it may be claimed at time of levy.
Tangible personal property: **Minn. Stat. Ann. § 550.37.** (Note that all dollar amounts, except for farm implements and combined farm implements plus tools of trade are indexed, and fluctuate periodically; amounts are adjusted on July 1 of even numbered years.)
Household goods: $8550. Household furniture and appliances, including sound systems, radios and televisions.
Motor vehicles: $3800. If modified for disability, at a cost of no less than $2840: $38,000.
Tools of trade: Farm implements, $13,000. Tools of trade $9500. Aggregate of these two exemptions may not exceed $13,000.

Clothing and jewelry: All clothing and one watch. $1225 in aggregate interest in wedding rings or other religious or culturally recognized symbols of marriage exchanged by debtor and spouse at time of marriage, and in the debtor's possession.
Miscellaneous and wildcard: Books and musical instruments; pew and burial place.

MISSISSIPPI

Has state opted out of federal bankruptcy exemptions? Yes. Miss. Code Ann. § 85-3-2.
Wages: **Miss. Code Ann. § 85-3-4.**
Scope: Wages, salaries or other compensation of laborers or employees.
Amount: Exempt for thirty days after date of service of writ of attachment, execution or garnishment; thereafter similar to federal.
Homestead: **Miss. Code Ann. §§ 85-3-21 through -27, and 85-3-1(e).**
Amount: Householder may claim $75,000 of 160 acres owned and occupied as a residence, subject to liens. $20,000 for mobile home used as debtor's residence.
Procedural requirements: Permitted but not required to record declaration of homestead. If this is not done, statute prescribes a formula for determining what land is homestead.
Tangible personal property: **Miss. Code Ann. § 85-3-1.**
Household goods: Tangible personal property of the following kinds to a total value of $10,000: household goods (definition similar to that of FTC rule restricting non-possessory security interests), wearing apparel, books, animals or crops, motor vehicles, implements, professional books or tools of a trade, cash on hand, professionally prescribed health aids, and any item of personal property worth less than $200.

MISSOURI

Has state opted out of federal bankruptcy exemptions? Yes. Mo. Ann. Stat. § 513.427.
Wages: **Mo. Ann. Stat. § 525.030.**
Scope: Aggregate earnings of an individual.
Amount: Garnishment limited to 10% for head of family; otherwise similar to federal.
Homestead: **Mo. Ann. Stat. §§ 513.430(6), .475, and .510.**
Amount: $15,000 in residence and land used in connection with it; exemption for multiple owners may not exceed, in aggregate, $15,000. Mobile home used as residence and not exceeding $5000 in value is exempt.
Procedural requirements: None stated. Homestead is acquired when deed recorded (or in case of inheritance, when new owner acquires title).
Tangible personal property: **Mo. Ann. Stat. §§ 513.430 and .440.**
Household goods: $3000 in household goods and furnishings, wearing apparel, appliances, books, animals, crops or musical instruments.
Motor vehicles: $3000.
Tools of trade: $3000.
Clothing and jewelry: Clothing included in $1000 household goods exemption. Wedding ring, $1500, other jewelry, $500.
Miscellaneous and wildcard: $600 any property. Additional $1250 wildcard for head of family, plus $350 for each unmarried, dependent, minor child; may not be used to exempt the non-exempt 10% of wages. Professionally prescribed health aids.

MONTANA

Has state opted out of federal bankruptcy exemptions? Yes. Mont. Code Ann. § 31-2-106.

Wages: **Mont. Code Ann. §§ 25-13-601, -610, -614.**

Scope: Same as federal.

Amount: Similar to federal.

Homestead: **Mont. Code Ann. §§ 70-32-101 through -107, -202, -216.**

Amount: $100,000 in dwelling house or mobile home and land thereunder. Claimant who owns undivided interest in property is limited to an exemption proportional to claimant's interest.

Procedural requirements: Declaration of homestead must be recorded. But it appears that homestead is protected against debts that precede recording, except mortgages and certain other liens. The main effect of recording a homestead declaration appears to be to require a spouse's signature on any sale or encumbrance thereafter.

Tangible personal property: **Mont. Code Ann. §§ 25-13-608, -609, -613, 35-15-404.**

Household goods: $600 per item, or $4500 in the aggregate in furniture, appliances, jewelry, wearing apparel, books, firearms and other sporting goods, animals, feed, crops and musical instruments.

Motor vehicles: $2500.

Tools of trade: $3000.

Clothing and jewelry: Included in $4500 household goods exemption.

Miscellaneous and wildcard: Health aids, burial place, property used to carry out government functions.

NEBRASKA

Has state opted out of federal bankruptcy exemptions? Yes. Neb. Rev. Stat. § 25-15,105.

Wages: **Neb. Rev. Stat. § 25-1558 and 25-1560 to -1563.**

Scope: Earnings paid or payable by an employer to an employee for personal services, whether called wages, salary, commission, bonus or otherwise, including periodic payments from pension or retirement program.

Amount: Head of family, 85% of disposable earnings exempt except for support obligations. Head of family is defined as anyone who actually supports and maintains one or more individuals related to him or her by blood, marriage, adoption or guardianship and whose right to exercise family control and provide for the dependent(s) is based on some moral or legal obligation. All others, similar to federal.

Homestead: **Neb. Rev. Stat. §§ 40-101, -102, -103, -111, -112, -113, -115, and -116.**

Amount: $12,500 in a dwelling located on up to 160 acres if not in city or village or two contiguous lots if in city or village; available only to heads of households, defined as married persons, surviving spouses, or anyone with a dependent residing with him or her.

Procedural requirements: None stated. May be claimed after judgment, anytime before confirmation of sale.

Tangible personal property: **Neb. Rev. Stat. §§ 25-1552, -1556.**

Household goods: Immediate personal possessions of debtor and family; $1500 household goods, appliances, computers, books and musical instruments.

Motor vehicles: Tools of trade exemption applies to motor vehicle used for work or for commuting.

Tools of trade: $2400.
Clothing and jewelry: All necessary clothing.
Miscellaneous and wildcard: $2500 any personal property except wages. Professionally prescribed health aids.

NEVADA

Has state opted out of federal bankruptcy exemptions? Yes. Nev. Rev. Stat. §§ 21.090.
Wages: **Nev. Rev. Stat. §§ 31.295 through 31.298.**
Scope: Earnings.
Amount: Garnishment may not exceed the lesser of 25% of disposable earnings for the workweek or the amount by which disposable earnings that week exceed 50 times the federal minimum wage.
Homestead: **Nev. Rev. Stat. §§ 21.090, .095, 115.005, .010, and .040.**
Amount: $350,000 in either land and a dwelling or a mobile home, subject to certain liens; land held in spendthrift trust for debtor is exempt. Unlimited exemption if "allodial title" has been established. (Nevada residents can acquire "allodial title" to their land by buying out the property tax right from the government. Then the landowner does not have to pay property tax on the land.) The primary dwelling, including a mobile home, and land may not be executed upon for a medical bill during the lifetime of the debtor, debtor's spouse, a joint tenant who was a joint tenant at the time judgment was entered, or debtor's disabled dependent adult child, or during the minority of any child of debtor.
Procedural requirements: Procedure available for filing declaration of homestead. Exemption available even without declaration. Once declaration is filed, spouse must join in any encumbrance or sale.
Tangible personal property: **Nev. Rev. Stat. §§ 21.080, .090, and .100.**
Household goods: $12,000 necessary household goods (FTC definition).
Motor vehicles: $15,000, no limit if specially equipped for disabled debtor or dependent.
Tools of trade: $10,000 tools of trade; $10,000 mining equipment; $10,000 farm equipment.
Clothing and jewelry: Not specified.

NEW HAMPSHIRE

Has state opted out of federal bankruptcy exemptions? No.
Wages: **N.H. Rev. Stat. Ann. §§ 161-C:11, 512:21.**
Scope: Wages.
Amount: Fifty times federal minimum wage is exempt.
Homestead: **N.H. Rev. Stat. Ann. §§ 480:1 and :4.**
Amount: $100,000. Manufactured housing explicitly included (but not the underlying land, if owned by another).
Procedural requirements: Procedure available for establishing homestead, but apparently not prerequisite to existence of exemption.
Tangible personal property: **N.H. Rev. Stat. Ann. § 511:2.**
Household goods: $3500 household furniture; beds and bedding; stove, utensils, refrigerator, heating unit; sewing machine; $400 provisions and fuel.

Motor vehicles: $4000.
Tools of trade: $5000.
Clothing and jewelry: Necessary clothing; $500 jewelry.
Miscellaneous and wildcard: Wild card exemption of $1000 plus up to $7000 from unused exemptions for furniture, provisions and fuel, library, tools of trade, motor vehicle and jewelry. Burial place; militia uniforms and arms; $800 in books; various livestock; a meeting-house pew.

NEW JERSEY

Has state opted out of federal bankruptcy exemptions? No.
Wages: **N.J. Stat. Ann. §§ 2A:17-50, 2A:17-56, -56.9, and -56.12.**
Scope: Wages, debts, salary, income from trust funds, or profits, due and owing or to become due and owing.
Amount: $48/week is exempt. 90% exempt if debtor's income does not exceed 250% of the poverty level
Homestead: None.
Tangible personal property: **N.J. Stat. Ann. §§ 2A:17-19, 2A:26-4, and 38A:4-8.**
Household goods: $1000 household goods and furniture.
Clothing and jewelry: All necessary clothing.
Miscellaneous and wildcard: $1000 all personal property except clothing. Pay and other benefits due as a result of participation in the state militia.

NEW MEXICO

Has state opted out of federal bankruptcy exemptions? No.
Wages: **N.M. Stat. Ann. § 35-12-7.**
Scope: Disposable earnings.
Amount: Greater of 75% of disposable earnings or 40 times minimum wage is exempt. Disposable earnings are those left after legally required deductions.
Homestead: **N.M. Stat. Ann. §§ 42-10-9 and -11.**
Amount: $30,000 in land or a dwelling if debtor owns, leases, or purchases the dwelling. Subject to certain liens. If property is jointly owned by two persons, each is entitled to a $30,000 exemption.
Procedural requirements: None specified.
Tangible personal property: **N.M. Stat. Ann. §§ 42-10-1, -2, -10, 53-4-28, and 53-10-2.**
Household goods: Furniture and books.
Motor vehicles: $4000.
Tools of trade: $1500.
Clothing and jewelry: Clothing; $2500 jewelry.
Miscellaneous and wildcard: $500 in personal property; married debtors or heads of households may take $500 in cash instead of the personal property; a resident without a homestead may exempt $2000 in real or personal property; health aids; the minimum amount of shares necessary for membership in certain cooperative associations; debtor's interest in the property of an unincorporated association.

NEW YORK

Has state opted out of federal bankruptcy exemptions? Yes. N.Y. Debt. & Cred. Law § 282.

Wages: **N.Y. C.P.L.R. §§ 5205(d), (e), 5252, and 5241; N.Y. Soc. Serv. Law § 137-a.**

Scope: Earnings for personal services.

Amount: 90% of earnings rendered 60 days before or any time after delivery of execution to the sheriff or a motion to apply the debtor's earnings to a judgment is exempt; wages received in addition to public assistance are exempt. Garnishment forbidden if debtor is receiving public assistance or would qualify for public assistance if the amount of the garnishment were subtracted from his or her wages. The pay of enlisted personnel and non-commissioned officers in the military is completely exempt, except for family support debts. Employer may not discipline or refuse to hire employee because of wage execution. Private right of action for six weeks lost wages, civil penalty of $500 ($1000 for repeat offense), court may order reinstatement or hiring. Private right of action if employer withholds income after being formally notified by social services official that worker is receiving or eligible for aid.

Homestead: **N.Y. C.P.L.R. § 5206.**

Amount: $10,000 in the following types of property owned as a principal residence: a lot with a dwelling, a cooperative apartment, a condominium, or a mobile home, unless the judgment was recovered wholly for the purchase price.

Procedural requirements: None specified in exemption statute.

Tangible personal property: **N.Y. C.P.L.R. § 5205; N.Y. Debt. & Cred. Law §§ 282 and 283(1).**

Household goods: All stoves and fuel for sixty days; one sewing machine; the family Bible; family pictures, family pew; domestic animals and feed for 60 days to a value of $450; a sixty-day supply of food for the debtor and family; all wearing apparel; household furniture, one refrigerator, one radio, one television, necessary tableware and cooking utensils; wedding ring; necessary working tools not exceeding $600. $5000 aggregate cap when exempting personal property from a bankruptcy estate.

Motor vehicles: $2400 in one vehicle.

Tools of trade: $600 (included in aggregate $5000 above).

Clothing and jewelry: Included in aggregate $5000 above.

Bank accounts: Bankruptcy only: the lesser of $2500 or the amount of certain unused exemptions.

Miscellaneous and wildcard: 90% of any unpaid proceeds from the sale of milk if the debtor is a farmer; security deposits; health aids and guide dogs; residential rental or utility security deposits.

Waiver: Not specified in exemption statute.

NORTH CAROLINA

Has state opted out of federal bankruptcy exemptions? Yes. N.C. Gen. Stat. § 1C-1601(f).

Wages: **N.C. Gen. Stat. § 1-362.**

Scope: Earnings for personal services within 60 days before date of court order.

Amount: Exempt to the extent needed for family support.

Homestead: **N.C. Const. art. X, § 2; N.C. Gen. Stat §§ 1C-1601(a)(1), (e).**

Amount: $18,500 (for unmarried debtor over age 65, who formerly owned the property in tenancy by entireties or joint tenancy with person now deceased, $37,000) in residence consisting of real or personal property, including a cooperative, subject to certain liens and support claims.

Procedural requirements: None specified in exemption statute.

***Tangible personal property:* N.C. Gen. Stat. § 1C-1601.**

Household goods: $5000 for debtor plus $1000 per dependent up to an additional $4000. Includes furniture, books, musical instruments, clothing, animals, crops.

Motor vehicles: $3500.

Tools of trade: $2000.

Clothing and jewelry: Clothing included in household goods exemption, above.

Miscellaneous and wildcard: Unused homestead exemption, up to $5000. Professionally prescribed health aids.

NORTH DAKOTA

Has state opted out of federal bankruptcy exemptions? Yes. N.D. Cent. Code § 28-22-17.

***Wages:* N.D. Cent. Code §§ 28-25-11 and 32-09.1-03.**

Scope: Compensation paid or payable for personal services, whether called wages, salary, commission, bonus or otherwise, including military retirement pay, or periodic payments pursuant to a pension or retirement program. Does not include Social Security benefits, or veterans' disability (except for child support garnishment).

Amount: Greater of 75% of disposable earnings or forty times federal minimum wage is exempt with an additional $20 for each dependent living with debtor; earnings for personal services received within sixty days preceding order are totally exempt if debtor can show earnings are necessary for use of a family supported in whole or in part by debtor. Disposable earnings are those left after legally required deductions.

***Homestead:* N.D. Cent. Code §§ 28-22-02, -03.1(1), 47-18-01, -04, -14, -16.**

Amount: $80,000 in land and dwelling but lots must be contiguous; or a house trailer or mobile home occupied as a residence; exemption subject to certain liens.

Procedural requirements: Procedure available for filing declaration of homestead, but homestead right not impaired by failure to do so.

***Tangible personal property:* N.D. Cent. Code §§ 28-22-01 through -05.**

Household goods: Fuel and provisions for one year. Head of family may exempt $1000 household and kitchen furniture.

Motor vehicles: $1200, or $32,000 if modified at cost of not less than $1500 to accommodate owner with permanent disability.

Tools of trade: Head of family may exempt $1000 tools of trade, $4500 farming implements and stock, and crops and grain from 160 acres of land occupied by debtor, either as tenant or owner but this exemption subject to certain liens.

Clothing and jewelry: All clothing.

Miscellaneous and wildcard: $7500 in lieu of homestead. Wildcard $2500 for single person, $5000 for head of family, i.e., married person or one who resides with certain dependents. Head of family may choose either the wildcard, or the listed head of family exemptions above, and $1500 in books and musical instruments. All family pictures, a pew, $100 in family library.

OHIO

Has state opted out of federal bankruptcy exemptions? Yes. Ohio Rev. Code Ann. § 2329.662.

Wages: **Ohio Rev. Code Ann. § 2329.66(A)(13).**

Scope: Personal earnings.

Amount: Similar to federal exemptions. Disposable earnings are those left after legally required deductions.

Homestead: **Ohio Rev. Code Ann. §§ 2329.66(1)(b) and .661.**

Amount: $5000 in one parcel of real or personal property used by debtor or dependent as residence, subject to certain liens. For debts for health care services or supplies, the exemption has no dollar limit; this does not preclude the creation of a lien, which may be enforced only when property is sold or otherwise transferred to someone other than a surviving spouse or surviving minor child of debtor.

Procedural requirements: Not specified in exemption statute.

Tangible personal property: **Ohio Rev. Code Ann. § 2329.66.**

Household goods: Up to $200 per item in all beds and bedding, up to $300 per item in one cooking unit and one refrigerator or similar unit, up to $200 per item in household goods and jewelry; but one item of jewelry in which debtor has a $400 interest may also be exempted; debtors exempting a homestead may only exempt a total of $1500 in cash, household items, exclusive of cooking unit and refrigerator, and jewelry; debtors not utilizing homestead exemption may exempt a total of $2000 in such items.

Motor vehicles: $1000.

Tools of trade: $750.

Clothing and jewelry: Up to $200 per item in clothing and jewelry, and one piece of jewelry up to $400 (clothing and jewelry are included in $1500 or $2000 caps above, under household goods).

Bank accounts: Bankruptcy only: $400 in cash, money due or to become due within 90 days, tax refunds, or bank deposits.

Miscellaneous and wildcard: $400; health aids; notary's seal and official register.

Waiver: Not specified in exemption statute.

OKLAHOMA

Has state opted out of federal bankruptcy exemptions? Yes. Okla. Stat. Ann. tit. 31, § 1(C).

Wages: **Okla. Stat. Ann. tit. 12, §§ 1171.1 and 1171.2; tit. 31, § 1.1.**

Scope: Money earned by a natural person as wages, salary, bonus or commission for personal services.

Amount: Follows federal scheme except debtor who is supporting dependent(s) may exempt a larger percentage on a showing of hardship.

Homestead: **Okla. Const. art. XII, § 1; Okla. Stat. Ann. tit. 31, §§ 1, 2, and 5.**

Amount: 160 acres not within any city or town, or annexed by a city or town after November 1, 1997, and owned, occupied and used for both residential and commercial agricultural purposes; urban homestead exemption shall not exceed $5000 if more than 25% of the square foot area of the improvements on the land is used for business purposes or if less than 75% of square foot area of the improvements on the land is used as principal residence.

Procedural requirements: None specified in exemption statute.
Tangible personal property: **Okla. Stat. Ann. tit. 31, § 1.**
Household goods: All household furniture, books, portraits and pictures.
Motor vehicles: $7500 in one vehicle.
Tools of trade: $10,000 aggregate in tools of trade and farming implements.
Clothing and jewelry: $4000 clothing, $3000 in wedding and anniversary rings.
Miscellaneous and wildcard: Health aids, a limited number of poultry and livestock, $2000 in guns and a year's supply of provisions; burial place.

OREGON

Has state opted out of federal bankruptcy exemptions? Yes. Or. Rev. Stat. § 18.300.
Wages: **Or. Rev. Stat. §§ 18.375 and .385.**
Scope: Compensation paid or payable for personal services, whether called wages, salary, commission, bonus or otherwise, including periodic payments pursuant to pension or retirement plan. Some independent contractors are covered.
Amount: Greater of 75% of disposable earnings or $170 is exempt. Disposable earnings are those left over after legally required deductions.
Homestead: **Or. Rev. Stat. §§ 18.395, .398, .402, .428.**
Amount: $30,000 in a residence; if two members of household are debtors whose interests in homestead are subject to execution, may not exceed $39,600; cannot exceed 160 acres if outside town or city; cannot exceed one block if within town or city; homestead exemption subject to certain liens; may exempt $23,000 in a mobile home and land used as residence; if two members of household are debtors whose interest in mobile home and land are subject to execution, the combined exemption may not exceed $30,000. If debtor owns a mobile home but not the land on which it stands, exemptions are $20,000 for individual or $27,000 for multiple owners. Mobile home definition explicitly includes a floating home.
Procedural requirements: None specified in exemption statute.
Tangible personal property: **Or. Rev. Stat. §§ 18.345, .362.**
Household goods: $3000 in household goods, a 60-day supply of fuel and provisions.
Motor vehicles: $2150 (joint debtors may stack).
Tools of trade: $3000 (joint debtors may stack).
Clothing and jewelry: $1800 in wearing apparel, jewelry and other personal items (joint debtors may stack).
Miscellaneous and wildcard: $400 which can be stacked by joint debtors and applied toward any personal property but which cannot be used to increase another exemption; $600 in books, pictures and musical instruments (joint debtors may stack), all health aids, $1000 in animals, poultry and 60-day supply of feed, a rifle or shotgun and one pistol, the combined value of which may not exceed $1000.

PENNSYLVANIA

Has state opted out of federal bankruptcy exemptions? No.
Wages: **23 Pa. Cons. Stat. Ann. § 3703; 42 Pa. Cons. Stat. Ann. § 8127.**
Scope: Wages, salaries and commissions of individuals.

Amount: Completely exempt in hands of employer, *except* for certain residential rent or damages, board for four weeks or less, family support, student loan, or criminal fine, restitution, costs. (Support 50%; landlord-tenant 10% or a sum not to place debtor's income below federal poverty guidelines, whichever is less; not specified for other exceptions.) Net wages are those left after legally required deductions, health insurance, and union dues. Garnishment for rent or damages not permitted if lessee is victim of domestic abuse.

Homestead: No statutory homestead exemption, but common-law doctrine of tenancy by the entireties protects property owned by husband and wife from debts owed just by one spouse. *See* Sterrett v. Sterrett, 401 Pa. 583, 166 A.2d (1960).

Tangible personal property: **42 Pa. Cons. Stat. Ann. §§ 8122, 8123, 8124, 8125, and 8127.**

Clothing and jewelry: All clothing.

Miscellaneous and wildcard: $300 in property including bank notes, money, securities, real property or money due the debtor; the exemption is inapplicable to claims for support, or for board for four weeks or less, or to foreclosure judgments or certain wage claims. Bibles and schoolbooks, sewing machines if not kept for sale or hire, and certain uniforms; tangible personal property on exhibition at any international exhibition held under the auspices of the federal government is exempt in the hands of the authorities of such exhibition or otherwise.

PUERTO RICO

Has state opted out of federal bankruptcy exemptions? No.

Wages: **32 P.R. Laws Ann. § 1130.**

Scope: Earnings for personal services within 30 days before levy of execution.

Amount: 75% exempt if debtor can show earnings are necessary for use of family supported wholly or in part by debtor's labor.

Homestead: **31 P.R. Laws Ann. tit. §§ 1851–1855.**

Amount: $1500 for heads of families, subject to certain mortgages and debts.

Procedural requirements: Head of family who acquires homestead should set forth this fact in the deed, but failure to do so does not destroy exemption.

Tangible personal property: **32 P.R. Laws Ann. § 1130.**

Household goods: $100 in chairs, tables, desks and books; necessary household furniture including one sewing machine; $200 in a stove, furniture, beds, bedding; provisions sufficient for one month; iceboxes; $200 in a washing machine, $100 in a radio, $250 in a television and an electric iron.

Motor vehicles: One motor vehicle used in debtor's occupation (except for purchase money and repair debts for the vehicle). Exemption is capped at $6000 for liability for injury to third person by the motor vehicle.

Tools of trade: $300 tools of trade. Various farm animals and their equipment and feed for one month; a water right not to exceed the amount used for land the debtor actually cultivates; $200 in seeds to be planted or sowed within six months; certain mining equipment, aggregate $500.

Clothing and jewelry: All clothing.

Miscellaneous and wildcard: Artwork done by the debtor, family portraits and their necessary frames; $500 in shares of a homestead association if the debtor has no homestead; uniforms the debtor is required to keep and one gun.

RHODE ISLAND

Has state opted out of federal bankruptcy exemptions? No.

Wages: **R.I. Gen. Laws § 9-26-4(8).**

Scope: Wages or salary.

Amount: $50 per week is exempt. All wages are exempt if debtor is, or within one year was, "an object of relief from any state, federal, or municipal corporation or agency." Wages due a sailor are completely exempt.

Homestead: **R.I. Gen. Stat. § 9-26-4.1.**

Amount: $200,000 in land or buildings which debtor has a right to possess by lease or otherwise and occupies or intends to occupy as a principal residence. Significant exceptions: certain liens, debts owed to a federally insured depository institution or a person regulated under title 19 (financial institutions), debt contracted prior to the purchase of the residence. Only one exemption per residence (whether single or multiple owners) and only one principal residence per family.

Procedural requirements: None. "Automatic by operation of law."

Tangible personal property: **R.I. Gen. Laws § 9-26-4.**

Household goods: Furnishings and family stores of a housekeeper, up to $8600.

Motor vehicles: Motor vehicles with aggregate value up to $10,000.

Tools of trade: Professional's library; tools of trade up to $1200.

Clothing and jewelry: Necessary clothing of debtor and family; $1000 jewelry.

Miscellaneous and wildcard: Books up to $300; one cemetery plot; debts secured by bills of exchange or promissory notes; $50 in holdings in consumer cooperative association.

SOUTH CAROLINA

Has state opted out of federal bankruptcy exemptions? Yes. S.C. Code Ann. § 15-41-35.

Wages: **S.C. Code Ann. §§ 15-39-410 and -420.**

Scope: Personal service earnings are exempt.

Amount: Fully exempt.

Homestead: **S.C. Code Ann. § 15-41-30(1); *see* S.C. Const. art. III, § 28.**

Amount: $5000 in real property or personal property used as residence or in cooperative used as residence or in burial plot. Multiple owners may exempt up to $10,000.

Procedural requirements: Not specified in exemption statute.

Tangible personal property: **S.C. Code Ann. § 15-41-30; *see* S.C. Const. art. III, § 28.**

Household goods: $2500 in household furnishings and goods, clothing, appliances, books, animals, crops, musical instruments.

Motor vehicles: $1200 in one motor vehicle.

Tools of trade: $750.

Clothing and jewelry: $500 in jewelry; clothing included in household goods exemption.

Miscellaneous and wildcard: $1000 in cash and liquid assets for those debtors without a homestead; health aids.

SOUTH DAKOTA

Has state opted out of federal bankruptcy exemptions? Yes. S.D. Codified Laws §§ 43-31-30 and 43-45-13.

Wages: **S.D. Codified Laws §§ 21-18-2.1, -51 through -53.**

Scope: Compensation paid or payable for personal services whether called wages, salary, commission, bonus or otherwise; includes periodic payments from pension or retirement plan.

Amount: Greater of 80% of disposable income or forty times minimum wage is exempt. Additional exemption of $25/week for each dependent residing with debtor.

Homestead: **S.D. Codified Laws §§ 43-31-1 through -6, -13, 43-45-3.**

Amount: Dwelling exempt, subject to certain exceptions; mobile home must be larger than 240 square feet at its base; $30,000 in sale proceeds are exempt for one year after receipt but exemption is $170,000 if debtor is 70 or older or the unremarried spouse of such a person; limit of one acre within a town plat and 160 acres outside a town plat; if outside a town plat and acquired under U.S. laws relating to mineral lands, limit is 40 acres; if acquired as a "lode mining claim," limit is five acres.

Procedural requirements: Homeowner may have homestead platted, but failure to do so does not destroy exemption.

Tangible personal property: **S.D. Codified Laws §§ 43-45-2, -4.**

Household goods: See Miscellaneous and wildcard, below; provisions and fuel for one year absolutely exempt.

Motor vehicles: See Miscellaneous and wildcard, below.

Tools of trade: See Miscellaneous and wildcard, below.

Clothing and jewelry: All clothing.

Miscellaneous and wildcard: Personal property head of family $6000, others $4000; burial plot; all family pictures, a pew, $200 in a family library.

TENNESSEE

Has state opted out of federal bankruptcy exemptions? Yes. Tenn. Code Ann. § 26-2-112.

Wages: **Tenn. Code Ann. §§ 26-2-102, -106, -107, -108.**

Scope: Compensation paid or payable for personal services, whether called wages, salary, commission or otherwise, including periodic payments pursuant to pension or retirement program.

Amount: Similar to federal, with additional $2.50 per week exemption for each dependent child under age 16. Disposable earnings are those left after legally required deductions.

Homestead: **Tenn. Const. art. 11, § 11; Tenn. Code Ann. §§ 26-2-301 through 26-2-306.**

Amount: $5000 in real property used as principal place of residence including leased property, if leased for more than two years; joint debtors may only exempt $7500 in shared home; subject to sale for payment of public taxes or satisfaction of debt for improvements. For an unmarried individual age 62 or older, the amount is $12,500. For a couple where one party is age 62 or over, the amount is $20,000. For a couple where both parties are 62 or older, the amount is $25,000. Exemption protects against some criminal law seizures.

Procedural requirements: None stated. Homestead may be set apart at time of levy.

Tangible personal property: **Tenn. Code Ann. §§ 8-36-111, 26-2-102 through -104, 26-2-111, 49-5-909.**

Household goods: See Miscellaneous and wildcard.

Motor vehicles: See Miscellaneous and wildcard.

Tools of trade: $1900.

Clothing and jewelry: Necessary and proper clothing.

Miscellaneous and wildcard: Personal property to the aggregate value of $4000 (includes cash or bank accounts); health aids; family portraits and pictures, Bible and school books.

TEXAS

Has state opted out of federal bankruptcy exemptions? No.

Wages: **Tex. Const. art. 16, § 28; Tex. Prop. Code Ann. § 42.001.**

Scope: Wages or commissions for personal services.

Amount: Current wages for personal service are exempt from garnishment. Commissions for personal services also protected, up to 25% of aggregate limitations ($60,000 for a family, $30,000 for an individual).

Homestead: **Tex. Const. art. 16, §§ 50 and 51; Tex. Prop. Code Ann. §§ 41.001 and 41.002.**

Amount: Rural homestead consists of not more than 200 acres for a family or 100 acres for an individual; an urban homestead consists of not more than ten acres (for property sold before January 1, 2000, the prior one-acre exemption applies); includes improvements; must be claimant's home which may include place of business; homestead is subject to certain liens. Urban is defined as within municipal limits and receiving certain municipal services.

Procedural requirements: Procedure available for designation of homestead, but may be done at time of levy.

Tangible personal property: **Tex. Prop. Code Ann. §§ 42.001 through .005.**

Household goods: Up to $60,000 for a family, $30,000 for a single adult, of the following: household furnishings, provisions, trade implements, clothing, two firearms, sporting equipment, certain animals, certain vehicles, and pets; exemptions not applicable to a child support lien under Family Code.

Motor vehicles: See above.

Tools of trade: See above.

Clothing and jewelry: See above. (Jewelry limited to 25% of aggregate amount.)

Miscellaneous and wildcard: See above. Health aids exempt and not included in cap.

UTAH

Has state opted out of federal bankruptcy exemptions? Yes. Utah Code Ann. § 78-23-15.

Wages: **Utah Code Ann. § 70C-7-103.**

Scope: Compensation for personal services, whether called wages, salary, commission, bonus or otherwise, including periodic payments pursuant to pension, disability or retirement plan.

Amount: Similar to federal. Disposable earnings are those left after legally required deductions.

Homestead: **Utah Const. art. XXII, § 1; Utah Code §§ 78-23-3, -4, and -9.**

Amount: Up to $20,000 for an individual or $40,000 for joint owners in the "primary personal residence" defined as a dwelling or mobile home (whether or not debtor owns the land on which mobile home is located) and up to one acre of land "as reasonably necessary to make use of the dwelling or mobile home."

Procedural requirements: Procedure available for filing declaration of homestead; may be filed up to time stated in notice of execution.

Tangible personal property: **Utah Code Ann. §§ 39-1-47, 78-23-5 through -11.**

Household goods: Washer, dryer, refrigerator, stove, microwave, sewing machine, carpets, 12 months of provisions, beds and bedding. In addition, $500 in other household furniture, books, musical instruments, animals or articles of sentimental value.

Motor vehicles: $2500; specifically excludes recreational or off-road vehicles, except for a motorcycle or van used for daily transportation.

Tools of trade: $3500.

Clothing and jewelry: All clothing, excluding furs and jewelry.

Miscellaneous and wildcard: Health aids; burial plot; military property; family pictures; works of art by debtor. Traceable proceeds of property sold, taken by condemnation, lost, damaged or destroyed remain exempt for one year.

VERMONT

Has state opted out of federal bankruptcy exemptions? No.

Wages: **Vt. Stat. Ann. tit. 12, §§ 3170 and 1372.**

Scope: Earnings.

Amount: Follows the federal scheme except for consumer credit claims where the greater of 85% of weekly disposable earnings or 40 times federal minimum wage is exempt. No garnishment if debtor was, within two months of the garnishment hearing, a welfare recipient. Court may reduce garnishment amount if debtor shows that weekly expenditures "reasonably incurred" for maintenance of self or dependents exceed the statutorily exempt amount. Garnishment orders may be modified from time to time. Discharge of employee because of garnishment forbidden; discharge within 60 days after garnishment rebuttably presumed to be violation; employee has private right of action for reinstatement, back wages, damages, costs and reasonable attorney fees.

Homestead: **Vt. Stat. Ann. tit. 27, §§ 101, 107, 109.**

Amount: $75,000 (increased from $30,000 as of January 1, 1997) in land and a dwelling, which may be a permanently sited mobile home, including the rents, issues and profits.

Procedural requirements: Deed or homestead must be recorded; exemption does not protect against debts which precede this declaration, except that new homestead acquired with proceeds of sale of former homestead is exempt as to any debts as to which former homestead was exempt.

Tangible personal property: **Vt. Stat. Ann. tit. 12, §§ 2740, 3023.**

Household goods: $2500 in aggregate value in household furnishings, goods or appliances, books, wearing apparel, animals, crops or musical instruments; one cooking stove, heating appliances, one refrigerator, one freezer, one water heater, sewing machines; various amounts of specified fuel; specified livestock and accessories; health aids; proceeds of exempt property.
Motor vehicles: $2500.
Tools of trade: $5000 tools of trade; $5000 in aggregate value in growing crops.
Clothing and jewelry: A wedding ring; $500 in aggregate value in other jewelry.
Bank accounts: $700.
Miscellaneous and wildcard: Proceeds of exempt property; $400 aggregate interest in any property plus up to $7000 of unused exemptions for motor vehicles, tools of trade, jewelry, household goods and crop; health aids.

VIRGIN ISLANDS

Has state opted out of federal bankruptcy exemptions? No.
***Wages:* 5 V.I. Code Ann. § 522.**
Scope: Wages, salary, commissions or other remuneration for services performed by an employee for his employer, including any remuneration measured partly or wholly by percentages or share of profits, or by other sums based upon work done or results produced and any drawing account made available to an employee by his employer.
Amount: 90% of gross wages in excess of $30 per week is exempt.
***Homestead:* 5 V.I. Code Ann. § 478.**
Amount: $30,000; rural homestead may not exceed five acres and urban homestead may not exceed 1/4 of an acre.
Procedural requirements: None stated. Homestead may be claimed at time of levy.
***Tangible personal property:* 5 V.I. Code Ann. § 479.**
Household goods: $3000.
Motor vehicles: None.
Tools of trade: Exempt so far as necessary to carry on trade, occupation or profession by which debtor habitually earns a living.
Clothing and jewelry: Clothing. (Watches and jewelry not exempt.)
Miscellaneous and wildcard: None

VIRGINIA

Has state opted out of federal bankruptcy exemptions? Yes. Va. Code Ann. § 34-3.1.
***Wages:* Va. Code Ann. §§ 34-29, -32, -33.**
Scope: Earnings of an individual.
Amount: Greater of 75% or 40 times federal minimum wage is exempt. Wages of minor fully exempt as to debts of parents.
***Homestead:* Va. Code Ann. §§ 34-4, -4.1, -6, -14, -18, and -22.**
Amount: $5000 in any property plus $500 for each dependent; profits derived from homestead property are exempt; exemption subject to certain liens. Additional $2000 in real or personal property for certain disabled veterans.
Procedural requirements: Homestead declaration must be recorded.

***Tangible personal property:* Va. Code Ann. §§ 34-4, -4.1, -6, -14, -18, -22, -26 through -28.**

Household goods: $5000.

Motor vehicles: $2000.

Tools of trade: $10,000. Does not cover motor vehicle used only for commuting. "Occupation" includes enrollment in school or college. For debtor engaged in farming, certain livestock and farming implements.

Clothing and jewelry: $1000 clothing; wedding and engagement rings.

Miscellaneous and wildcard: See homestead exemption above (any real or personal property); family bible; $5000 family portraits and heirlooms; burial place; pets.

WASHINGTON

Has state opted out of federal bankruptcy exemptions? No.

***Wages:* Wash. Rev. Code Ann. § 6.27.150.**

Scope: Compensation paid or payable for personal services, whether called wages, salary, commission, bonus or otherwise, including periodic payments pursuant to a non-governmental pension or retirement program.

Amount: Similar to federal.

***Homestead:* Wash. Const. art. XIX, § 1; Wash. Rev. Code Ann. §§ 6.13.010 through 6.13.040, .070, and .080.**

Amount: $40,000 for dwelling house or mobile home (whether or not permanently affixed) and land, or unimproved land on which debtor intends to place dwelling house or mobile home. If debtor is married, may consist of community property or separate property of either spouse, provided that the same premises cannot be claimed separately by the husband and wife with the effect of increasing the exemption in excess of the amount specified by law; homestead exemption subject to certain liens.

Procedural requirements: Homestead is automatic in land occupied as residence; declaration of homestead required to exempt unimproved land on which owner intends to build residence. Declaration of non-abandonment must be recorded if owner who wishes to retain homestead will be absent for more than six months.

***Tangible personal property:* Wash. Rev. Code Ann. §§ 6.15.010 through .040.**

Household goods: $2700 ($5400 for marital community) household goods, appliances and furniture.

Motor vehicles: $2500 motor vehicle used for personal transportation (two vehicles, aggregate $5000, for community).

Tools of trade: $5000.

Clothing and jewelry: All clothing (but $1000 per individual limit for furs, jewelry or ornaments).

Bank accounts: $200.

Miscellaneous and wildcard: $1500 books; all family pictures and keepsakes; health aids. $2000 wildcard: may not be used for earnings, not more than $200 for cash, not more than $200 for bank accounts, stocks, or the like.

WEST VIRGINIA

Has state opted out of federal bankruptcy exemptions? Yes. W. Va. Code § 38-10-4.

Wages: **W. Va. Code §§ 38-5A-3 and -9, 38-5B-12.**

Scope: Salary and wages are given their ordinary meaning, but include compensation measured partly or wholly by commissions, percentages or share of profits, or by other sums based upon work done or results produced, whether or not debtor is given a drawing account.

Amount: Greater of 80% of wages or 30 times federal minimum hourly wage per week is exempt.

statute.

Homestead: **W. Va. Const. art. 6, § 48; W. Va. Code §§ 38-9-1 through -6 and 38-10-4.**

Amount: Bankruptcy only: $25,000 in real or personal property or a cooperative that debtor or dependent uses as a residence, or in a burial plot of debtor or dependent. Non-bankruptcy: $5000, which may be claimed by a "husband, wife, parent or other head of household." For all debts and liabilities for hospital or medical expenses incurred for a catastrophic illness or injury as defined, the exemption is $7500. (Enhanced exemption does not apply to debts incurred before July 1, 1996.)

Procedural requirements: None stated. Homestead available "by operation of law."

Tangible personal property: **W. Va. Code §§ 38-8-1, -3, -10, -15, 38-10-4 and 46A-2-136.**

Household goods: Bankruptcy: household goods and furnishings, clothing, books, animals, musical instruments, up to $400 in any item to an aggregate of $8000. Non-bankruptcy: $8000. For consumer credit transactions and consumer leases, all the property listed in § 38-8-1, plus all children's books, pictures, toys and other such personal property of children, and all "medical health equipment used for health purposes" by consumer, spouse or dependent.

Motor vehicles: Bankruptcy: $2400. Non-bankruptcy: $5000.

Tools of trade: Bankruptcy: $1500. Non-bankruptcy: $3000.

Clothing and jewelry: Bankruptcy: $1000 in jewelry. (Clothing included in household goods exemption).

Bank accounts: Non-bankruptcy: "[F]unds on deposit in a federally insured financial institution, wages or salary, not to exceed" the greater of $1000 or a figure based on 125% of poverty level.

Miscellaneous and wildcard: Bankruptcy: $800 plus any unused household goods exemption; health aids. Non-bankruptcy, head of household: $1000 any personal property. $15,000 cap on non-bankruptcy personal property exemptions including certain bank accounts.

WISCONSIN

Has state opted out of federal bankruptcy exemptions? No.

Wages: **Wis. Stat. Ann. §§ 812.30, .34, .38.**

Scope: Compensation paid or payable for personal services whether called wages, salary, commission, bonus or otherwise, including periodic payments under a pension or retirement program.

Amount: Greater of 80% of disposable earnings or the amount of the federal poverty line adjusted for family size is exempt. Disposable earnings are those left after legally required deductions. Garnishment is forbidden if debtor is eligible to receive need-based public assistance or has received it within six months or if the debtor's household income is below the poverty line. If a 20% garnishment would result in household income below the poverty line, garnishment limited to the amount by which household income exceeds the poverty line. Debtor may petition for relief, if the exemption is "insufficient to acquire the necessities of life for the debtor and his or her dependents." *See also* Wis. Stat. Ann. § 815.18(3)(h) (exempting 75% of wages or 30 times minimum wage from execution).

***Homestead:* Wis. Stat. Ann. §§ 815.20 and 990.01(14).**

Amount: $40,000 except for mortgages, taxes and certain mechanics liens. Not less than ¼ acre, nor more than 40 acres, so far as reasonably necessary to use the dwelling as a home, subject to the value limitation. Married couple may not stack exemptions.

Procedural requirements: None stated. Homestead may be set apart at time of levy.

***Tangible personal property:* Wis. Stat. Ann. §§ 425.106 and 815.18.**

Household goods: $5000: household goods, wearing apparel, firearms, Bible, library, pew. For debts that arise from a consumer credit transaction, certain specified household goods are exempt.

Motor vehicles: $1200, plus any unused household goods exemption.

Tools of trade: $7500.

Clothing and jewelry: Clothing and jewelry are included in household goods exemption.

Bank accounts: $1000 in bank account, but only to extent account is for personal rather than business use. Tuition units purchased under Wis. Stat. Ann. §§ 14:63 or 14:64.

Miscellaneous and wildcard: Provisions for burial.

Waiver: Contractual waiver is void.

WYOMING

Has state opted out of federal bankruptcy exemptions? Yes. Wyo. Stat. Ann. § 1-20-109.

***Wages:* Wyo. Stat. Ann. §§ 1-15-408(b), 1-15-511.**

Scope: Accrued and unpaid earnings for personal services.

Amount: Similar to federal.

***Homestead:* Wyo. Const. art. 19, § 9; Wyo. Stat. Ann. §§ 1-20-101 through -104.**

Amount: $10,000, each occupant entitled to separate exemption; $6000 for a mobile home.

Procedural requirements: Not specified in exemption statute.

***Tangible personal property:* Wyo. Stat. §§ 1-20-105 and -106.**

Household goods: $2000. May be stacked if two or more persons in residence.

Motor vehicles: $2400 in one vehicle.

Tools of trade: $2000.

Clothing and jewelry: $1000 in necessary clothing; no jewelry except wedding rings.

Miscellaneous and wildcard: Family library and pictures.

APPENDIX F

Summaries of Key State Utility Consumer Protections

F.1 TERMINATION TIMEFRAMES BY STATE

Alabama

Payment Period: 10 days
Termination Notice Period: 5-day termination notice
Notice Void: No provision
Applicable Regulatory Provisions: Alabama PSC Gen. Rule 12

Alaska

Payment Period: 40 days
Termination Notice Period: 15-day termination notice
Notice Void: No provision
Applicable Regulatory Provisions: Alaska Admin. Code tit. 3, § 52.45

Arizona

Payment Period: 15 days
Termination Notice Period: 5-day termination notice
Notice Void: No provision
Applicable Regulatory Provisions: Ariz. Admin. Code §§ 14-2-2-210 and 14-2-2-211

Arkansas

Payment Period: 14 days (22 days if late charge is imposed)
Termination Notice Period: 5-day termination notice; 8 days if mailed
Notice Void: A utility must suspend service within 30 days after the last day to pay.
Applicable Regulatory Provisions: 126-03-003 Ark. Code R. §§ 5.03 and 6.03 (Weil)

California

Payment Period: 19 days
Termination Notice Period: 10-day termination notice; 15 days if mailed
Notice Void: No provision
Applicable Regulatory Provisions: Cal. Pub. Util. Code § 779.1

Colorado

Payment Period: 10 days
Termination Notice Period: Electric: 10-day termination notice; Gas: 7-day termination notice
Notice Void: No provision
Applicable Regulatory Provisions: 4 Colo. Code Regs. § 723-5-13(b)

Connecticut

Payment Period: 33 days
Termination Notice Period: 13-day termination notice
Notice Void: If service is not terminated within 120 days of notice, company shall mail another notice at least 13 days before termination.
Applicable Regulatory Provisions: Conn. Agencies Regs. §§ 16-3-100(a)(5) and 16-3-100(d)

Delaware

Payment Period: 20 days
Termination Notice Period: 14-day termination notice
Notice Void: No provision
Applicable Regulatory Provisions: 10-800-003 Del. Code of Regs. § 3.1 (Weil)

District of Columbia

Payment Period: 20 days
Termination Notice Period: 15-day termination notice
Notice Void: No provision
Applicable Regulatory Provisions: D.C. Mun. Regs. tit. 15, §§ 306.1, 311.3 (Weil)

Florida

Payment Period: 20 days
Termination Notice Period: 5-day termination notice
Notice Void: No provision
Applicable Regulatory Provisions: Fla. Admin. Code Ann. r. 25-6.101, 25-6.105

Georgia

Payment Period: Electric: 45 days; Gas: 20 days
Termination Notice Period: Electric: 5-day termination notice; Gas: 15-day termination notice
Notice Void: No provision
Applicable Regulatory Provisions: Ga. Comp. R. & Regs. 515-3-2.0, 515-3-2.02, 515-3-3.02(B), 515-7-6.02

Hawaii

Payment Period: 15 days
Termination Notice Period: Reasonable notice of termination
Notice Void: No provision
Applicable Regulatory Provisions: Haw. Code R. § 6-60-8 (Weil)

Idaho

Payment Period: 15 days of date of issuance
Termination Notice Period: 8-day termination notice
Notice Void: Notice requirements shall be repeated if termination does not occur 21 days after the scheduled termination date.
Applicable Regulatory Provisions: Idaho Admin. Code r. 31.21.01.202, 31.21.01.304, 31.21.01.305

Illinois

Payment Period: 21 days (considered delinquent after 23 days)
Termination Notice Period: 5-day termination notice ; 8-day termination notice if mailed.
Notice Void: Disconnection notice remains effective for two consecutive 20-day periods, provided personal contact (in-person or phone) is made.
Applicable Regulatory Provisions: Ill. Admin. Code tit. 83, §§ 280.90, 280.130

Indiana

Payment Period: 17 days
Termination Notice Period: 14-day termination notice
Notice Void: No provision
Applicable Regulatory Provisions: 170 Ind. Admin. Code 4-1-13, 4-1-16

Iowa

Payment Period: 20 days
Termination Notice Period: 12-day termination notice
Notice Void: No provision
Applicable Regulatory Provisions: Iowa Admin. Code r. 199-19.4(11), 19.4(15)

Kansas

Payment Period: Payment due upon receipt. Bill is delinquent if payment is not received in time to be credited before the next billing cycle.
Termination Notice Period: 10-day termination notice
Notice Void: No provision
Applicable Regulatory Provisions: Kansas Consumer Information Rules §§ II and IV

Kentucky

Payment Period: 27 days
Termination Notice Period: 10-day termination notice
Notice Void: No provision
Applicable Regulatory Provisions: 807 Ky. Admin. Regs. 5:006 § 14

Louisiana

Payment Period: 20 days
Termination Notice Period: 5-day termination notice
Notice Void: No provision
Applicable Regulatory Provisions: General Order U 9-10-57

Maine

Payment Period: 25 days
Termination Notice Period: 14-day termination notice
Notice Void: Disconnection notices shall expire 10 days after the scheduled date of disconnection and shall require the utility to repeat notification procedures.
Applicable Regulatory Provisions: 65-407-81 Code Me. R. § 9

Maryland

Payment Period: 20 days
Termination Notice Period: 14-day termination notice; 7-day termination notice (obtaining service using fraudulent means)
Notice Void: No provision
Applicable Regulatory Provisions: Md. Code Regs. 20.31.02.04-.05

Massachusetts

Payment Period: 45 days
Termination Notice Period: 3-day termination notice
Notice Void: No provision
Applicable Regulatory Provisions: 220 Mass. Code Regs. § 25.02

Michigan

Payment Period: 17 days
Termination Notice Period: 10-day termination notice; 30-day termination notice for single-metered residence containing 5+ families
Notice Void: Utility must send final termination notice 72 hours to 14 days before termination.
Applicable Regulatory Provisions: Mich. Admin. Code r. 460.2116, 460.2163

Minnesota

Payment Period: Payment due by next scheduled billing date which must not be less than 25 days from current billing date.
Termination Notice Period: 5-day termination notice
Notice Void: No provision
Applicable Regulatory Provisions: Minn. R. 7820.5300, 7820.2300

Mississippi

Payment Period: No provision
Termination Notice Period: 5-day termination notice
Notice Void: No provision
Applicable Regulatory Provisions: 26-000-02 Miss. Code R. § 8 (Weil)

Missouri

Payment Period: Payment due 21 days from the date of billing
Termination Notice Period: 4-day termination notice when hand-delivered; 10-day when mailed

Notice Void: No provision
Applicable Regulatory Provisions: Mo. Code Regs. Ann. tit. 4 §§ 240-13.020, 240-13.050

Montana

Payment Period: No provision
Termination Notice Period: 10-day initial termination notice; 10-day second termination notice if no response to first notice.
Notice Void: No provision
Applicable Regulatory Provisions: Mont. Admin. R. 38.5.1405

Nebraska

Payment Period: No provision
Termination Notice Period: 7-day termination notice; if customer is welfare recipient termination notice must be sent by certified mail.
Notice Void: No provision
Applicable Regulatory Provisions: Neb. Rev. Stat. §§ 70-1603, 70-1605

Nevada

Payment Period: 15 days (4-day grace period for payments made by first class mail)
Termination Notice Period: 10-day termination notice
Notice Void: No provision
Applicable Regulatory Provisions: Nev. Admin. Code §§ 704.339, 704.360

New Hampshire

Payment Period: 25 days
Termination Notice Period: 14-day termination notice
Notice Void: No provision
Applicable Regulatory Provisions: N.H. Code Admin. R. Ann. PUC 1201.08, 1203.11

New Jersey

Payment Period: 15 days
Termination Notice Period: 10-day written notice
Notice Void: No provision
Applicable Regulatory Provisions: N.J. Admin. Code § 14:3-7.12

New Mexico

Payment Period: 20 days (35 days—delinquent)
Termination Notice Period: 15 day-termination notice; 3-day termination notice when termination due to refusal of customer to allow utility access
Notice Void: No provision
Applicable Regulatory Provisions: N.M. Code R. §§ 17.5.410.13, 17.5.410.29 (Weil)

New York

Payment Period: 3 days
Termination Notice Period: 15-day termination notice after bill is 20 days past due; Note:

if utility is aware that a customer subject to service termination receives public assistance or SSI, it shall notify the assisting organization 3–5 days prior to termination.

Notice Void: No provision

Applicable Regulatory Provisions: N.Y. Comp. Codes R. & Regs. tit. 16, § 11.4

North Carolina

Payment Period: 25 days

Termination Notice Period: Electric: 5 day-termination notice; Gas: 10-day termination notice

Notice Void: No provision

Applicable Regulatory Provisions: 4 N.C. Admin Code 11.R.12-10, 11.R.12-8

North Dakota

Payment Period: No provision

Termination Notice Period: 10-day termination notice by first class mail or in person

Notice Void: No provision

Applicable Regulatory Provisions: N.D. Admin. Code 69-09-01-18.1

Ohio

Payment Period: 14 days

Termination Notice Period: 14-day termination notice

Notice Void: No provision

Applicable Regulatory Provisions: Ohio Admin. Code 4901:1-18-05

Oklahoma

Payment Period: 20 days

Termination Notice Period: 10-day termination notice

Notice Void: Disconnection may occur the date of or 30 days after scheduled disconnection.

Applicable Regulatory Provisions: Okla. Admin. Code §§ 165:35-19-40, 165:35-21-20

Oregon

Payment Period: 15 days

Termination Notice Period: 15-day first termination notice; 5-day final notice

Notice Void: No provision

Applicable Regulatory Provisions: Or. Admin. R. 860-021-0125, 860-021-0405

Pennsylvania

Payment Period: 20 days

Termination Notice Period: 10-day termination notice; in hazardous/emergency conditions, a utility may not interrupt/terminate without personally contacting the occupant at least 3 days prior to interruption/termination.

Notice Void: No provision

Applicable Regulatory Provisions: 52 Pa. Code §§ 56.21, 56.91, 56.93

Rhode Island

Payment Period: 30 days
Termination Notice Period: Electric: 10-day termination notice; Gas: 5-day termination notice
Notice Void: No provision
Applicable Regulatory Provisions: 90-060-002 R.I. Code R. § 1 through Appx. D (Weil)

South Carolina

Payment Period: 25 days
Termination Notice Period: 10-day termination notice (5-day termination notice for termination due to delinquent payment plan)
Notice Void: No provision
Applicable Regulatory Provisions: S.C. Code Ann. Regs. §§ 103-339, 103-352

South Dakota

Payment Period: 20 days
Termination Notice Period: 10-day termination notice certified mail)
Notice Void: No provision
Applicable Regulatory Provisions: S.D. Admin. R. 20:10:20:03

Tennessee

Payment Period: No provision
Termination Notice Period: 7-day termination notice
Notice Void: No provision
Applicable Regulatory Provisions: Tenn. Comp. R. & Regs. 1220-4-4-.19

Texas

Payment Period: 16 days
Termination Notice Period: 10-day termination notice
Notice Void: No provision
Applicable Regulatory Provisions: 16 Tex. Admin. Code §§ 25.28 and 25.29

Utah

Payment Period: 20 days
Termination Notice Period: No provision
Notice Void: No provision
Applicable Regulatory Provisions: Utah Admin. Code r. R746-200-4

Vermont

Payment Period: 30 days
Termination Notice Period: Notice of delinquency and disconnection shall be no more than 40 days after delinquency, but notice shall not be more than 20 days or less than 14 days prior to the first date of disconnection.
Notice Void: Notice shall not be more than 20 days prior to the first date of disconnection.
Applicable Regulatory Provisions: 30-000-03 Vt. Code R. § 3.301

Virginia

Payment Period: 20 days
Termination Notice Period: 10-day termination notice
Notice Void: No provision
Applicable Regulatory Provisions: 20 Va. Admin. Code §§ 5-10-10, 56-247.1

Washington

Payment Period: No provision
Termination Notice Period: 8-day termination notice
Notice Void: Disconnection not occurring within 10 days of scheduled date voids the initial notice and requires notice requirements to be repeated.
Applicable Regulatory Provisions: Wash. Admin. Code 480-90-128

West Virginia

Payment Period: Service may be terminated 30 days after due date.
Termination Notice Period: 10-day termination notice; 5-day for violation of payment plan
Notice Void: Notice void if service not terminated within 30 days.
Applicable Regulatory Provisions: W. Va. Code R. § 150-3-4.8

Wisconsin

Payment Period: 20 days
Termination Notice Period: 10-day termination notice
Notice Void: If service is not disconnected within 10 days after disconnection date, notice procedures shall be repeated.
Applicable Regulatory Provisions: Wis. Admin. Code PSC § 113.0301

Wyoming

Payment Period: No provision
Termination Notice Period: 7-day termination notice
Notice Void: No provision
Applicable Regulatory Provisions: 023-0020-2 Wyo. Code R. § 242 (Weil)

F.2 ILLNESS, AGE AND DISABILITY TERMINATION PROTECTIONS BY STATE

Alabama

Serious Illness: Utilities shall adopt and follow reasonable tariff rules for discontinuing service when life or health may be threatened by termination. Alabama PSC Gen. Rule 12.

Age/Disability: No provision

Alaska

Serious Illness: Electric utilities must provide the notice of intent to discontinue service at least 30 days before the scheduled termination date if the electric utility knows that a person who is seriously ill, elderly, disabled lives in the customer's residence. Electric utilities must postpone the scheduled disconnection date for 15 days and notify the customer if a customer notifies the utility that a person who is seriously ill, elderly, disabled or dependent on human life support systems lives in the customer's residence after the notice of intent to discontinue service is issued. Alaska Admin. Code tit. 3, § 52.450.

Age/Disability: No provision

Arizona

Serious Illness: Service shall not be terminated for non-payment when termination would threaten the well-being of an occupant of the residence due to medical condition, illness, age, disability or weather. Said customers will be provided with information concerning assistance and/or may be required to enter into payment plan to avoid termination. Ariz. Admin. Code § 14-2-211

Age/Disability: No provision

Arkansas

Serious Illness: Utilities must honor a physician's certificate in prescribed form that a customer/permanent resident has a serious medical condition and stating that suspension of service would result in substantial risk of death or grave impairment. Certificate can be given by telephone by doctor, nurse, R.N., or public or private agency providing mental health care services, but must be confirmed within 7 days by a physician's writing. 126-03-003 Ark. Code R. § 6.17 (Weil).

Age/Disability: When informed that elderly/disabled customer cannot pay a bill on time, utility shall offer delayed payment agreement, arrange for levelized billing (gas and electric); explain right to third party notice; provide names of potential sources of assistance. Heightened termination notice requirements. 126-03-003 Ark. Code R. § 6.18 (Weil).

California

Serious Illness: Customer who provides certification from licensed physician and surgeon that service termination will be life-threatening and who is unable to pay in normal period shall be permitted to amortize over a period not to exceed 12 months. Cal. Pub. Util. Code § 779 (West). Master-meters: A utility may not terminate service when a public health or building officer certifies that termination would result in a significant threat to the health or safety of the occupants or the public. Cal. Pub. Util. Code § 777.1(e) (West).

Age/Disability: No provision

Colorado

Serious Illness: Service may not be discontinued or must be restored during any period when discontinuance would aggravate an existing medical condition or create a medical emergency for the customer or a permanent resident of the customer's household; certification of licensed doctor or health practitioner required; Initial certification by phone acceptable. Utility may require written confirmation within 10 days. Certification effective for 60 days with one 30-day extension period. Customer may invoke med cert provisions only once during 12-month period. Customers who secure service under this provision may enter or renegotiate installment plan. Those who have broken installment agreement may not renegotiate and must become current by expiration of certification period. 4 Colo. Code Regs. § 723-3-13(f).

Age/Disability: No provision

Connecticut

Serious Illness: Company may not terminate service if resident is or becomes seriously ill or in a life threatening situation as certified by registered physician. Certification must be renewed every 15 days if physician doesn't specify length of illness. Initial cert can be made by telephone subject to company's right to written confirmation. If service continued under this section, customer shall enter amortization agreement. Conn. Agencies Regs. § 16-3-100(e)

Age/Disability: No provision

Delaware

Serious Illness: Utility may not disconnect service upon receipt of certification from licensed physician or Christian Science practitioner that a named occupant is so ill that termination would adversely affect the occupant's safety. 10-800-003 Del. Code Regs. § 3.2 (Weil)

Age/Disability: No provision

District of Columbia

Serious Illness: Utility shall postpone termination of service for up to 21 days if the customer provides a physician's certificate or notice from a public health official stating that termination would be detrimental to the health/safety of a person occupying the premises, provided that the customer enters into a deferred payment plan. The postponement may be extended for additional periods of not more than 21 days by renewal of the certificate or notice. D.C. Mun. Regs. tit 15, § 311.1

Age/Disability: No provision

Florida

Serious Illness: Each utility shall submit a procedure for discontinuance of service when

that service is medically essential. Fla. Admin Code. Ann. r. 25-6.105
Age/Disability: No provision

Georgia

Serious Illness: Utility (gas) shall postpone termination for 10 days upon receiving notice form a customer followed by notice within 10 days from a licensed physician or health official that termination of service would be especially dangerous to the health of someone living at the residence. Postponement of termination shall be for 30 days and may be extended and additional 30 days. Ga. Comp. R. & Regs. 515-3-2.03
Age/Disability: No provision

Hawaii

Serious Illness: No provision
Age/Disability: Termination of service to elderly or disabled customers may not commence without a written report and investigation by the utility to the PUC submitted not less than 5 days before the intended termination. Elderly customers must provide proof that they are 62+ by appearing in person at the utility office or by verifying date of birth in a personal written statement. disabled customers can qualify by certification of physical condition by either a registered physician or and appropriate state agency. Haw. Code R. § 6-60-8 (Weil).

Idaho

Serious Illness: A utility shall delay disconnection an additional 30 days upon receipt of a certificate from a physician or social service agency that a medical emergency exists with an option for an additional thirty-day delay. If a customer whose service has been disconnected is eligible for a medical delay, service shall be restored within 24 hours with the limit beginning on the day of restoration. Idaho Admin. Code r. 31.21.01.308.
Age/Disability: No provision

Illinois

Serious Illness: When certified by either a physician or Board of Health, termination may not occur if it would aggravate an existing medical emergency. Certification must be renewed every 30 days. Ill. Admin. Code tit. 83, § 280.130.
Age/Disability: No provision

Indiana

Serious Illness: Utility shall delay disconnection an additional 10 days upon receipt of a certificate from a physician or social service agency that a medical emergency exists. 170 Ind. Admin. Code 4-1-16.
Age/Disability: No provision

Iowa

Serious Illness: Utility shall delay disconnection an additional 30 days upon receipt of a certificate from a physician or social service agency that a medical emergency exists.

Medical professional may initially notify the utility, but shall provide written cert within 5 days of initial notice. Iowa Admin. Code r. 199-19.4(15).

Age/Disability: No provision

Kansas

Serious Illness: Service may not be discontinued when it would adversely affect a serious illness. Kansas Consumer Information Rule IV.

Age/Disability: No provision

Kentucky

Serious Illness: Utility shall postpone termination for 30 days upon receiving notice from a licensed physician or public health official that termination of service would be especially dangerous to the health of someone living at the residence. Postponement may be extended an additional 30 days. 807 Ky. Admin. Regs. 5:006, § 14.

Age/Disability: No provision

Louisiana

Serious Illness: No provision

Age/Disability: No provision

Maine

Serious Illness: Utility shall not terminate for 3 days when notified that a medical emergency exists. Disconnection shall be delayed 30 days when a medical emergency, as certified by a medical doctor, orally or in writing exists. Written confirmation is required 7 days after oral notification. Certificate renewable in intervals of 30 days; Customer must enter into payment plan. 65-407-81 Me. Code R. § 10 (Weil).

Age/Disability: No provision

Maryland

Serious Illness: Subject to physician certification, electric or gas service, or both shall not be terminated for an initial period of up to 30 days beyond the scheduled date of service termination when the termination will aggravate an existing serious illness or prevent the use of life support equipment of nay occupant of the premises; payment plans for past due bills; certification renewable. Md. Code Regs. § 20.31.03.01.

Age/Disability: If utility is aware that termination is to occur at residence of an elderly (65+) or disabled person, utility shall attempt to make personal contact on at least two occasions and shall inform customer of any financial assistance available to avoid termination. Md. Code Regs. § 20.31.03.02.

Massachusetts

Serious Illness: Utilities cannot terminate or refuse to restore a customer's service if the customer or someone living in the customer's house is seriously ill. Utilities cannot terminate or refuse to restore a customer's service if there's a child under the age of 12 months and service hasn't terminated for non-payment before the child's birth. Customer can begin claim for infant protection by phoning the Dept. A registered physician/local board of health official shall return official cert form within 7 days. Serious illness cert renewal due monthly. 220 Mass. Code Regs. 25.03.

Age/Disability: Utilities cannot terminate or refuse to restore a customer's service if there's a child under the age of 12 months and service hasn't terminated for non-payment before the child's birth. Customer can begin claim for infant protection by phoning the Dept. 220 Mass. Code Regs. § 25.03. Utilities cannot discontinue service to a household where all residents are 65+. 220 Mass. Code Regs. § 25.05

Michigan

Serious Illness: Termination may not occur for an additional 21 days if it would aggravate an existing medical emergency or condition that has been certified. Certification may be renewed an additional 42 days. Customer may notify utility of an existing medical emergency by telephone and shall have 7 days to produce certification. Mich. Admin. Code r. 460.2153.

Age/Disability: Elderly (65+) and low-income (150% of poverty line or recipient of means-tested benefit) customer shall not have service terminated for non-payment of bills during the winter protection period (December 1–March 31) if they agree and satisfy terms of payment program. Mich. Admin. Code r. 460.2174.

Minnesota

Serious Illness: No provision

Age/Disability: No provision

Mississippi

Serious Illness: If customer subject to termination of service, demonstrates a medical emergency from December through March, the utility shall not terminate service without offering a levelized plan. Customers demonstrating a medical emergency shall not have service terminated after April 1st if the customer agrees to a levelized billing plan. Mississippi PSC Rule 8.

Age/Disability: No provision

Missouri

Serious Illness: Discontinuance shall be postponed for 21 days due to the medical condition of an occupant. Mo. Code Regs. Ann. tit. 4, § 240-13.055.

Age/Disability: With respect to termination for heat-related service during cold weather months, the methods of notification and discontinuance are increased when occupants within the premises are either disabled, elderly, or eligible or receiving low-income energy assistance. Mo. Code Regs. Ann. tit. 4, § 240-13.055

Montana

Serious Illness: When certified by either a physician or the Board of Health, termination may not occur if it would aggravate an existing medical emergency. Certificate must be renewed every 30 days. Mont. Admin. R. 38.5.1411.

Age/Disability: No provision

Nebraska

Serious Illness: Termination would be postponed upon receipt of certification by licensed physician that such termination would worsen a resident's illness or disability; a 30-day extension is available. Neb. Rev. Stat. § 70-1606.

Age/Disability: No provision

Nevada

Serious Illness: Utility shall postpone termination for 30 days upon receiving notice from licensed physician or public health official that service termination would be especially dangerous to the health of someone living at the residence. Postponement can be extended 30 days. Nev. Admin. Code § 704.370.

Age/Disability: Utility shall not terminate service of a residence where an elderly or disabled person resides unless it's notified some adult resident, in persons or by phone, 48 hours prior to termination. Nev. Admin. Code § 704.390

New Hampshire

Serious Illness: During winter regulation rules, if utility is notified by a licensed physician that a medical emergency would be caused by disconnection, or the utility receives a guarantee from a welfare office, service shall not be disconnected. N.H. Code Admin. R. Ann. PUC 1203.11.

Age/Disability: No provision

New Jersey

Serious Illness: No provision

Age/Disability: No provision

New Mexico

Serious Illness: No provision

Age/Disability: No provision

New York

Serious Illness: No utility shall terminate or refuse to restore service for 30 days when a medical emergency, as certified by a medical doctor or local board of health, orally or in writing, exists. A demonstration of the customer's inability to pay charges for service shall be required before a certificate of medical emergency can be renewed. If the medical condition is likely to continue beyond the expiration of the initial certification, a certificate may be renewed for 60 days or, subject to commission approval, a longer period. Customers remain liable for charges incurred while certificate is in effect. Once certificate expires, utility shall abide by notification and termination requirements. N.Y. Comp. Codes R. & Regs. tit. 16, § 11.5.

Age/Disability: No termination or refusal to restore service where a customer is blind, disabled, or 62 years of age or older, and all the remaining residents of the household are 62+, under 18, or blind or disabled without a diligent effort to make phone or personal contact at least 72 hours prior to termination of service for the purpose of devising a payment plan. If a plan cannot be implemented, the utility shall delay termination for 15 days and notify and request that social services assist in devising a plan. N.Y. Comp. Codes R. & Regs. tit. 16, § 11.5.

North Carolina

Serious Illness: No provision
Age/Disability: No provision

North Dakota

Serious Illness: 30-day termination stay is available if a resident is elderly, disabled, or a medical emergency would result from terminating service. N.D. Admin. Code 69-09-01-18.1.
Age/Disability: 30-day termination stay is available if a resident is elderly, disabled, or a medical emergency would result from terminating service. N.D. Admin. Code 69-09-01-18.1.

Ohio

Serious Illness: If customer can establish that disconnection would result in danger to resident's health, the utility shall inform the customer of the disconnection postponement options and use this information in its considerations when offering a payment plan. Ohio Admin. Code 4901:1-18-05.
Age/Disability: No provision

Oklahoma

Serious Illness: A delay of at least 30 days when other circumstances would endanger the life, health or property of the consumer shall be allowed upon verification. Okla. Admin. Code § 165:35-21-10.
Age/Disability: No provision

Oregon

Serious Illness: Disconnection shall be delayed upon oral or written confirmation that disconnection would significantly endanger the physical health of the customer or a member of the customer's household. Oral notification shall be confirmed within 14 days. Delay shall be valid for duration of condition but may not exceed 6 months for non-chronic conditions and 12 months for chronic ones. Customer shall enter into payment arrangement for an overdue balance and may renegotiate if a financial hardship is shown. Or. Admin. R. 860-021-0410.
Age/Disability: No provision

Pennsylvania

Serious Illness: Utility may not terminate or refuse to restore service to a premise when an occupant therein is certified by a physician to be seriously ill or affected with a medical condition that will be aggravated by a cessation of service or failure to restore service. If, prior to service termination, the utility employee is informed that an occupant is seriously ill or is affected with a medical condition which will be aggravated by a service cessation and that a medical certification will be procured, termination may not occur for at least 3 days. Certification may be renewed for 2 additional 30-day periods. 52 Pa. Code §§ 56.111, 56.112, 56.114.

Age/Disability: No provision

Rhode Island

Serious Illness: Utility shall postpone termination for 21 days upon receiving notice from licensed physician or public health official that termination of service would be especially dangerous to the health of someone living at the residence. Postponement of termination may be extended after review. 90 060 002 R.I. Code R. (Weil).

Age/Disability: Disconnection is also restricted when services are provided to the elderly, disabled, or customers eligible under RI hardship exception. 90 060 002 R.I. Code R. (Weil).

South Carolina

Serious Illness: 30-day delay option for certified medical reasons during winter protection months (December-March). S.C. Code Ann. Regs. § 103-352.

Age/Disability: No provision

South Dakota

Serious Illness: Utility shall delay disconnection an additional 30 days upon receipt of a certificate from a physician or social service agency that a medical emergency exists. S.D. Admin. R. R.20:10:20:1.

Age/Disability: No provision

Tennessee

Serious Illness: Upon receiving written notification from a physician, public health official, or social service agency that a medical condition would be aggravated due to termination of service, termination shall be postponed for 30 days and the utility shall refer the customer to a social service agency. Tenn. Comp. R. & Regs. 1220-4-4-.19.

Age/Disability: No provision

Texas

Serious Illness: If, upon physician verification, a person residing in the unit would become seriously ill or more seriously ill as a result of disconnection, disconnection shall be delayed. 16 Tex. Admin. Code § 25.29.

Age/Disability: No provision

Utah

Serious Illness: Upon receipt of a physician's written notification that a medical condition may be aggravated due to termination or that a health hazard exists, service shall be restored or termination delayed for a period indicated in the physician's certification or 1 month, whichever is less. Utah Admin. Code r. R.746-200-6.

Age/Disability: No provision

Vermont

Serious Illness: No utility shall terminate or refuse to restore service for 30 days when a medical emergency, as certified by a medical doctor or local board of health, orally or in writing, exists. If the medical condition is likely to continue beyond the expiration of the initial certification, a certificate may be renewed for 60 days or, subject to commission approval, a longer period. Customers remain liable for charges incurred while certificate is in effect. VT PSB Rule 3.302.

Age/Disability: Service shall not be disconnected between November 1–March 31 when the temperature will be below 32° Fahrenheit during the following 48 hours at the time of disconnection if someone 62 years + resides within the residence. VT PSB Rule 3.303.

Virginia

Serious Illness: No provision

Age/Disability: No provision

Washington

Serious Illness: When utility is notified of a medical emergency related to disconnection, the utility shall reconnect service at least by the next business day without requiring a deposit or a reconnection fee, or disconnection shall be delayed for an additional 5 days pending written physician certification. Written certification shall delay disconnection for 60 days and may be renewed for additional 60 days. During the delay period, the utility may require the customer to keep the account current, pay 10% of any outstanding balance and enter into a payment plan that reconciles the account within 120 days. Wash. Admin Code 480-90-128.

Age/Disability: No provision

West Virginia

Serious Illness: Termination shall be delayed and a payment plan offered in some circumstances if termination would be dangerous to the health and safety of a household member (medically or from December through February). Medical certification must be received 10 days after utility notification and shall be renewed every thirty days unless a physician states to a reasonable degree of medical certainty that the condition is permanent. W. Va. Code R. § 150-3-4.8.

Age/Disability: Service shall not be terminated to residential customers 65+ unless the customer refuses to enter into a payment plan. W. Va. Code R. § 150-3-4.8.

Wisconsin

Serious Illness: Disconnection shall be delayed for 21 days and utility shall negotiate special payment arrangements when a licensed physician, public health, social service, or law enforcement official certifies that a medical or protective emergency would result from disconnection. Wis. Admin. Code PSC § 113.0301

Age/Disability: No provision

Wyoming

Serious Illness: Utility must notify residence subject to termination of service that an additional 15-day delay is available if it can be documented that a resident is disabled or seriously ill. An additional 30 days' notice is required if household resident is dependent on utility for life support services. 023-020-002 Wyo. Code R. § 242 (Weil).

Age/Disability: No provision

F.3 HARSH WEATHER TERMINATION PROTECTIONS BY STATE

(Source: LIHEAP Clearinghouse)

Alabama

Date-Based: No
Protection Dates: No provision
Temperature-Based: Yes
Temperature: 32° Fahrenheit or below
Seasonal Policy: Ban for special circumstances such as extreme weather or life-threatening situation.

Alaska

Date-Based: No
Protection Dates: No provision
Temperature-Based: No
Temperature: No provision
Seasonal Policy: No disconnect for seriously ill, disabled.

Arizona

Date-Based: No
Protection Dates: No provision
Temperature-Based: Yes
Temperature: 32° Fahrenheit or below and 95° Fahrenheit or higher
Seasonal Policy: Temperature-based

Arkansas

Date-Based: Yes
Protection Dates: November 1–March 31
Temperature-Based: Yes
Temperature: 32° Fahrenheit or below and 95° Fahrenheit or higher
Seasonal Policy: No disconnect for elderly or disabled, 95° Fahrenheit or higher, or medical emergency. No disconnect if customer agrees to deferred or extended payment agreement.

California

Date-Based: No
Protection Dates: No provision
Temperature-Based: No
Temperature: No provision
Seasonal Policy: No special seasonal protections.

Colorado

Date-Based: No
Protection Dates: No provision
Temperature-Based: No
Temperature: No provision
Seasonal Policy: No special seasonal protections.

Connecticut

Date-Based: Yes
Protection Dates: November 1–April 15
Temperature-Based: No
Temperature: No provision
Seasonal Policy: No disconnect for hardship customers to include: public assistance recipients, one source of income from Social Security, Veteran's or unemployment compensation benefits income at less than 125% of the federal poverty guidelines, ill, disabled, unemployed with income less than 200% of the federal poverty guidelines, or would be without necessities if bill was paid.

Delaware

Date-Based: Yes
Protection Dates: November 15–April 15
Temperature-Based: Yes
Temperature: 20° or below
Seasonal Policy: Temperature based

District of Columbia

Date-Based: No
Protection Dates: No provision
Temperature-Based: Yes
Temperature: 32° Fahrenheit or below
Seasonal Policy: Temperature based

Florida

Date-Based: No
Protection Dates: No provision
Temperature-Based: No
Temperature: No provision
Seasonal Policy: No special seasonal protections.

Georgia

Date-Based: Yes
Protection Dates: November 15–March 15
Temperature-Based: Yes
Temperature: 32° Fahrenheit or below

Seasonal Policy: Total ban when 32° Fahrenheit or below; protection if payment arrangement is made. No disconnect if illness would be aggravated, statement from doctor.

Hawaii

Date-Based: No
Protection Dates: No provision
Temperature-Based: No
Temperature: No provision
Seasonal Policy: No special seasonal protections

Idaho

Date-Based: Yes
Protection Dates: December 1–February 29
Temperature-Based: No
Temperature: No provision
Seasonal Policy: Disconnect ban for households with children under 18, elderly age 62 or older, or infirm.

Illinois

Date-Based: Yes
Protection Dates: December 1–March 31
Temperature-Based: Yes
Temperature: 32° Fahrenheit or below
Seasonal Policy: Total ban when 32° Fahrenheit or below. Utilities must offer payment plan of 10% down payment and equalized billing over the next 4 to 12 months. Customer can earn credits to apply to overdue bill by working at a nonprofit organization or by attending school.

Indiana

Date-Based: Yes
Protection Dates: December 1–March 15
Temperature-Based: No
Temperature: No provision
Seasonal Policy: Total ban for customers receiving or applying for LIHEAP or WAP (125% of the federal poverty guidelines).

Iowa

Date-Based: Yes
Protection Dates: November 1–April 1
Temperature-Based: Yes
Temperature: No provision
Seasonal Policy: Ban for LIHEAP- or WAP-eligible customers (150% of the federal poverty guidelines) when temperature 20° Fahrenheit or below, utility must offer payment plan after moratorium.

Kansas

Date-Based: Yes
Protection Dates: November 1–March 31
Temperature-Based: Yes
Temperature: 35° Fahrenheit or below
Seasonal Policy: Ban when 35° Fahrenheit or below, to avoid disconnect when temperature is above 35° customers must make payment schedule and meet payments and apply for aid if eligible.

Kentucky

Date-Based: Yes
Protection Dates: November 1–March 31
Temperature-Based: No
Temperature: No provision
Seasonal Policy: 30-day extension if eligible for energy assistance (less than 130% of the federal poverty guidelines), must agree to pay plan. Must reconnect if customer proves need and pays lower of $200 or one-third of bill and makes payments on time. Cannot disconnect if payment agreement is in effect.

Louisiana

Date-Based: No
Protection Dates: No provision
Temperature-Based: No
Temperature: No provision
Seasonal Policy: No provision

Maine

Date-Based: Yes
Protection Dates: November 15–April 15
Temperature-Based: No
Temperature: No provision
Seasonal Policy: Not permitted if eligible customer (less than 185% of the federal poverty guidelines) agrees to payment plan or if account is less than 3 months overdue or less than $50; requires PUC approval.

Maryland

Date-Based: Yes
Protection Dates: November 1–March 31
Temperature-Based: No
Temperature: No provision
Seasonal Policy: Utility must provide affidavit to the Commission that disconnect will not endanger the health of any household member.

Massachusetts

Date-Based: Yes

Protection Dates: November 15–April 30(electric) November 15–April 30 (gas)
Temperature-Based: No
Temperature: No provision
Seasonal Policy: Disconnect not permitted if customer's income is less than 150% of the federal poverty guidelines or if household includes child less than 12 months, seriously ill member or all residents are 65 or older. For 2003, the Dept. of Telecommunications and Energy approved a 4–6 week extension of the shut-off moratorium.

Michigan

Date-Based: Yes
Protection Dates: December 1–March 31
Temperature-Based: No
Temperature: No provision
Seasonal Policy: Winter Protection Plan for low income (less than 150% of the federal poverty guidelines), elderly 65 years or older or recipient FIA cash assistance, food stamps or Medicaid. Must be enrolled in a payment plan.

Minnesota

Date-Based: Yes
Protection Dates: October 15–April 15
Temperature-Based: No
Temperature: No provision
Seasonal Policy: Disconnect ban if customer declares inability to pay and income is less than 50% state median income and agrees to payment plan; if eligible customer pays 10% of income or the full amount of current bill (whichever is less) or if customer agrees and adheres to payment plan.

Mississippi

Date-Based: Yes
Protection Dates: December 1–March 31
Temperature-Based: No
Temperature: No provision
Seasonal Policy: Prohibited for customers who can prove extreme financial difficulty or medical emergency and agree to payment plan.

Missouri

Date-Based: Yes
Protection Dates: November 1–March 31
Temperature-Based: Yes
Temperature: 32° Fahrenheit or below
Seasonal Policy: No disconnect if unable to pay, must apply for assistance and enter payment plan. No disconnect if 32° Fahrenheit or below. Elderly and disabled with incomes at 150% or less of the federal poverty guidelines can avoid disconnection if they pay at least 50% of their bill between November 1 and March 31. Utilities are required to reconnect service if a customer pays at least 80% of bill.

Montana

Date-Based: Yes
Protection Dates: November 1–April 1
Temperature-Based: No
Temperature: No provision
Seasonal Policy: Prohibited for customers receiving public assistance or if household member is age 62 or older or disabled. PUC approval needed for shut-off.

Nebraska

Date-Based: No
Protection Dates: No provision
Temperature-Based: No
Temperature: No provision
Seasonal Policy: No state-mandated policies.

Nevada

Date-Based: No
Protection Dates: No provision
Temperature-Based: No
Temperature: No provision
Seasonal Policy: No provision

New Hampshire

Date-Based: Yes
Protection Dates: December 1–April 1
Temperature-Based: No
Temperature: No provision
Seasonal Policy: PUC approval needed to shut-off elderly 65 or older. Disconnect is not allowed unless arrears are more than $175 for non-heating, more than $300 for gas and steam heating or more than $400 for electric heating. Must allow customers to pay balance over next 6 months after winter moratorium.

New Jersey

Date-Based: Yes
Protection Dates: November 15–March 15
Temperature-Based: No
Temperature: No provision
Seasonal Policy: Ban on disconnection for customers receiving Lifeline, LIHEAP, TANF, SSI, PAAD or GA or households unable to pay overdue amounts because of unemployment, medical expenses, or recent death of spouse. Customers eligible for the Winter Termination Protection Program are placed on a budget plan and cannot be disconnected as long as they make good faith payments. During the heating season, a utility may not ask for a security deposit.

New Mexico

Date-Based: Yes
Protection Dates: November 15–March 15
Temperature-Based: No
Temperature: No provision
Seasonal Policy: Disconnection is delayed for 15 days if customer is eligible for or receiving LIHEAP.

New York

Date-Based: Yes
Protection Dates: November 1–April 15
Temperature-Based: No
Temperature: No provision
Seasonal Policy: 15-day shut-off protection; no disconnection if a doctor certifies that there is a medical emergency.

North Carolina

Date-Based: Yes
Protection Dates: November 1–March 31
Temperature-Based: No
Temperature: No provision
Seasonal Policy: No disconnect for elderly, disabled, and customers who are eligible for the Energy Crisis Assistance Program.

North Dakota

Date-Based: No
Protection Dates: No provision
Temperature-Based: No
Temperature: No provision
Seasonal Policy: No disconnect for customers who enter into a payment plan.

Ohio

Date-Based: Yes
Protection Dates: November 1–April 15
Temperature-Based: No
Temperature: No provision
Seasonal Policy: Winter Protection adds 10 days to shut-off notice. No disconnect year-round if customer is below 150% of the federal poverty guidelines, is enrolled in a percentage of income payment plan and applies for all energy assistance. Customers are required to pay no more than $175 in arrears from October 22 to April 12 to maintain service or reconnect under the state's Winter Reconnection Order.

Oklahoma

Date-Based: Yes
Protection Dates: November 15–April 15
Temperature-Based: Yes
Temperature: 32° Fahrenheit or below (daytime), 20° Fahrenheit or below (night) or 103° Fahrenheit or higher
Seasonal Policy: No disconnect if temperatures are 32° Fahrenheit or below (daytime), 20° Fahrenheit or below (night) or if predicted heat index is 103° Fahrenheit or higher or if customer enters into a deferred payment plan. 30-day delay and 30-day extension possible in case of life threatening condition. Commission may order a ban on all disconnections if severe weather or if dangerous to health of the customer.

Oregon

Date-Based: No
Protection Dates: No provision
Temperature-Based: No
Temperature: No provision
Seasonal Policy: No provision

Pennsylvania

Date-Based: Yes
Protection Dates: December 1–March 31
Temperature-Based: No
Temperature: No provision
Seasonal Policy: PUC approval needed for disconnection, in practice no approvals are granted during winter months.

Rhode Island

Date-Based: Yes
Protection Dates: November 1–March 31
Temperature-Based: No
Temperature: No provision
Seasonal Policy: Disconnect ban for elderly, ill, disabled, unemployed or those eligible for public assistance or if arrears are less than $375 for primary source of heat or less than $110 if not primary.

South Carolina

Date-Based: Yes
Protection Dates: December 1–March 31
Temperature-Based: No
Temperature: No provision
Seasonal Policy: 31-day shut-off delay for seriously ill with medical certificate, can be renewed up to 3 times during the winter protection period.

South Dakota

Date-Based: Yes
Protection Dates: November 1–March 31
Temperature-Based: No
Temperature: No provision
Seasonal Policy: Additional notice of 30 days.

Tennessee

Date-Based: No
Protection Dates: No provision
Temperature-Based: Yes
Temperature: 32° Fahrenheit or below
Seasonal Policy: Disconnect postponed for medical emergency or if temperature 32° Fahrenheit or below

Texas

Date-Based: No
Protection Dates: No provision
Temperature-Based: Yes
Temperature: 32° Fahrenheit or below or during heat advisory
Seasonal Policy: No disconnect during heat advisories or if the previous day's temperature was 32° Fahrenheit or below or if a serious illness exists in the household.

Utah

Date-Based: Yes
Protection Dates: November 15–March 15
Temperature-Based: No
Temperature: No provision
Seasonal Policy: No disconnect if customer has written statement from utility that states that a payment plan could not be agreed upon, if applied for HEAP and Red Cross energy assistance, has an income less than 125% of the federal poverty guidelines, medical emergency or becomes unemployed or income is cut by 50% or more. During winter moratorium customer must pay at least 5% of income towards utility costs (10% for electric heat).

Vermont

Date-Based: Yes
Protection Dates: November 1–March 31
Temperature-Based: No
Temperature: 10° Fahrenheit or below
Seasonal Policy: No disconnect if temperature is 10° Fahrenheit or below or 32° Fahrenheit or below for households with elderly age 62 or older.

Virginia

Date-Based: No
Protection Dates: No provision
Temperature-Based: No
Temperature: No provision
Seasonal Policy: No state-mandated policies. Terms and conditions concerning disconnection shall be set forth in each local distribution company's tariff approved by the State Corporation Commission.

Washington

Date-Based: Yes
Protection Dates: November 1–March 31
Temperature-Based: No
Temperature: No provision
Seasonal Policy: Protection for hardship customers (less than 125% of the federal poverty guidelines) who qualify or apply for energy assistance, and enter into payment plan.

West Virginia

Date-Based: Yes
Protection Dates: December 1–February 28
Temperature-Based: No
Temperature: No provision
Seasonal Policy: Disconnections during protection dates are considered detrimental to the health of the customer's household and are prohibited.

Wisconsin

Date-Based: Yes
Protection Dates: November 1–April 15
Temperature-Based: Yes
Temperature: No provision
Seasonal Policy: No disconnect during extreme weather unless last resort after all other legal means of collection have been attempted and only if greater than 250% of the federal poverty guidelines and health and safety would not be endangered due to presence of elderly, small children, or mentally disabled. Prohibited when heat advisory from the National Weather Service is in effect.

Wyoming

Date-Based: Yes
Protection Dates: November 1–April 30
Temperature-Based: Yes
Temperature: No provision
Seasonal Policy: Temperature-based restrictions if unable to pay and has exhausted available assistance or is actively seeking assistance, or can pay, but only in installments.

F.4 PAYMENT PLAN REQUIREMENTS BY STATE

Alabama

Payment Plans: Utility shall give the power to extend payment deadlines and to enter into installment agreements to at least one employee in each of its offices. Alabama PSC Gen. Rule 12.

Effect of Breaching Payment Plan: No provision

Alaska

Payment Plans: Service shall note be terminated due to non-payment when the customer agrees to enter and enters into deferred payment plan. Alaska Admin. Code tit. 3, § 52.450. Deferred Payment Plans for economic hardship (1/3 outstanding balance at time of agreement with remainder to be paid within 12 months); deferred payment plans can include a finance charge. Levelized billing also available. Alaska Admin. Code tit. 3, §§ 52.440, 52.445.

Effect of Breaching Payment Plan: Electric utilities may discontinue or refuse to restore service to residential customers who do not follow a deferred payment plan. Alaska Admin. Code tit. 3, § 52.445.

Arizona

Payment Plans: Utility shall not be required to offer a subsequent plan if a customer is in violation of one already. Ariz. Admin. Code § 14-2-210.

Effect of Breaching Payment Plan: Utility shall not be required to offer a subsequent plan if a customer is in violation of one already. Ariz. Admin. Code § 14-2-210.

Arkansas

Payment Plans: Levelized billing available; deferred payment agreements available to customers whose average bill for last 12 months was less than $200; Utilities must offer extended due-date policy to persons receiving AFDC, AABD, SSI, persons whose primary income is from SS or VA disability or retirement benefits. 126-03-003 Ark. Code R. § 6.13 (Weil).

Effect of Breaching Payment Plan: Service may be suspended without prior written notice for failure to pay under delayed payment or extension agreement. 126-03-003 Ark. Code R. §§ 6.04B, 6.13 (Weil). If a customer can show a change in ability to pay due to a serious medical condition or the loss of a major source of income, the utility must document a good faith effort to renegotiate a delayed payment agreement once during the term. The customer loses the right to renegotiate for failure to keep any term of the agreement. 126-03-003 Ark. Code R. § 6.13 (Weil).

California

Payment Plans: Customers unable to make payment may be eligible for amortization agreements not to exceed 12 months

Effect of Breaching Payment Plan: If a customer does not comply with an amortization agreement, the corporation shall not terminate service without giving notice at least

48 hours prior to cessation of the conditions required to avoid termination. Cal. Pub. Util. Code § 779.1.

Colorado

Payment Plans: Installment payment plans available. Such plans may consist of equal monthly installments not to exceed 6 months. 4 Colo. Code Regs. §§ 723-3-10(e), 723-3-13(e), 723-3-13(e)(5)(b) (budget billing).

Effect of Breaching Payment Plan: If a customer defaults on monthly installment payment or a new bill becomes past due, utility must notify them that service may be discontinued if the monthly installment payment is not received within 10 days after its due date. 4 Colo. Code Regs. § 723-3-13(e).

Connecticut

Payment Plans: Gas/electric service may not be terminated for a delinquent amount until co. first offers the customer an opportunity to enter into an amortization agreement. Company may charge simple interest on the unpaid balance of the delinquent acct at the rate of 6% per annum. Conn. Agencies Regs. § 16-3-100(b)(3). *See also* Conn. Agencies Regs. § 16-3-100(f) review of amortization agreements and hardship cases.

Effect of Breaching Payment Plan: Service may be terminated if a customer is paying under an amortization agreement and either fails to comply with it or to stay current on current charges. If a customer makes payments or payments amount to 20% of the balance due, then notice is required of the condition the customer must meet to avoid termination. Conn. Agencies Regs. § 16-3-100(b)(2).

Delaware

Payment Plans: Installment Agreements—customer pays both current bills as they become due and past arrearages in monthly installments over a period not less than the period that the unpaid bills were incurred. 10-800-003 Del. Code of Regs. § 3.2 (Weil).

Effect of Breaching Payment Plan: If a customer fails to comply with an initial installment agreement, the limitation on the minimum duration installment period shall not apply to any subsequent installment agreement. 10-800-003 Del. Code of Regs. § 3.2 (Weil).

District of Columbia

Payment Plans: Level payment billing program; Deferred Payment Plan

Effect of Breaching Payment Plan: No provision

Florida

Payment Plans: Payment plans available. Fla. Admin. Code Ann. r. 25-6.105.

Effect of Breaching Payment Plan: No provision

Georgia

Payment Plans: No provision

Effect of Breaching Payment Plan: No provision

Hawaii

Payment Plans: No provision
Effect of Breaching Payment Plan: No provision

Idaho

Payment Plans: Utilities shall offer reasonable payment arrangements to customers who cannot pay a bill. Idaho Admin. Code r. 31.23.01.313.
Effect of Breaching Payment Plan: Additional notice is not required if a customer violates a payment plan or tenders payment with a dishonored check or from an account with insufficient funds. Idaho Admin. Code r. 31.21.01.304.

Illinois

Payment Plans: Present residential customers who are indebted to a utility for past due utility service shall have the opportunity to negotiate a deferred payment agreement. Ill. Admin. Code tit. 83, § 280.60. Customer whose primary income is received 10 days following their billing due and whose income qualifies (SSI, VCA, AADB, Unemployment etc) shall be eligible for the preferred payment date program. Ill. Admin. Code tit. 83, § 290.90. Deferred payment agreement: initial 25% payment followed by 2-12 month payment period. Ill. Admin. Code tit. 83, § 280.110. Budget Payment plan. Ill. Admin. Code tit. 83, § 280.120.
Effect of Breaching Payment Plan: Customers shall have the right to renegotiate the payment plan should their financial circs change provided the customer notifies the utility within 14 days of defaulting on plan. If the customer defaults on a deferred payment agreement but has not yet had service discontinued by the utility, the utility shall permit such customer to be reinstated on the deferred payment agreement if the customer pays in full the amounts which should have been paid up to that date pursuant to the original payment plan. Ill. Admin. Code tit. 83, § 280.110.

Indiana

Payment Plans: Disconnection may be avoided if the customer agrees to pay a portion of the bill and enter into a payment agreement or for cause (financial hardship). 170 Ind. Admin. Code 4-1-16.
Effect of Breaching Payment Plan: No provision

Iowa

Payment Plans: Customers who cannot pay for services rendered shall be offered a reasonable payment plan. See Iowa Admin. Code r. 199-19.4(10) for reasonableness factors.
Effect of Breaching Payment Plan: No provision

Kansas

Payment Plans: Customers may receive a 14-day due-date extension in exchange for 1% service charge; Customers with delinquent balances shall be offered levelized payment plans allowing equal payments over a 12-month period. Kansas Consumer Information

Rules § II]. Budget payment plans also available. Kansas Consumer Information Rules § I.

Effect of Breaching Payment Plan: No provision

Kentucky

Payment Plans: Deferred payment arrangements and budget billing available. 807 Ky. Admin. Regs. 5:006 § 13.; See reg. for specific eligibility and payment plan requirements. 807 Ky. Admin. Regs. 5:006 § 14.

Effect of Breaching Payment Plan: No provision

Louisiana

Payment Plans: No provision

Effect of Breaching Payment Plan: No provision

Maine

Payment Plans: Utility shall continue to service a customer who expresses an inability to pay bill if customer is eligible and agrees to a reasonable payment plan. 65-407-81 Code Me. R. § 6.

Effect of Breaching Payment Plan: 3-day termination notice for breach of payment plan. 65-407-81 Code Me. R. § 9. A utility is not required to negotiate a second payment plan if the customer has breaches a payment plan. 65-407-81 Code Me. R. § 6.

Maryland

Payment Plans: Utility shall make good faith effort to negotiate a payment plan with customers and low-income customers who cannot pay; utility will consider circumstances and financial condition of customer. Md. Code Regs. 20.31.01.08.

Effect of Breaching Payment Plan: If a customer fails to adhere to a payment plan, the utility shall notify the customer that termination procedures may begin. Md. Code Regs. 20.31.01.08. Utility is not required to offer a payment plan to customers who have failed to meet the terms and conditions of any alternate payment plan during the past 18 months, committed fraud or theft against the utility, or refused the utility access to equipment at the customer's residence. Md. Code Regs. 20.31.01.08.

Massachusetts

Payment Plans: Payment plans available where customer meets financial hardship criteria. 220 Mass. Code Regs. §§ 25.02, 25.03.

Effect of Breaching Payment Plan: No provision

Michigan

Payment Plans: Budget billing available. Mich. Admin. Code r. 460.2114.

Effect of Breaching Payment Plan: No provision

Minnesota

Payment Plans: See Winter Protection. Minn. R. 7820.1900, 7820.2000. Every residential customer (**regardless of ability to pay**), who receives a termination notice during the winter months, shall have the right to a payment schedule. Minn. R. 7820.2100.

Effect of Breaching Payment Plan: No provision

Mississippi

Payment Plans: If customer subject to termination of service demonstrates an "extreme financial difficulty" or a medical emergency from December–March the utility shall not terminate service without offering the customer a levelized payment plan. Utilities may require a customer to accept a payment plan that requires payment of amounts due that accrued before November 11 with the remaining balance to be paid in installments of 133% (levelized monthly bill + 33% of past due amount). However, the utility is not prevented from negotiating a plan that is more acceptable to the customer. Customers shall not be allowed to carry forward an unpaid balance beyond December 1st of the following winter season. 26-000-02 Miss. Code R. § 8 (Weil).

Effect of Breaching Payment Plan: No provision

Missouri

Payment Plans: No provision

Effect of Breaching Payment Plan: No provision

Montana

Payment Plans: When a customer is unable to pay a bill a utility may negotiate a reasonable payment plan taking into account a customer's ability to pay, the size of the unpaid balance, the customer's payment history, and the amount of time and reasons the debt is outstanding. Mont. Admin. R. 38.5.1115.

Effect of Breaching Payment Plan: No provision

Nebraska

Payment Plans: No provision

Effect of Breaching Payment Plan: No provision

Nevada

Payment Plans: Equalized billing available; deferred payment plan for delinquent bills available unless customer has already entered into one in previous 11 months. Nev. Admin. Code § 704.341. Utilities shall provide a program to assist customers who have difficulty paying their bills due to financial hardship. Nev. Admin. Code § 704.342.

Effect of Breaching Payment Plan: Failure to fulfill payment agreement may result in termination without notice. Nev. Admin. Code § 704.339.

New Hampshire

Payment Plans: Reasonable payment arrangements available to customers unable to pay bills. N.H. Code Admin. R. Ann. PUC 1203.07.

Effect of Breaching Payment Plan: No provision

New Jersey

Payment Plans: Budget billing and payment plans available upon request. N.J. Admin. Code § 14:3-7.11A.

Effect of Breaching Payment Plan: No provision

New Mexico

Payment Plans: Budget payment plans available. N.M. Code R. § 5.410.11 (Weil). If an unreasonable hardship with no reasonable alternative exists, a customer may request a temporary or permanent exemption from this title. N.M. Code R. § 5.410.9 (Weil).

Effect of Breaching Payment Plan: Service may be terminated for noncompliance with payment agreement. N.M. Code R. § 5.410.29 (Weil).

New York

Payment Plans: Utility shall offer a deferred payment plan and may postpone termination for 10 days to negotiate with customer. Utility may require proof of financial statements to determine payment plan eligibility/amounts and to determine whether down payment is required. N.Y. Comp. Codes R. & Regs. tit. 16, § 11.10. Budget/levelized billing available. N.Y. Comp. Codes R. & Regs. tit. 16, § 11.11.

Effect of Breaching Payment Plan: If a customer's payment plan becomes delinquent, the utility shall send notification of delinquency at least 8 days before termination notice; notice shall inform customers that payment is due within 20 days and that payment plan may be altered if customer contacts utility and demonstrates changed financial situation. N.Y. Comp. Codes R. & Regs. tit. 16, § 11.10.

North Carolina

Payment Plans: Payment plan shall be offered and may require the customer to accept a plan that will bring his account into balance within 6 months. N.C. Admin Code 11.R.12-10.

Effect of Breaching Payment Plan: No provision

North Dakota

Payment Plans: Deferred payment plans available. N.D. Admin. Code 69-09-01-18.1.

Effect of Breaching Payment Plan: No provision

Ohio

Payment Plans: Utility shall offer payment plans to customers who express an inability to pay their bills; payment plans shall allow a customer to pay outstanding balance over 3-6 months. Levelized payment plans shall be offered to any customer not in default on payment plans. Ohio Admin. Code 4901:1-1804.

Effect of Breaching Payment Plan: No provision

Oklahoma

Payment Plans: Budget payment plans available. Okla. Admin. Code § 165:35-19-31. Disconnection for nonpayment shall be delayed 20 days if, upon notification to the utility, a consumer has applied and is waiting for financial assistance from a federal, state, or local agency and said agency verifies the application, and the consumer enters into a payment plan arrangement to pay any amount not covered by assistance in order. Okla. Admin. Code § 165:35-21-10.

Effect of Breaching Payment Plan: General disconnection provision states that service may be disconnected for non-payment. Okla. Admin. Code § 165:35-21-2.

Oregon

Payment Plans: Equal-payment plans available to customers with no outstanding balance. Or. Admin. R. 860-021-0414. A utility may not disconnect residential service for nonpayment if a customer enters into a written time-payment plan. A utility will offer customers a choice of payment agreements such as levelized payment plan and equal-pay arrearage plans. Or. Admin. R. 860-021-0415.

Effect of Breaching Payment Plan: General disconnection provision states that service may be disconnected for non-payment. Or. Admin. R. 860-021-0305.

Pennsylvania

Payment Plans: Equalized billing available. 52 Pa. Code § 56.12.

Effect of Breaching Payment Plan: Service shall not be terminated for noncompliance with a payment agreement prior to the due date of the bill which forms the basis of the agreement. 52 Pa. Code § 56.83.

Rhode Island

Payment Plans: Customers expressing payment problems shall be offered reasonable payment plans. 90-060-002 R.I. Code R. § 1 through Appx. D (Weil).

Effect of Breaching Payment Plan: General disconnection provision states that service may be disconnected for non-payment. 90-060-002 R.I. Code R. § 1 through Appx. D (Weil).

South Carolina

Payment Plans: Payment plans available

Effect of Breaching Payment Plan: Notice of termination due to a delinquent payment plan account shall be given at least 5 days prior to termination if by mail and/or at least 2 days if given in person or by phone. S.C. Code Ann. Regs. § 103-352.

South Dakota

Payment Plans: Equal monthly billing available. S.D. Admin. R. 20:10:17:10.

Effect of Breaching Payment Plan: No provision

Tennessee

Payment Plans: No provision

Effect of Breaching Payment Plan: No provision

Texas

Payment Plans: Utilities shall offer customers who express an inability to pay their bills alternative payment plans and info concerning disconnection moratoriums for the ill and any payment or energy assistance programs. 16 Tex. Admin. Code § 25.28.

Effect of Breaching Payment Plan: No provision

Utah

Payment Plans: Customers unable to pay outstanding balances in full shall be offered payment plans as a method of obtaining or continuing service. Utah Admin. Code r. R746-200-3. Service shall be provided if the customers enters into a written deferred payment plan to pay all past due amounts (within 12 months).

Effect of Breaching Payment Plan: Termination may proceed after a payment agreement is breaches and a utility is not obligated to renew the agreement. Utah Admin. Code r. R746-200-5.

Vermont

Payment Plans: When establishing a reasonable repayment plan the company shall consider the income and income schedule of the customer, the customer's payment history, the size of the arrearage and current bill, the amount of time and reason for the outstanding bill and whether the delinquency was caused by unforeseen circumstances. 30-000-03 Vt. Code R. § 3.302. A utility shall restore service if the customer has paid 1/2 of delinquent bill and agrees to a payment plan that reconciles the account within 3 months. 30-000-03 Vt. Code R. § 3.307. Levelized billing available. 30-000-03 Vt. Code R. § 3.302.

Effect of Breaching Payment Plan: If disconnection is due to a failure to abide by the terms of a payment plan, notice shall be given prior to disconnection either 5 days (mail) or 72 hours (phone). A customer is within substantial compliance with payment plan if customer has paid at least 75% of plan payment. Service will be terminated for failure to remain in substantial compliance with plan. 30-000-03 Vt. Code R. § 3.304.

Virginia

Payment Plans: No provision

Effect of Breaching Payment Plan: No provision

Washington

Payment Plans: Utility shall offer all customers an opportunity to enter into equalized payment agreements. The utility may deny the equalized payment option to customers who have been removed from a payment plan within the last 6 months for non-payment or have an outstanding balance of at least two months. Wash. Admin. Code 480-90-138.

Effect of Breaching Payment Plan: No provision

West Virginia

Payment Plans: Termination shall be delayed and a payment plan offered in some circumstances if, prior to termination, the utility is notified that the reason for termination is being disputed, termination would be dangerous to health and safety of a household member, or the customer can only pay the bill in monthly installments. When calculating a plan, utility shall consider amount due, ability to pay, payment history, and the time and reason for non-payment. Utility may assess a 6% carrying fee on a payment plan. W. Va. Code R. § 150-3-4.8.

Effect of Breaching Payment Plan: Utilities shall renegotiate payment plans should the existing plan create a financial hardship due to a change in the customer's finances. W. Va. Code R. § 150-3-4.8. A shorter 5-days termination notice will be provided where payment plan is violated. W. Va. Code R. § 150-3-4.8.

Wisconsin

Payment Plans: Deferred payment plans shall be offered to customers having difficulty paying bills and accepted as means of avoiding disconnection of service if the customer agrees to pay a reasonable initial payment followed by reasonable payments. All payment plans shall also consider a customer's ability to pay, amount of and time period of delinquent bill, payment history, and reason for delinquency. Wis. Admin. Code PSC § 113.0404.

Effect of Breaching Payment Plan: Utilities may disconnected services for failure to abide by payment plan terms and are not obligated to renegotiate a payment plan. Wis. Admin. Code PSC § 113.0404.

Wyoming

Payment Plans: No provision

Effect of Breaching Payment Plan: No provision

F.5 SECURITY DEPOSITS REQUIREMENTS BY STATE

Alabama

Deposit/Guarantee Requirement: Utilities may require deposit before beginning or continuing service; deposit not to exceed the amount of an estimated bill for 2 billing periods. Alabama PSC Gen. Rule 8.

Alaska

Deposit/Guarantee Requirement: Utilities may require deposit before beginning or continuing service; deposit not to exceed the amount of an estimated bill for 2 billing periods. Alaska Admin. Code tit. 3, § 52.415.

Arizona

Deposit/Guarantee Requirement: Utilities may require deposit before beginning or continuing service for issues relating to non-payment; deposit not to exceed estimated bill for two months. Ariz. Admin. Code § 14-2-203.

Arkansas

Deposit/Guarantee Requirement: Utilities may require deposit before beginning or continuing service for issues relating to non-payment of this or prior bills or misrepresentation; deposit not to exceed specified amount. Such amount increases if there is evidence of tampering; deposit payable in 2 installments; instead of deposit, utility may allow guaranty of a qualified third party. 126-03-003 Ark. Code R. §§ 4.01, 4.02, 4.03, 4.04 (Weil).

California

Deposit/Guarantee Requirement: May require deposit before commencing service; deposit not to exceed estimated bill for 3 months. Cal. Pub. Util. Code § 394.4(g).

Colorado

Deposit/Guarantee Requirement: Utility may require applicants and customers to make cash deposit, not to exceed estimated 90 days' bill. 4 Colo. Code Regs. § 723-3-11.

Connecticut

Deposit/Guarantee Requirement: **New customers:**company may require deposit if customer cannot provide specified info; **Other customers**: company may require deposit if company has terminated prospective customer's utility service during past 2 years for non-payment; A customer from whom a security deposit is required shall be informed that service will not be denied if the customer lacks the financial ability to pay it; deposit shall not exceed 3/12 of a year's estimated billing and may be paid in installments. Conn. Agencies Regs. § 16-262j-1(b).

Delaware

Deposit/Guarantee Requirement: Utility may require a deposit from any customer or prospective customer for purpose of guaranteeing payment, and the deposit may be retained as long as necessary to ensure payment; deposit not to exceed the max. estimated charge for service of the lesser of 2 consecutive billing periods or 90 days. 10-800-003 Del. Code of Regs. § 10 800 007.8 (Weil).

District of Columbia

Deposit/Guarantee Requirement: Utility shall not require a cash deposit or guarantee from a person who has never been a customer of the utility; utility shall not require a cash deposit from a person who has been a customer of a utility before, except in certain circs; utility shall not require a cash deposit as a condition of continued service except in limited circs; deposit not to exceed lesser of $100 or twice the estimated maximum monthly bill. D.C. Mun. Regs. tit. 15, § 307.

Florida

Deposit/Guarantee Requirement: A new or existing customer may be required to pay a deposit or provide a guarantee of payment if they fail to meet the tariff's criteria for establishing credit. Deposits not to exceed 2 months actual estimated bill. Fla. Admin. Code Ann. r. 25-6.097.

Georgia

Deposit/Guarantee Requirement: Utility may require deposits from customers before beginning or continuing service if they judge the deposit necessary. Deposit not to exceed the amount of an estimate bill for 2.5 billing periods (gas deposits not to exceed $150). Ga. Comp. R. & Regs. 515-3-1.10.

Hawaii

Deposit/Guarantee Requirement: Deposits may not be less than $10 for electric or $5 for gas and may not exceed twice the maximum estimated charge for 2 consecutive months.

Idaho

Deposit/Guarantee Requirement: Deposit shall not be required unless there is proof that the applicant or customer is a credit risk or is likely to damage utility property. A deposit may be required due to issues relating to non-payment for service (4 year look-back pd), misrepresentation or providing false information, lack of credit history combined with a lack of 12 consecutive months of previous service within the last 4 years, 2 or more final termination notice within last 12 months, or filing for bankruptcy relief; deposit not to exceed 1/6 of annual usage; when gas is primary source of heat, deposit shall not exceed a total of 2 months of the highest monthly bills from the previous 12. Deposits can be paid in two installments. Idaho Admin. Code r. 31.21.01.101 and 31.21.01.105.

Illinois

Deposit/Guarantee Requirement: A utility may request a deposit from a present residential customer during the first 24 months(and beyond in cases of tampering) that the customer receives utility service from that utility if certain conditions are met (repeated late payment; tampering). Deposit shall not exceed 1/6 annual charges for service. Ill. Admin. Code tit. 83, § 280.60. Utility shall not require a deposit from applicant is eligible for LIHEAP. Ill. Admin. Code tit. 83, §280.50.

Indiana

Deposit/Guarantee Requirement: Deposit may be required to receive or continue to receive due to issues related to non-payment of services for past and present utility service. 170 Ind. Admin. Code 4-1-15. Deposit not to exceed 1/6 of actual/estimated billing (gas: 1/3); deposit/guarantee shall not be required if an applicant/customer can demonstrate a consistent employment history, purchase or long-term rental of residence to be service, a graduate student, or is being discharged from the military. 170 Ind. Admin. Code 4-1-15.

Iowa

Deposit/Guarantee Requirement: Deposit or guarantee may be required as a condition for receiving, or continuing to receive service. Deposit not to exceed actual/estimated bill for one month of service from previous 12 months. Iowa Admin. Code r. 199-19.4(2). Service shall not be denied for failure to pay a deposit during the winter protection months. Iowa Admin. Code r. 199-19.4(16).

Kansas

Deposit/Guarantee Requirement: New or existing customers may be required to pay a deposit or provide a guarantee; deposit not to exceed an estimated bill for two billing periods; deposits can be paid in monthly installments. Kansas Consumer Information Rules § III.

Kentucky

Deposit/Guarantee Requirement: Deposit or guarantee may be required as a condition for receiving, or continuing to receive service. Deposit not to exceed 2/12 of annual actual/estimated bill where bills are rendered monthly. 807 Ky. Admin. Regs. 5:006 § 7.

Louisiana

Deposit/Guarantee Requirement: Utility may required deposit not to exceed 2.5 months of actual/estimated service.

Maine

Deposit/Guarantee Requirement: Utility may require deposit due to poor utility payment history, customer is deemed a credit risk, lack of employment or income or bankruptcy filing. Deposit not to exceed 2 of the highest consecutive billing periods; deposit may be paid with an initial 50% payment followed by 2 equal payments in 30-day intervals. 65-407-81 Code Me. R. § 5.

Maryland

Deposit/Guarantee Requirement: Utility may require deposit; deposit not to exceed 2.5 months of estimated charges for ensuing 12 months. Md. Code Regs. 20.30.02.04.

Massachusetts

Deposit/Guarantee Requirement: No provision

Michigan

Deposit/Guarantee Requirement: Utility may require deposit for issues relating to non-payment within last 6 years; misrepresentation of or failure to provide credit info; unauthorized access or diversion of service; inability to provide utility history from past 6 years; an appointment of a receiver or bankruptcy filing. Mich. Admin. Code r. 460.2131. Deposit not to exceed twice the peak usage rate or 4 times that rate if unauthorized use is at issue. Mich. Admin. Code r. 460.2134.

Minnesota

Deposit/Guarantee Requirement: Deposits permitted where payment cannot be assured or where existing customer's service has been disconnected. Minn. R. 7820.4300. No utility shall charge deposit to a residential customer who has declared to the utility inability to pay and is income eligible. Minn. R. 7820.1750. A customer may assure payment by written guarantee. Minn. R. 7820.4500.

Mississippi

Deposit/Guarantee Requirement: Utility may require a deposit where necessary to assure payment except from those who are 60+ years old; deposit not to exceed one month's estimated bill for residential service. 26-000-02 Miss. Code R. § 9 (Weil).

Missouri

Deposit/Guarantee Requirement: New/existing customers may be required to make a deposit where necessary to assure payment; deposit amounts vary depending on billing cycle; when assessed November–January, deposits may be paid in 6 installments. Mo. Code Regs. Ann. tit. 4 § 240-13.030.

Montana

Deposit/Guarantee Requirement: Utility may require deposit or guarantee. Mont. Admin. R. 38.5.1103. Deposit not to exceed 1/6th the annual estimated billing. Mont. Admin. R. 38.5.1105.

Nebraska

Deposit/Guarantee Requirement: No provision

Nevada

Deposit/Guarantee Requirement: Deposit may be required. Deposit not to exceed 150% (or 50% for an elderly customer) of an average estimate monthly bill for an applicant or 150% of the highest monthly bill for existing customers. The elderly may have to pay additional deposit in case of delinquency. Nev. Admin. Code §§ 704.327, 704.328. Deposit not required where there is a guarantor. Nev. Admin. Code § 704.329. Deposit may be payable in 3 installments. Nev. Admin. Code § 704.331.

New Hampshire

Deposit/Guarantee Requirement: New applicants may be required to pay deposit or provide guarantee for non-payment within 3 years of application; existing customers may be required to pay deposit for numerous disconnection notices within past 12 months; deposit not to exceed total for two months high usage. N.H. Code Admin. R. Ann. PUC 1203.02.

New Jersey

Deposit/Guarantee Requirement: Utilities may require deposit as requirement for service if customer hasn't established credit; deposit approx 2 months average billing. N.J. Admin. Code § 14:3-7.1. May require deposit for existing customers in default. N.J. Admin. Code § 14:3-7.3.

New Mexico

Deposit/Guarantee Requirement: Deposit/Guaranty may be required for unsatisfactory credit, chronic delinquency or unauthorized use of utility service. N.M. Code R. § 17.5.410.16 (Weil). Deposit may not exceed 1/6 annual estimated bill or 1.5 times an estimated monthly bill. N.M. Code R. § 17.5.410.18 (Weil).

New York

Deposit/Guarantee Requirement: Customers already receiving service, who aren't delinquent in payment or had services terminate within the previous 6 months shall not be required to pay a deposit. A delinquent payment is 2 consecutive months of arrears without making reasonably payment (1/2 of total arrears) or failure to make a reasonable payment on a bimonthly bill within 50 days after the bill is due; deposits shall not be required of customers or applicants receiving public assistance or SSI or for elderly customers (62+) unless service ha been terminated within previous 6 months. N.Y. Comp. Codes R. & Regs. tit. 16, § 11.12.

North Carolina

Deposit/Guarantee Requirement: Deposit or guarantee may be required for new/existing customers. N.C. Admin. Code 11.R.12-2.

North Dakota

Deposit/Guarantee Requirement: Gas: deposit or guarantee may be required for new/existing customers; deposit not to exceed 1.5 times estimate for monthly billing. N.D. Admin. Code 69-09-01-17.

Ohio

Deposit/Guarantee Requirement: Applicant or customer with previous disconnection or late payments, regardless of actual disconnection, may be required to pay a deposit. Ohio Admin. Code 4901:1-17-04. Deposit not to exceed 1/12 plus 30% of the estimated monthly charge. Ohio Admin. Code 4901:1-17-05.

Oklahoma

Deposit/Guarantee Requirement: Deposit may be required for new/existing customers; deposit not to exceed 1/6 estimated annual bill; deposits may be made in installments. Okla. Admin. Code § 165:35-19-10.

Oregon

Deposit/Guarantee Requirement: Customer/applicant may be required to pay deposit to ensure ability to pay. Deposit not to exceed 1/6 annual estimated usage. Deposits payable in installments of $30 or 1/3 whichever is greater. Or. Admin. R. 860-021-0200, 860-021-0205.

Pennsylvania

Deposit/Guarantee Requirement: May require deposit or third party guarantor for applicants and existing customers; deposit not to exceed estimated bill for 2 months; payable in installments. 52 Pa. Code §§ 56.38, 56.41, 56.51.

Rhode Island

Deposit/Guarantee Requirement: Deposit may be required for new and existing customers; not to exceed 2 months of estimated billing. 90-070-005 R.I. Code R. (Weil).

South Carolina

Deposit/Guarantee Requirement: Deposit may be required for new and existing customers; not to exceed 2 months of estimated billing. S.C. Code Ann. Regs. §§ 103-332, 103-333.

South Dakota

Deposit/Guarantee Requirement: Credit may be established by paying a deposit or providing a guarantee of no more than 1/6 an annual estimated bill. S.D. Admin. R. 20:10:19:02. Deposits may be paid in 4 equal monthly installments. S.D. Admin. R. 20:10:19:04.

Tennessee

Deposit/Guarantee Requirement: Deposits to insure payment of services shall not exceed the lesser of an estimated billing period or 90 days. Tenn. Comp. R. & Regs. 1220-4-4-.15.

Texas

Deposit/Guarantee Requirement: Applicant or customer may be required to pay deposit if their credit is not sufficiently established. Deposit not to exceed 1/6 of annual estimated billing. 16 Tex. Admin. Code § 25.24.

Utah

Deposit/Guarantee Requirement: Deposit or guarantee may be required to receive or continue receiving service. Customers shall have right to pay deposit in 3+ monthly installments if the first payment is made when required. Utah Admin. Code r. R746-200-3.

Vermont

Deposit/Guarantee Requirement: Deposit may be required from customers and applicants deemed a credit risk or who have had previous utility service disconnected or sent 2 disconnection notices within previous 24 months; may be paid in 3 monthly installments; deposit not to exceed 2.5 times actual/estimated monthly usage. 30-000-03 Vt. Code R. §§ 3.202–3.204.

Virginia

Deposit/Guarantee Requirement: Deposit shall not exceed 2 months estimated usage and customer shall have right to pay deposit greater than $40 in 3 consecutive installments. 20 Va. Admin. Code § 5-10-20.

Washington

Deposit/Guarantee Requirement: Deposit/guaranty not to exceed 2.5 estimated annual billing may be required from an applicant or existing customer. Utility shall allow a customer or applicant to pay deposit in installments: 50% initial payment with the remaining 50% to be paid in 2 equal monthly installments. Wash. Admin. Code 480-90-113.

West Virginia

Deposit/Guarantee Requirement: Deposit not to exceed 1/12 estimated annual charges. W. Va. Code R. § 150-3-4-2.

Wisconsin

Deposit/Guarantee Requirement: Deposit or guarantee shall not be required if the customer or applicant provides the utility with information showing that his or her gross quarterly income is at or below 200% of the federal income poverty guidelines. Deposit/guarantee shall not be required unless a customer has an outstanding account balance with any Wisconsin electric utility which accrued within last 6 years and for which there is not a payment agreement or dispute. Wis. Admin. Code PSC § 113.0402. Deposit not to exceed two estimated consecutive billing periods. Wis. Admin. Code PSC § 113.0402.

Wyoming

Deposit/Guarantee Requirement: Applicant or customer may be required to ensure payment. Deposit not to exceed 90 days estimated or actual billing. 023-0020-2 Wyo. Code R. § 241 (Weil).

APPENDIX G

Status of Payday Lending

LEGAL STATUS OF PAYDAY LENDING BY STATE

Alabama
Ala. Code §§ 5-18A-1 through 5-18A-22
Payday loan law

Alaska
Alaska Stat. §§ 06.50.400 through 06.50.560
Payday loan law

Arizona
Ariz. Rev. Stat. Ann. §§ 6-1251 through 6-1263
Payday loan law

Arkansas
Ark. Code. Ann. §§ 23-52-101 through 23-52-117; Ark. Const. art. 19, § 13
Payday loan law

California
Cal. Fin. Code §§ 23000 through 23106 (West)
Payday loan law

Colorado
Colo. Rev. Stat. §§ 5-3.1-101 through 5-3.1-123
Payday loan law

Connecticut
Payday lending prohibited

Delaware
Del. Code Ann. tit. 5, §§ 2227 through 2238; Del. Code. Ann. tit. 5 § 2744
Payday lending permitted under small loan act or licensing law
Check cashers cannot accept postdated checks

District of Columbia

D.C. Code §§ 26-301 through 26-323
Payday loan law
Check cashers cannot accept postdated checks

Florida

Fla. Stat. §§ 560.401 through 560.408; Fla. Admin. Code Ann. r 3C-560.901 through 3C-560.912
Payday loan law

Georgia

Ga. Code Ann. §§ 16-17-1 through 16-17-10
Payday lending prohibited

Hawaii

Haw. Rev. Stat. §§ 480F-1 through 480F-7
Payday loan law

Idaho

Idaho Code Ann. §§ 28-46-401 through 28-46-413
Payday loan law

Illinois

815 Ill. Comp. Stat. § 122/1-1 (eff. 12/6/05)
Payday loan law

Indiana

Ind. Code §§ 24-4.5-7-101 through 24-4.5-7-414
Payday loan law

Iowa

Iowa Code §§ 533D.1 through 533D.16
Payday loan law

Kansas

Kan. Stat. Ann. § 16a-2-404, *as amended by* 2005 Kansas Legis. 144 (eff. April, 2005)
Payday loan law

Kentucky

Ky. Rev. Stat. Ann. §§ 368.010 through 368.120 (West)
Payday loan law

Louisiana

La. Rev. Stat. Ann. §§ 9:3578.1 through 9:3578.8
Payday loan law

Maine
Me. Rev. Stat. Ann. tit. 9-A, § 2-401; tit. 32 § 6138
Check cashers cannot accept postdated checks
Payday lending prohibited

Maryland
Payday lending prohibited

Massachusetts
Payday lending prohibited

Michigan
Mich. Comp. Laws §§ 487.2121 through 487.2173
Payday loan law

Minnesota
Minn. Stat. § 47.60
Payday loan law

Mississippi
Miss. Code Ann. §§ 75-67-501 through 75-67-539
Payday loan law

Missouri
Mo. Rev. Stat. §§ 408.500 through 408.510; Mo. Code Regs. Ann. tit. 4, §§ 140-11.010 through 140-11.040
Payday loan law

Montana
Mont. Code Ann. §§ 31-1-701 through 31-1-725
Payday loan law

Nebraska
Neb. Rev. Stat. § 45-904
Payday loan law

Nevada
Nev. Rev. Stat. §§ 604A.010 through 604A.940
Payday loan law

New Hampshire
N.H. Rev. Stat. Ann. §§ 399-A:1 through 399-A:19
Payday loan law

New Jersey
Check cashers cannot accept postdated checks
Payday lending prohibited

New Mexico
Payday lending permitted under small loan act or licensing law
New regulations essentially prohibiting payday lending subject to court challenge
Regulations announced in 2006 impose some restrictions

New York
Check cashers cannot accept postdated checks
Payday lending prohibited

North Carolina
Check cashers cannot accept postdated checks
Payday lending prohibited

North Dakota
N.D. Cent. Code §§ 13-08-01 through 13-08-15, *as amended by* 2005 N.D. Laws Ch. 127 (H.B. 1321)
Payday loan law

Ohio
Ohio Rev. Code Ann. §§ 1315.35 through 1315.99 (West)
Payday loan law

Oklahoma
Okla. Stat. tit. 59, §§ 3101 through 3119
Payday loan law

Oregon
Or. Rev. Stat. §§ 725.600 through 725.625
Payday loan law

Pennsylvania
Check cashers cannot accept postdated checks
Payday lending prohibited

Puerto Rico
Check cashers cannot accept postdated checks
Payday lending prohibited

Rhode Island

R.I. Gen. Laws §§ 19-14.4-1 and 19-14.4-4, *as amended by* 2005 RI Laws 05-230 (05-H6-3A)

Payday loan law

South Carolina

S.C. Code Ann. §§ 34-39-110 through 34-39-260

Payday loan law

South Dakota

S.D. Codified Laws §§ 54-4-36 through 54-4-72

Payday lending permitted under small loan act or licensing law

Tennessee

Tenn. Code Ann. §§ 45-17-101 through 45-17-119 and Tenn. Comp. R. & Regs. 0180-28-.01

Payday loan law

Texas

Tex. Fin. Code Ann. §§ 342.251 through 342.259 and 342.601 through 342.605; 7 Tex. Admin. Code § 1.605

Payday loan law

Utah

Utah Code Ann. §§ 7-23-101 through 7-23-110

Payday loan law

Vermont

Check cashers cannot accept postdated checks

Payday lending prohibited

Virgin Islands

Payday lending prohibited

Virginia

Va. Code Ann. §§ 6.1-444 through 6.1-471

Payday loan law

Washington

Wash. Rev. Code §§ 31.45.010 through 31.45.900

Payday loan law

West Virginia

Check cashers cannot accept postdated checks
Payday lending prohibited

Wisconsin

Payday lending prohibited

Wyoming

Wyo. Stat. Ann. §§ 40-14-362 through 40-14-364
Payday loan law

Survey of State Payday Loan Laws prepared by the National Consumer Law Center (November, 2005)

Index

NOTES

NOTES

NOTES

NOTES

NOTES

NOTES

HELP US HELP YOU

We appreciate your feedback.

Let us know what you think of the book and how to make it better by going to www.nclc.org\publications\dveval.html.

ORDER FORM

☐ The NCLC Guide to Consumer Rights for Domestic Violence Survivors (2006 ed.) . . . . $15 ppd.
(SAVE! $10 each for 5 or more, $7 for 100 or more.)

☐ The NCLC Guide to Surviving Debt (2006 ed.) . . . . $20 ppd.
(SAVE! $14 each for 5 or more. $12 for 20 or more, $8 for 100 or more.)

☐ The NCLC Guide to the Rights of Utility Consumers (2006 ed.) . . . . . $15 ppd.
(SAVE! $10 each for 5 or more. $7 each for 100 or more.)

☐ **20 copies** Surviving Credit Card Debt Workbooks with CD-Roms (2005 ed.) . . . . $80 ppd.
(Minimum order of 20 copies; $4 for each additional copy over 20)

☐ The NCLC Guide to Mobile Homes (2002 ed.) . . . . $12 ppd.

☐ Return to Sender: Getting a Refund or Replacement for Your Lemon Car (2000 ed.) . . . . $16 ppd.

☐ **Please send me more information about NCLC books for lawyers.**

Name ______________________

Organization ______________________

Street Address ______________________

City ______________ State ________ Zip ________

Telephone ______________________

E-mail ______________________

Mail to: National Consumer Law Center, Inc.
Publications Department
77 Summer Street, 10th Floor
Boston, MA 02110-1006

Telephone orders
(617) 542-9595
or fax (617) 542-8028
for credit card orders

☐ Check or money order enclosed, payable to the National Consumer Law Center

☐ MasterCard ☐ VISA ☐ American Express Cards

Card# ☐☐☐☐☐☐☐☐☐☐☐☐☐☐☐☐

Exp. date ☐☐☐☐ Signature ______________________

(card number, expiration date, and signature must accompany charge orders)

NATIONAL CONSUMER LAW CENTER
77 Summer Street, 10th Floor • Boston, MA 02110-1006
Tel. (617) 542-9595 • FAX (617) 542-8028 • publications@nclc.org

Order securely online at
www.consumerlaw.org